Prose: Essays and Letters

C. Liegh McInnis

Psychedelic Literature/Jackson, Mississippi

Psychedelic Literature ®

203 Lynn Lane
Clinton, MS 39056
(601) 383-0024
psychedeliclit@bellsouth.net

LCCN: 99-70269
ISBN: (13 digit) 978-0-9655775-5-7
ISBN: (10 digit) 0-9655775-5-4

Other Works by C. Liegh McInnis

Matters of Reality: Body, Mind & Soul (Poetry, 1997)
The Lyrics of Prince (Lyrical Criticism, 1997, 2001)
Scripts: Sketches and Tales of Urban MS (Fiction, 1998)
Confessions: Brainstormin' from Midnight 'til Dawn (Poetry, 1998)
Searchin' 4 Psychedelica (Poetry, 1999)
Da Black Book of Linguistic Liberation (Poetry, 2001)
Poetic Discussions (Interviews, DVD 2005)
Introduction of a Blues Poet (Poetry, CD 2005)

Acknowledgments

<u>To Monica Taylor-McInnis, My Wife (Soul of My Soul)</u>: How many tires have we patched or replaced on the Highway to Psychedelica? Each one has brought us closer to each other, closer to Psychedelica, closer to God.

<u>To My Family</u>: The Foundation of my life. Thanks for the Love and the Food.

<u>To Claudette McInnis (Momma)</u>. Thanks...I Love you.

<u>To. Claude Sr. (Pops)</u>. Thanks, man...I Love you.

<u>To David Brian Williams</u>. My Mentor. Thanks for giving me a nest. Whatever it is, Whatever we find...Mississippi will give it to us.

<u>To Jolivette Anderson aka The Poet Warrior</u>. Your spirit is my motivator. You are our Eshu.

<u>To Charlie Braxton</u>. The Bridge. You are an anthology. Thanks for letting me read you.

<u>To Derrick Johnson</u>. You are a Civil Rights Attorney in any day. We all need vision. Thanks for teaching us all.

<u>To. Dr. Jerry Ward</u>. The Master. There is no Mississippi scene without you. Thanks for teaching us all.

<u>To Dr. Hillery Knight</u>. The Beautiful Poet. In your verse we find what God wants us to do...Love, enjoy, and celebrate each other.

<u>To Dr. Marie O'Banner Jackson</u>. For the one thousandth time, thanks!!!

To Ezra Brown (EB). Mr. Jazzoetry. Thanks for laying it down every Thursday night. Your spirit moves us to greater levels.

To Terry Miller. Rainy nights and smooth horns...Play brotha.

To Tri-Tone (Rhonda R., Nellie M., and Rufus M.). We need you back. The students need a school.

To Ahmos Zu-Bolton. Thank you for your life and your work. You are the eternal spring from which all poets flow.

To Kalamu ya Salaam. I promise I will not talk while hip music is playing nor when masters are speaking.

To the JSU and Tougaloo poets. Too Funky. I'm just glad that I'm here to watch y'all grow. Thanks for your dedication and your sharing.

To Chris Burkett. Thanks for letting your house be our crib.

To Sandy Smith-Vantz. Thanks for letting us hang at your place.

To Stan Branson. Thanks for the support. You are an angel to all Mississippi artists.

To Karen Allen, Netti Ravick, Cecil Fountain, and Jeffery Jamison. Thanks for your eyes and your insight. They are invaluable.

And to you. Psychedelica is a woman. Let her give birth to your Utopia. Peace, rain and sunshine...rainbows forever.

Table of Contents

Writing as Theory and Art Form

Writing as with any form of art is merely a physical manifestation of human genius. The product of writing is the combination of the idea and the method used for articulating the idea. The manner in which those two elements are combined creates the artistry. Thus, if we are going to discuss creative writing (poetry or fiction), we must first discuss art because poetry and fiction are aspects or segments of art, and art is merely the use of skill or talent for the specific purpose of creating meaning and beauty. In all forms of art, there are common denominators or characteristics that tie these forms together, binding them to each other, to us, and to the universe, making art the thread that houses humanity's DNA. Therefore, it should be understood that to study any particular art form, such as literature, music, painting, or any other form, without studying the general aspects and principles of art as well as the culture that has produced the art, is narrowing and meaningless. So then, if you want to master your particular medium, you must learn artistic principles in general as well as gain an understanding as to how environment or culture affects the production of an art form such as writing. We must realize that with any form of art, such as writing, the structure of the art tells us as much about the creator as the subject or message, but it is the message that is driving the structure. Organic to human evolution is the evolution of our languages, which is the medium and representation of our critical thinking abilities. So for humanity to evolve, our mastery of language must evolve, which includes our willingness and ability to understand and embrace the languages and cultures of those not like us. Mastering the balance between structure, subject, and socio-political context allows us to create art that helps humanity to understand the world in which we live thus allowing us to live better.

If we date ourselves to the Sudan area of Africa about six thousand BC, we find the first rock markings. Prior to this, the ruling literature was oral literature, and even oral literature was seen as an aspect of several activities combined to produce the artistic expression. Or to put it another way, prior to six thousand BC, art was not segmented into various forms or genres but was one creation or activity created from an amalgamation of human activities. The first cave and temple drawings were simultaneously aesthetic and informative, a dual collaboration of painting and writing. In ancient African civilization, which is the birth place and foundation of civilization, there can be no distinction made between different artistic genres. Art was a combination of vocal expression, body movement, and body and object painting working as one cohesive form for the purpose of ritual or ceremony. Even hieroglyphics, the first writing, is a combination of at least two forms of art, painting and writing, because it is picture art. Thus, many of the rules that govern language and many of the rules that govern painting and sculpting were and are the same. Even today, techniques such as metaphor/imagery and onomatopoeia are used to evoke visual and auditory sensations. Yet, hieroglyphics should be seen as the first step toward writing becoming something distinctly separate from drawing because "hieroglyphic writing developed in Egypt [around 3100 BC] greatly aided the new administrators in knitting their new country together" (Damrosch and Pike 2). However, it is not until the ninth or eighth century BC when the Greeks receive an alphabet that writing begins its final evolution to a separate, autonomous form of art. And in writing's earliest stages, it is clear that the expression, the message, the articulation of information is far more important than the medium or form. In fact, it is not until the European Renaissance that we have this dividing of genres creating the so called age of specialization. (Yet we must note that the Renaissance's categorization of writing into various forms is based on the work done by Horace

7

fifteen hundred years earlier.) It is Horace's so called scientific approach to writing that creates the dissection and categorization of art forms into tiny boxes. Prior to this, expression and message, not form, were the primary concern. Prior to Horace, all art, even writing, was seen as a gift from the gods, and man was merely a vessel for the articulation of the gods' will. And it was also during the Renaissance when art was wrestled away from ritual to be allowed to exist as purely an entertainment or leisure activity.

Yet, it is during the Medieval era (410 – 1492) that writing and art in general begins to mutate or diverge into two simultaneous paths of the sacred and the profane. During the Middle Ages art was still considered a useful tool for religious, social, and political propaganda but not merely for religious or cultural ritual. There exist many tales and poems dedicated to the lives and adventures of knights, samurai, merchants, and missionaries because it was a period of growth in international trade, which is also accompanied by international struggle for place and power. And at the same time, Medieval writers become the first writers who are exclusively paid and controlled by royal patrons. This means that the propaganda poetry of the past, such as Egypt's "Hymn to the Aton," which is a blend of religious and political propaganda, is replaced by poems and stories that become mostly political propaganda. So, works, such as *Gawain and the Green Knight*, *The Seven Samurai*, and *The Thousand and One Nights* become almost devoid of religious propaganda and are used to celebrate and market their respective cultures and sensibilities. While the Middle Ages is a time of growth, it is also a time of war and disease. Even the courtly love poetry that grows from the romance is as much a commentary/criticism of class oppression as it is a declaration of love. However, it is the rise of the urban city and its universities, such as those in Bologna, Paris, Oxford, Cambridge, Heidelberg, and Salamanca, which finally wrestles creative writing from its sole purpose of ritual.

> "This 'clerkly' culture was instrumental in the philosophical and literary movement known as the twelfth century renaissance: a renewed interest in classical philosophy and literature paired with an increased investment in rational argumentation and the study of the physical world...The newly intellectual focus on rationality and experience was seen by many religious figures to come at the expense of the basic tenets of the Christian faith" (Damrosch and Pike 898, 899).

The Medieval man was a multicultural man whose world was influenced by the cultures and sensibilities of others because the ability to trade with others for profit so deemed it. Thus the man who saw and experienced the world changed because how he saw and understood the world changed.

> "One of the reasons that so many different uses and contradictions could coexist in the same place and in a single person is that the medieval mind preferred analogy to symbolism. Symbolic thinking typically attaches a unique and unchanging meaning to a specific word or object (the cathedral as a sacred place of worship), and an individual to a single, fixed identity from cradle to grave. By contrast, medieval thought tended to conceptualize the world in terms of a complex network of parallel relations...To approach the world allegorically is to regard it as simultaneously possessing a multitude of meanings. Just as the medieval person was accustomed to juggling several languages and several different cultures, so was she or he accustomed to keeping multiple meanings in mind simultaneously, or to singing sacrilegious songs in

the tavern while piously praying in church, without feeling obligated to choose irrevocably between any of the several apparently contradictory possibilities" (Damrosch and Pike 899).

The Early Modern Period (1400 – 1640) and the Age of Enlightenment (1641 - 1799) are the periods where art is finally separated from ritual/religion and allowed to exist on its own as a "thing" with its own unique rules and sensibilities that are in service to the man's leisure or play time. This transformation is driven, of course, by the global embrace of the scientific approach to life where "old traditions came newly into question [and] writers sought modes of expression that would reflect the changing reality around" (Damrosch and Pike 1437). It was a circular development where commerce and industry were advanced by science, and science, in turn, advanced commerce and industry. This development and accomplishment of science created new classes of people which led to the decline of the aristocracy and the rise of a new merchant class that not only had more money but more leisure time. From France to Russia to India there developed a new class of people between aristocracy and peasantry that became the middle-class. And this new middle-class not only embraced science and leisure, but it also embraced the notion of applying the science and rational planning to social ills and problems so that the art that they embraced was not only for leisure but articulated the change from man handing his problems to God to man attempting to solve his problems with his own will and intellect. Now, I must state that this attack on religion's lack of empirical thought was as much an attack on aristocracy. Scholars such as John Locke, Gottfried Wilhelm Leibniz, Voltaire, Jean-Jacques Rousseau, and Immanuel Kant argued that "reason must also master the passions that drove the wars of religion by fostering religious tolerance alongside intellectual experimentation and argument." Therefore, scientific inquiry should cause humanity to achieve "fundamental human equality" (Damrosch and Pike 1804). Thus, when we study the rise of mass printing, what Damrosch and Pike call "print culture," we must also understand that what truly drove the demand for mass printing was that the universities and the rising merchant class were creating a generation of intellectual beings with the time to read and explore on a daily basis. And this also includes the rise in popularity of the theaters in England and Spain as evidenced by the popularity of Shakespeare. With the age of specialization creating more leisure time for man, art becomes, for the first time, merely a leisure activity. And as leisure activity became associated with the upper class, the arts were also segmented into fine arts and common arts or high and low art, with fine or high art placing as much emphasis on the form as on the subject matter. And this division has remained the primary battle or tension in art, especially writing, the discussion in regards to subject versus technique. This tension is best seen when white critics attempt to analyze and value art by people of color. Placing their own culture, values, or standards on the form and structure of the art created by non-whites has created a tradition or legacy of whites marginalizing African and African American art. What the art says about the artists and the community is the focal point of African and African American art, and this is also true of all art. When we study art, we are studying a people's desire to say something about themselves and their experiences as well as the tension that exists between what a people want to say and the means, tools, and abilities to articulate that message.

Many scholars will say that this statement makes form and structure far too secondary to message, for it is the form and structure that allows the message to be articulated. This is true. But before you have form and structure, you must have something to say or show. In fact, it is the message that dictates to the form or structure. Forms and structures change because times and messages change. This has been the primary misunderstanding of art. This is why, very often, academies and universities are not always the best place for an artist to develop. The university addresses what has been. It is a museum. To be blunt, the only way to study something is if it is dead or no longer evolving. We can not dissect living animals. It is difficult to dissect living art. This is the problem with overly applying the scientific approach to art. Critics are scientists not artists. To paraphrase Friedrich Von Schiller in his poem "Human Knowledge," the scientist can only group. They can only tell you when, where, and how. They can not tell you why. Critics are not philosophers. Critics are scientists. For as Aristotle puts it, the true philosopher is the poet because the poet addresses meaning; I extend this definition to all artists. Universities typically produce scientists not artists. The streets produce artists. All streets produce artists, the streets of Africa, the streets of Asia, the streets of Europe, the streets of the Americas. A university can not make you an artist. Yet, they do serve their purpose even in the minor development of an artist.

Dr. Iely Mohamed and Dr. Rosalie Daniels, both professors at Jackson State University, constantly stressed to me that before you can break the rules, you must show that you can follow and master the rules. This is where an artist first gains his respect. As much as the vernacular and the individuality in me wishes to disagree, I must agree. All artists create in some form. We all have a particular calling. This is not to say that some do not have more callings than others or can not master more than one medium. This is to say that when we do create, we create in a form. It is the form that gives order and structure to the work. It is the form that makes it palatable or accessible to the receiver. Form also makes it easier for a receiver to begin getting his brains around the artist's work. When a receiver approaches a particular work, certain bells and alarms are sounded, preparing the receiver for the work. Just the utterance of certain forms, poetry, fiction, music, painting, and sculpture, causes an immediate reaction in the body. Form allows us to prepare ourselves for a work. The problem arises when form begins to regulate how we feel about a certain piece. When a particular piece breaks form, it tends to cause us trouble with digesting it. That is, critics are not able to categorize is so they marginalize it. When I first read *Cane* by Jean Toomer, I could not get my brain around it because it was not of a particular form. It engaged and incorporated many forms. It adhered to no form. Possibly, then, it is a form in and of itself. Even today when I read criticism on the piece, I am still bothered when critics call it a novel. It is not a novel in any terms or definitions of a novel that I have read. And yet, I will admit that I am basing my definitions of a novel on a Westernized, Eurocentric definition of novel that comes after the age of specialization. What Toomer does with *Cane* seems to be acceptable by ancient African traditions of improvisation, which, of course, continues today as evident in jazz and what rap performers call free-styling. Unfortunately, in the literary world, especially the academic world, critics tend to marginalize or minimize works if they do not adhere to a certain form. Rather than aiding us, criticism, as it is understood, often restricts us because it restricts the artist based on subjective, cultural notions.

Now, I am not blind to the game of academy based/controlled scholarship. I understand that most critics are artists. And with the production of criticism they are merely doing what T.S. Elliot did in his essay "Tradition and the Individual Talent." All critics want to etch or carve a place for themselves and their likes. Criticism serves to create and maintain a canon. It assigns where one is and what one is. So to say that criticism is not subjective is absurd. It is probably the most subjective form of science if not a pseudo-science because usually the end desire is to assign value. When you assign value to art, you assign value to the artist, thus assigning value to the artist's race, community, nation, and lineage. The problem is that we do not say or admit this in the university classroom. We pretend that this is all objective reasoning and that objective reasoning alone brought us to the particular anthology of a class. The truth is that criticism is the highest form of cultural warfare. From the moment Hegel proclaims "Africa had nothing to do with civilization," cultural warfare through the arts was waged. From this moment, intellects of European descent and African descent have been studying and writing to win the battle of race superiority through artistic superiority.

> "James Weldon Johnson states explicitly that African people must create literature because it is, inevitably, a fundamental aspect of their larger struggle for civil rights, and it can never escape this role because it serves as *prima facie* evidence of the Negro's intellectual potential. A people become great through many means, but there is only one measure by which greatness is recognized and acknowledged. The final measure of the greatness of all peoples is the amount and standard of the literature and art they have produced. The world does not know that a people is great until that people produces great literature and art. No people that has produced great literature and art has ever been looked upon by the world as distinctly inferior" (Gates and McKay xxxv).

Johnson's statements seem to sound contradictory to those of Booker T. Washington when he uttered "No race can prosper till it learns that there is as much dignity in tilling a field as in writing a poem" (Gates and McKay, 514). But Washington is articulating a sense of utilitarianism that is an organic or innate or inherent part of African artistry. When you understand the phrase "as much dignity," you understand that for Washington, W.E.B. Du Bois, and Marcus Garvey, artistic expression was a key to racial dignity and survival. Even Du Bois in his essay "Two Novels" asserts the notion that African artists have a duty and responsibility to create art that moves beyond merely being beautiful to being useful. In fact, as Larry Neal, Hoyt W. Fuller, and Maulana Karenga will articulate forty years after Du Bois, in order for art to be beautiful it must first be useful. And, this is why artistic criticism is the highest form of cultural warfare. As Aristotle asserts that the beauty of the play is man's recognition of himself, it is the nature of every artist to create the "talking book" for his people. Seeing ourselves in a positive and beautiful light is beautiful. Art is the magnifying glass of a people, of a culture.

Yet, often the discussion of art is not about showing beauty but is often an attack on a particular culture by attacking the art that the culture produces. Instead of saying what a piece is not, critics should say what it is. Critics are quick to say that a piece is not something as if that, in itself, makes it a bad or ineffective piece. I am often intrigued when a piece is not like something that has been. Immediately, I begin to wonder, what circumstances in the universe conspired to make this new or different thing occur or exist. Of course, we know that nothing under the sun is totally new. But times, spaces, and places allow new formations of familiar things in such a way that the amalgamated thing is new. Unfortunately, the creators or patrons of the older, more established style dislike the new creation because it is new. Newness represents evolution and a need for man (different generations of man) to produce something that is his own, that makes a particular and specific statement about his certain existence. We must understand that whatever we do not like about the art, there is something in that particular culture that we do not like. So if a piece of art does not suit your fancy, this often occurs because something in that particular culture does not suit your fancy. In discussing a work of art we should primarily be concerned with how well the work reflects the culture, what it says about the culture, and the writer's mastery and use of his particular cultural artifacts, including language. It must be understood that we can not do the latter of these three if we do not have a clear and objective understanding of the culture. I often wonder if the critic does not do this because he does not believe that the receiver will understand the message because he is not culturally astute enough to understand, appreciate, and articulate that understanding to a receiver. Or, is it just that the critic is a failed, bitter artist who can not affect change with his art and now attempts to affect change with his criticism. We forget that value judgments are subjective and should be resigned to the personal taste of each individual and are counter-productive in any discussion of art where the attempt is to gain an understanding of the art—what it is. If we are truly going to have this scientific approach to art, let us not be hypocritical. The literary scientists (critics) should only give us the properties of the art, and we, the patronizing public, can decide its value to us based on how it relates to our individual lives and existences. Some people want good (useful) art. Some people want art purely for pleasure. Both of these are still value judgments. A critic's job is to tell the receiver what the art is to the best of his historical understanding. If I want revolutionary art that causes a catharsis in me, then so be it. If I want escapism that allows me to forget my pain, then so be it. It is not for the critic to decide what is best for the public. The critic only studies, dissects, and presents his "objective" findings to the public. But, this will not truly happen until criticism becomes a means of informing, enlightening, and educating receivers with an earnest attempt to be a receiver's aid in understanding all art and not the mouth piece of cultural warfare.

Far too often when we categorize art, we tend to leave out the human element of change or evolution. Man lives in a circular relationship with his environment. His environment affects him, and he affects his environment. The events in his environment affect him, causing him to affect change in the art. Art, also, affects change in man. Then, these changes in man, again, affect changes in the environment which affect changes in art, and so on. As one of my former professors at the University of Southern Mississippi, Mr. Michael May, once said, "It is an 'I push you-you pull me' relationship between cultures and men that directs and drives art." So, then, form and structure are created from the lives of men. Thus, I assert that form and structure should be taught with a more existentialistic perception of culture. The value of form and structure amounts to what is effective in achieving a desired effect for artists and for their generation. So, when that form and structure ceases to be affective in articulating a message, then that form and structure becomes obsolete. Though I know that this sounds extremely pragmatic, we must realize that effective art is a practical art. For what good is art for art's sake if no one can understand it other than the artists and those who believe that good art is art which is difficult for the lay person or non artist to understand?

So, then, what is art? Art is the conscious use of skill and creative imagination used to create beauty, represent some aspect of life, be useful to mankind, and express one's personal individuality. Art is not necessarily what you do, but how and why you do what you do. When art is created, man is reacting to and attempting to order his world. Yet, the act of ordering his world through art is what creates the circular relationship between environment, man, and art. We begin with people. Once there is a certain amount of people living in an area, then that area becomes a community and takes on certain communal characteristics based on their particular needs and desires. These characteristics develop into behavior patterns. These behavior patterns have to do with how the people in this area decide to govern the social, political, economic, and religious aspects of their lives. All of this is called social theory which governs the people's hierarchy of needs. Art then grows from this social theory, these behavior patterns. When an artist creates, he is only making one of two statements. He is saying, "I like my environment, and I want to celebrate and share it with you." Or, he is saying, "There are some problems with my environment, and these are the specific issues that we need to address." Every thing that an artist says and does falls under these two statements. Yet, the argument can be made for a third category which would be called skepticism, the questioning of everything. This is when an artist, not in an attempt to assign a value judgment, creates art that rises from his questioning of the happenings and occurrences in his environment that seem to defy logic or the logic of his environment. Yet, since skepticism seems to always be attempting to get at what things are not, it might be placed in the second category since skepticism is generally used to disprove certain beliefs. I am open, however, to leaving this as a third, autonomous category. The final point to be plotted on this circle is artistic theory. Artistic theory is the governing principles which evolve from the particular culture of the art that we use to create art that best articulates or represents the particular culture. This is our form and structure of art. When all of these points are plotted, we have the art circle as represented below.

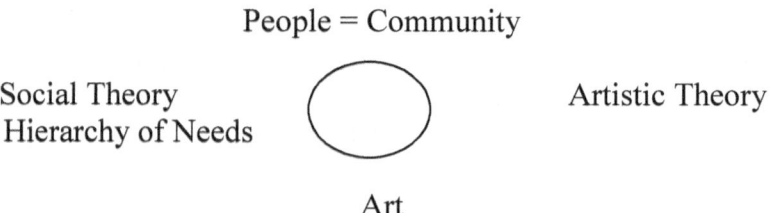

People = Community

Social Theory   Artistic Theory
Hierarchy of Needs

Art

It is important to understand this evolution or relationship that art has to people so that we are better able to produce a more effective art as artists, teach others how to produce effective art, and teach others how best to read and interpret the art. And yet while we need to understand form, we must also understand that form is only half of the equation. Writing or the activity of writing is merely a form of art, an art form. To put it another way, it is merely one of the forms in which art becomes manifest. Art exists in the mind and the soul of man. It is metaphysical by nature. Yet, this metaphysical thing, which is art, needs an outlet, a medium through which it can be expressed and shared. This too is the nature of art. To understand this, we must change our primary understanding of man as a physical being with a soul to man as a spiritual being having a physical experience. The soul or spirit man has some experience which produces art: it reads a book, it hears a sound, it hears music, it sees something happen, or something happens to it. These occurrences in our lives cause us to create art. Art is our reaction and commentary to our existence and experience. So, the spirit man, the soul of the person, receives and formulates art. This is the first nature of art. The second nature of art is that it demands to be shared. The need to share our art has to do with our relationship to God and/or the universe. I take and rework Plato's notion of reality inasmuch as I believe that the physical world is merely a copy of some Ideal. The physical world is the manifestation of some metaphysical Ideal. For instance, when God creates man, he constructs a body from earth, but man is not living until God Breathes life into him. If that life that is in man is the breath of God, then our spirit man is a part of God, is God. Art then is our making sense of the universe. It is God's attempt to rejoin himself inside us. So the art that is given to man is God's attempt to talk to man or man's attempt to make sense of this world/life that he has been given. Art, then, is the work of God, is the work of the universe. Yet, I must go further than a reworking of Plato's notion of reality and art to affirm my belief in Aristotle's notion of reality and art. Man is the only physical being created by the hands of God. Everything else is created by the word, is spoken into being. The artist, in this case the poet, is God-like in that

19

he, as Aristotle would put it, completes reality. So not only are we expressing and sharing our art when we make it manifest in the physical, we are helping to recreate or redefine reality, thus, giving us the notion that art both reflects and affects life. For the poet, writing becomes his tool to reflect, affect, and recreate or complete life. The form is merely the manner in which we manifest our ideas.

There are, in a real sense of language, only two forms of writing, poetry and the essay. A poem is a riddle elevated to its highest forms. It is a three dimensional puzzle layered in form, imagery, and style. What separates poetry from prose is ambiguity. Fiction, then, is poetry. The term poetry was always used to represent both fiction and poetry. When Plato demands the banning of poets in his *Republic*, it is understood that this includes everyone having to do with the creation of imaginative literature. So then, there are really only two kinds of literary works, poetry and the essay. The difference is that the essay is never intended to be ambiguous. The essay is always written to be taken literally. Furthermore, the essayist whose work is not to be taken or understood literally is either a poor writer or purposely hiding his message and intent for some certain reason. These essayists who are not poor writers are cowards. For they propose to a receiver some literal articulation on a subject, but hide their message from fear of reproach from society or their peers.

So why is it important to understand the various aspects and purposes of writing? "Writing, many philosophers argued in the Enlightenment, stood alone among the fine arts as the most salient repository of 'genius,' the visible sign of reason itself. In this subordinate role, however, writing, although secondary to reason, was nevertheless the medium of reason's expression" (Gates and McKay xxx). Writing is there before everything else is in place to have an advanced, centralized, and ordered civilization. Before you can have a form of government, laws, treaties on science, medicine, and agriculture, you need writing. Writing is the form that makes all of these other ideas tangible. Once they are tangible, they can be evolved even further. This is the importance of writing, and this notion of writing's importance dates back even further to the great Egyptian civilization. Much of the reason why Egypt is still a mystery is because of the believed sacredness of writing. Writing, in Egypt, as in many other civilizations to follow, was a highly sacred and guarded skill with a very few and select members of the society, namely the priests, being allowed to know all of the alphabet, let alone being able to read.

> "Dating back to the Meroe whose civilization was probably anterior to Egypt...secret societies, actually societies of secrets, often had their own scripts. As symbol systems for sacred occasions, these scripts are often under the control of specially trained and consecrated priests. Ancient Africans believed that the deity Djehuti, who became the Greek Hermes, invented writing...Writing brought with it so much power and influence that the ancient Africans reserved the knowledge and the skill for priests and kings" (Asante and Abarry 2).

So when Egypt is finally conquered by the Roman Empire in 3 BC and again by the Arabs in the seventh century AD, its culture is destroyed from the top. Thus, the priests, guardians of the written word, are killed and enslaved, leaving the Egyptian language and its culture to remain locked away as hidden treasures of the world. Yet, this idea of the sacredness of language perpetuates itself into the Yoruba culture with Eshu and the signifying monkeys. Eshu, the God of writing, is a type of middle man who acts as a liaison for the gods and for man. Eshu's presence demonstrates the power, purpose, and responsibility that humanity has to use language to create an effective world.

21

The importance of writing, particularly poetry, can also be found in the ancient Chinese government. Influenced by the teachings of Confucius, the Chinese implemented a set of examinations which became the first civil service tests. These examinations were entirely literary and required knowledge of the ancient classics and the technique of writing poetry. So, the very government of China was founded on respect for poetic skill as evident by one of the highest offices one could hold, Member of the Forest of Pens. Even further, this whole notion of the sacredness of writing is the entire essence of Martin Luther's attack on the Church of England and Luther's desire to share this society of secrets to the common man. It even lays the foundation for European scholars, such as David Hume and Immanuel Kant and even Thomas Jefferson, to wage war against the intellect of the African by denying their historical accomplishments in writing. Writing, more than any other medium, allows for preciseness in emotional and mental articulation that other genres can not deliver. Other forms of art such as painting or sculpture capture moments in time. And while a picture may be worth a thousand words, it merely reflects a mood or an event. Writing allows you to get within the mood, thoroughly explaining the mood. With phonemes, language becomes less subjective than any other art form. Thus, to create literature is to demonstrate a higher form of intellect, which includes the ability to shape and remake the world.

It must be argued that all art forms can be both literal and figurative. Yet writing is different in that it attempts to assign specific meaning to singular utterances. Even in the complex world of music where notes and chords have understood meaning, a note or a chord will never always have some fixed or attached meaning to it. Even when a language dies or evolves, a language can, at any point or period, be open to empirical study because of a fixed assignment to each individual utterance. So, writing is the most specific, by nature, making it the most scientific medium for sharing and expressing thought. Take for instance the word "gay." Before the 1960s the word "gay" was primarily used to identify someone as being happy. Even though this word's denotation and connotation have evolved or changed, we can specifically plot this word on some language graph that allows us to gain an understanding of it as it relates to a certain time period and cultural use. Since we understand the specific relationship of culture to language and language to culture, we know that words have denotative and connotative meanings that change and evolve as culture changes and evolves. Yet, because every root word has some basic, dare I say indigenous definition in a particular culture, we can plot the changes. Probably the most vivid example of this is the word "nigger." This word continues to befuddle the world. It totally perplexes so many African Americans because they can not understand how a word of such a negative and derogatory origin and nature became a word of endearment to those for whom the word was used, from their inception and indoctrination into the American culture, to degrade them and place them into a permanent psychological illusion of inferiority and second class citizenship to everyone else. Probably James Baldwin explains this happenstance best in his book with Margaret Mead, *A Rap on Race*, when he asserts that the term "nigger" became a badge of honor and courage for many African Americans as an affront to the consistent debasement of African American being. This is much in the way that Frederick Douglass discusses how "we cooked the chicken and they gave us the skin." African Americans have learned to fashion an existence from the discarded scraps of White America. So, the attempt to capture and redefine the word "nigger" is an attempt by some African Americans to gain power through the language, which culminates with the Rap group, Nigga's with Attitudes (NWA) and Tupac Shakur's remolding and refashioning of the term "thug" and his "Thug Life" ideology.

23

This whole notion of a word being defined one way by one group of people and then being redefined in just the opposite way by a second group of people gets at the very nature of writing and language. As a noun, language, itself, is a thing as much as it is a concept, which causes it to be an ongoing discourse which emerges from the lives of people to order their world. We begin with a notion, concept, or happenstance and need words to define and discuss the notion, concept, or happenstance. Every other art form is used to express and share, but only writing meticulously articulates what the "it" is. Yet, the problem lies in the fact that only language is used to discuss itself. We do not use painting to discuss poetry. We do not use music to discuss poetry. We use language to discuss poetry. We use language to discuss painting. We use language to discuss music. Language is the thing created to articulate (make physical) the simple and complex essence of who we are, and writing is its tool. Yes, I am separating language from writing. It is important to understand that language, as with art, begins in the metaphysical. Language has the same origin and inception as described herein for art. This is because language is first poetry or in the least poetic by nature. It is poetic by nature because it is tropical. Although language evolves from an arbitrary system of naming as Plato attempts to show in *Cratylus* when he asserts "that the knowledge of things is not to be derived from names. No, they must be studied and investigated in themselves" (Adams 47), second and third generation words, words coined or evolved after the establishment of a culture and not a part of the indigenous or original language which help to establish the culture, are generally not truly arbitrary. They are not arbitrary in that they are created from words with fixed definitions and new occurrences in the culture where something new is needed to effectively and specifically represent the new and unique occurrence. The term "downsize" best fits this category of second and third generation words. Both "down" and "size" have origins outside the American culture, but the term "downsize" is a second or third generation term that is indigenous to this capitalistic society used to represent some happenstance that is unique to this culture. Now some will argue, as Plato did in *Cratylus* that "downsizing" is an arbitrary term because its root words are arbitrary. That is, the term/sign "down" has no organic relationship to the notion of "down," and the same holds true for the term "size." With the notion of "down" and "size" as separate terms, I agree. But, the new word "downsize," which is based on embedded, cultural definitions, is not arbitrary because it is a real attempt to get at what the terms name or signify. "Downsize" names an action that can be discussed in this culture by the terms "down" and "size." Therefore language, even though it has arbitrary beginnings, comes closest to the specific representation of the thoughts and emotions of man and its changes and evolutions. In fact, in its nature, it is the perfect balance between arbitrary, symbolic, and objective signifying. This is why we can say that language is tropical. A word or term is not only concerned with what the thing or action is, but also with the thing's or action's relationship to man and his world. Thus if either an artist or a scientist is truly concerned with precisely articulating what the world is he must be concerned with a mastery of the preciseness of language for ideas must be carried in the vessel of language, and a flawed vessel creates a flawed/ineffective message.

Language is a symbol, a tool used to represent the notions, ideas, and concepts of man. Man is not slave to the tool. Language is slave to man. Language is a systematic means of communicating ideas or feelings by the use of conventionalized signs, sounds, gestures, or marks having understood meaning. There are three key words to this definition of language which help us to understand that language is tropical and that the arbitrary nature of language poses no real problem for man because language exists for the fancy of men and not vice versa. These terms are systematic, conventionalized, and understood. These three terms implicitly inform us that language is based on an agreement which develops over time and place. It grows from man's need to order his world. And when the commonly used language no longer orders his world or is able to adequately represent his world, it is either discarded like old clothes or is changed, modified, or evolved. For instance, many, such as Amiri Baraka, have held that the name of the language that Americans speak needs to be changed from English to American or American English or American Vernacular even. The English that was spoken here when the first English settlers arrived was changed immediately because it was not the indigenous language of this land. It was placed on top of Spanish, French, the language of the Native Americans, and the various languages of all of the Africans who either came before Columbus or who were brought here as uprooted slaves. The language of the English settlers was never allowed to grow roots here in its purest form. English became the unofficial language of the colonies, but even then there was an ongoing redefining of the language because of the need to communicate with other settlers as well as with Native Americans and Africans. A slave can not do anything unless you tell him what to do. What begins to happen is that we have English semantics placed within the context of the syntax of another language. So, English words would be placed within an African sentence structure and produce something new. So then, V.F. Calverton, a Marxist critic, is correct when he asserts that "the Negro's music and folk art were never 'purely imitative,' and that black vernacular cultural forms were 'definitely and unequivocally American,' the only 'original' American culture yet created" (Gates and McKay xxxiv). And I go further where both Calverton and Gates stop short to assert that black vernacular is the second language created on the lands of the Americas, the first being the languages of the Native Americans. So, Baraka is right when he asserts that we need to begin retraining ourselves and the country in the

26

notion of the black vernacular. "[Richard] Wright, too, would repeat this claim. If black writers turned to their own vernacular traditions, he concluded, black literature could be as original and as compelling as black music and folklore" (Gates and McKay xxxiv). African novelist Chinua Achebe articulates it best when he asserts:

"What I do see is a new voice coming out of Africa, speaking of African experience in a world-wide language. So my answer to the question *Can an African ever learn English well enough to be able to use it effectively in creative writing?* is certainly yes. If on the other hand you ask: *Can he ever learn to use it like a native speaker?* I should say, I hope not. It is neither necessary nor desirable for him to be able to do so. The price of a world language must be prepared to pay submission to many different kinds of use. The African writer should aim to use English in a way that brings out his message best without altering the language to the extent that its value as a medium of international exchange will be lost. He should aim at fashioning out an English which is at once universal and able to carry his peculiar experience. I have in mind here the writer who has something new, something different to say. The nondescript writer has little to tell us, anyway, so he might as well tell it in conventional language and get it over with. If I may use an extravagant simile, he is like a man offering a small, nondescript routine sacrifice for which a chick, or less, will do. A serious writer must look for an animal whose blood [language] can match the power of his offering" (Asante and Abarry 383).

These statements, coming from Wright and Achebe, are not to be taken lightly. When Wright releases *Native Son* in 1940, he becomes the most noted, celebrated writer on the planet as attested to by both Theodore Dreiser and William Dean Howells. When Achebe releases *Things Fall Apart* (1958) and *Arrow of God* (1964), he perfects the fiction following in the line of the Negritude Movement that articulates the notion that there are both exterior and interior forces working to evolve or change cultures, and it is up to the artists to adequately articulate, specifically, what these forces are and how they are changing the culture. They become the best writers not by copying, mimicking, or imitating someone else's language and culture but by creating from their own language pool. This is not to say that Negro, Black, African American language and culture are some completely separate creatures from the standard language of American whites. In fact, very few Caucasian Americans speak the language that is commonly referred to as standard English. This is to say that the language spoken by most Americans is organic to their unique American existence. Even Hawthorne and Melville understood this when they were imploring the writers of the American colonies to write about the new world. Because the African American existence is uniquely different from that of Caucasian Americans, it must be understood that this difference produces a different culture and a different type of American language. If we understand that the best art is art produced in earnest that shows its organic relationship to the artist and the environment, we understand that language is merely a tool of man to best relate this experience and relationship to the receiver. Yet, if one is from one existence and attempts to produce art from an existence that is foreign to his, the art will be merely a shell with no essence. For he has reversed the process and placed the emphasis on the structure and the form and not on the essence of the life, making the art that he produces dead on arrival because it has no soul, only a body which is the form. Wright and Achebe become the best writers of their eras because they understand the relationship of language and culture. Their accomplishment is the best example of the best intentions and accomplishments of the Negritude Movement.

The Negritude Movement grows from the need of Africans to have their work studied and critiqued on its own merits and culture and not by the merits and culture of Europeans. The first time that I read *Arrow of God* by Achebe, I completely missed the messages and the poetics from being consumed by the social structure of the Africans, more specifically the marriage structure. By going to an Achebe work with a very Westernized, Eurocentric mind set, I was unable to get beyond certain basic social differences in the book which hindered me from judging the book on its artistic merits. All my life I had heard of the notion of bigamy only in a negative manner. The notion of a man having more than one wife was wrong. So, because the book's central character is a man married to several wives, I judged the work negatively because of my ill feelings about bigamy and anyone involved in bigamy. The same held true for the notion of ancestor worship. Again, to my Westernized and Christianized mind, this pagan activity was too foreign for my narrow scope. The combination of bigamy and ancestor worship caused me to discontinue my initial reading of *Arrow of God*. This is what the Negritude Movement of the 1930s sought to change. Lead by writers such as Leopold Sedar Senghor, "Negritude was an anti-assimilationist African literary movement that promoted a return to Africa's distinctive values and culture" (Rosenberg 340). Its goal was to promote the beauty and value of Africa, causing Africans and African Americans to look toward a more Africentric way of creating their art. The works often "speak of the beauty of Africa and its women, the protective guidance of the dead in the lives of the living, the destructive effect of European colonization on African culture, the need for cultural interdependence, and the world's need for Africa's special qualities of passion and spontaneity" (Rosenberg 340). The champions of Negritude understood that as long as African writers are judged by standards and cultures other than African, their works will always be received and viewed negatively. Thus one of the duties of the cultural critic is to teach others outside the particular culture how the philosophies of the culture are influencing the art created by that culture.

Although there always will be cultural differences which separate and make for diversity in writing and reading, the writer is warned not to use Negritude or any other cultural theory or understanding to justify being overly self indulgent. Self indulgence in writing is writing for the sake of writing. It is creating art for the sake of creating art. It is creating art in a vacuum that relates and connects to no one but the writer in some vague, obtuse, abstract way that even he fails to be able to articulate or ascertain some understanding. Poetry, more so than fiction, has oft times fallen prey to this, that notion of if you do not understand it, then it must be great art. All art will begin as some specific, individual form of expression. This is because events, problems, or issues do not truly gain our attention or raise our interest until it happens to one of us on a personal level. Conservative African Americans generally do not become revolutionaries until injustice happens along their path. Racism is not an issue until it is you who are denied the job or admittance into a university on the basis of race. Then, race is a problem with which "WE" must deal. So, then, the writer has to experience something to produce art. In the production of the art, the artist must make it manifest in the physical in some manner that he effectively articulates the message of the art to the receiver. If not, the artist has failed. Self indulgence usually occurs when a writer becomes selfish or too overly impressed with his own skill, work, or his own life. (This, I must admit, is my greatest failing, my inability to balance my individual whims and concerns with the concerns of the receiver.) This causes his work to be guided by the whims of his fancy and not the desires and needs of the receiver.

This is not to say that the artists does not have the right and duty to follow the voices in his head and heart, but the artist must understand that to chart a course too far away from what the masses want is often artistic suicide or, at the best, delayed or deferred appreciation of his work.

This of course begs the question *Is art well crafted because it is popular?* Art is generally popular when it comments on or shows the lives of a certain group or number of people. Art does well or is accepted by a mass audience when it defines or effectively articulates some truth about a certain group of people. Thus, all great work will at some time be popular. The term "great," however, unlike the term "well-crafted" is a more subjective term. How is a work judged to be great? Somebody, somewhere, at some time decides that it is great based on certain arbitrary and subjective factors and standards. Yet, almost always one of the factors will be the artist's or work's ability to speak to and express the lives of a particular group. This will generally be the group that has economic, political, and social power and autonomy. This means two things. You do not have to be considered great or popular in your time to be judged great or popular by following generations. Also, there have been and always will be those artists, who were popular or judged to be great during their time, who have lost their appeal and influence over following artists. So, then, maybe influence is our key term. Besides general popularity, an artist will be judged as being great or well crafted by the influence that he has over his peers and artists who follow. True greatness is one's ability to influence. The number of artists following in that particular artist's footsteps determines greatness. Thus, an artist can be good (useful) to his times, but not great because of the limited amount of influence he has on others following his generation. Does this mean that an artist can single-handedly define a particular time and not be great? Yes. Greatness is only achieved when generations continuously look to you for guidance. So, then, does this make the European writers such as Shakespeare and Milton the greatest poets of all time. This is a question that can not be answered because criticism is cultural warfare based on subjective notions of race and intellect. Shakespeare may not be the greatest, but merely one of several shining White Knights used to etch into the minds of the global community the superiority of Europe. That is, only when Africans are given their true credit for their role in founding global civilization, and African writers are taught with the same clarity, enthusiasm, and consistency of European writers will we be able to have an intelligent/objective (earnest discourse) discussion on world cultures and the rightful place of certain writers. I have a great admiration for much of the work of Shakespeare, but it is only because I have an appreciation of his work which comes from a consistent, systematic, and thorough education of him and his culture. I hesitate to discuss his greatness in relation to the global community because no other writer or writer's culture has been or is now given the same treatment in American culture or in the American public school system. So the question is not just whether or not a writer influences others but what is the cause of that influence, and is that influence due to something other than the writer's ability. So, using literary criticism as cultural warfare actually taints Shakespeare in a similar way that Ty Cobb and Babe Ruth's legacies are tainted. Because Cobb and Ruth were kept from competing against the best in an open and objective forum, then we can never fully judge the greatness of their accomplishments. Similarly, because other writer's cultures have been marginalized merely for being non-white, then we have also limited our ability to fully understand the place of Shakespeare and Milton.

There is also a group of writers whom we cannot forget, those writers who achieve some form of greatness not because of their skill but because of their place in time and history. Phyllis Wheatley was not a great writer. She was an effective writer, a writer who did deserve to be published. She was a skilled writer whose work adequately reflects a particular group and their time. Yet, Wheatley is not immensely popular with most African Americans today. Her poem, "On Being Brought from Africa to America," is not a very popular poem among African Americans. The fact that it seems to justify the means of slavery for her ends of becoming a Christian has never sat well with the core of African Americans. And additionally, Wheatley seems to be more concerned with pouring herself and her work into the mold of whiteness to prove or justify her humanity. By doing this, she is erasing that quality of which Achebe and Wright spoke, that creative uniqueness that all writer's must explore for a key element in being well crafted is in exploring and presenting something different or unique. Yet, Wheatley achieves some form of greatness because she is the first African American to publish a collection of poetry in English with her *Poems on Various Subjects, Religious and Moral* (1773). Being first makes her great because she broke new ground and opened doors for others. Whether it is style, form, subject matter, or some racial or cultural uniqueness, being first means that in some way one influences all others who may come later.

This questioning of good (useful) and great art gets us to the notion of the proper purpose of art. The inception of all art is to inform. If you date back all civilizations, the initial art is doing some sort of informing, recording, and myth making. The literature of every culture begins with the creation narrative or some form that deals with how man was created. So art begins with a very practical purpose. The next evolution of art has to do with social or community rituals. Again, this is another practical purpose. So, where, then, does our whole aesthetic notion of art begin? This is tricky because we can say that art has always had an aesthetic value because of the need to accurately reflect life, accurately reflect the truth. Remember Plato's "copy of a copy" theory. Even with the creation narratives and the social rituals, there is a need and a desire for the artist to accurately reflect what they know or believe to be the truth. So, we then affirm Keats' notion that Beauty is Truth and Truth is Beauty. Aristotle asserted to us that the beauty of the play is man seeing himself in the work. This is why even bawdy folklore ballads such as "The Sinking of the Titanic" and "Shine and the Titanic" have a resonating effect and reaction from African Americans. The beauty is the truth that these poems speak about the relationship between African Americans and white Americans. On the surface, they are stories about the supposedly illiterate Negro who has enough "common" sense to out think the whites who attempt to make a fool of him. Underneath the story is a commentary about the daily existence of African Americans and their daily cat and mouse relationship with white Americans, having constantly to do certain things to pacify the fears and angers of white America in order to survive. Little Richard would comment that when the white men saw his big, black buck musicians coming into the club, the white men would get on their guard until they saw that those big black bucks were with him. Shine is the embodiment of the African American masquerade of being less intelligent and passive in order to survive. At the same time, Shine is a celebration of the African American intellect because he always outsmarts the whites and is the only one left surviving. A modern version of this intellectual cat and mouse game is the *Jack Bennie Show*. It is understood throughout the series that Rochester, Bennie's servant, is always one step ahead of Bennie for the sake of the survival of his job, as well as for the sake and survival of Bennie and the household. The difference between the two is that Shine, written from an Africentric point of view, reflects the anger of African Americans because the whites always die in a Shine poem. The beauty, for African Americans, is in the presenting of the true feelings that art allows them to do with less repercussions.

So art informs and entertains, yet its true power lies in its ability to direct, influence, or persuade. Thus, art is by nature propaganda. If we date ourselves back to the time of the Egyptian King Zoser (Netjerikhet Djoser), when hieroglyphics and art had evolved to their apex, there already seems to be this notion of art's ability and purpose to influence humanity's thought and behavior. And this is especially true of a poem such as "The Hymn to the Aton" by King Akhenaton, which was written for the specific purpose of changing the national religion from polytheistic to monotheistic which would also allow Akhenaton to gain greater political power. Understanding that since hieroglyphics is picture writing, the Egyptians chose to emphasize the best of man or the best of their people, which is an act of propaganda. Many of their principles that govern painting and sculpture also govern their writing process. So we find that the principles of visibility, straightness of line to indicate youth and health, symmetry which relates to balance, ephebism which relates to the idealized age, smoothness which relates to the showing of the body in the idealized form, and hypermimesis which relates to showing the general resemblance of the body are all, in various forms, incorporated into writing through hieroglyphics. By the time of Zoser, the statues of the rulers were created as a way to show them in an ideal state, and the inscriptions were used to promote the divinity of the rulers. Following that trend, the Egyptian artists of the twenty-five thirties BC were not interested in showing movement as this term is understood today. Standing figures are not posed as if they are walking but rather at rest, in a more serene or ideal state. From the beginning of the dynastic period, human anatomy was understood but given an ideal form. The same is true with hieroglyphics which became a combination of recording events as well as the Egyptians crafting themselves into a more idealized state. And four thousand years later Du Bois, in his essay "The Criteria of Negro Art," attempts to affirm that "all art is propaganda" (Gates and McKay 757). When he makes this statement, it must be understood that Du Bois is in the midst of waging a war for the first class citizenship of African Americans. He views art as a vital tool for fixing the negative image of African Americans. This is obvious when he blasts Claude McKay's *Home to Harlem*.

> "Claude McKay's 'Home to Harlem'...for the most part nauseates me, and after the dirtier parts of its filth I feel distinctly like taking a bath...it looks as though,...McKay has set out to cater for that prurient demand on the part of white folk for a portrayal in Negroes of that utter licentiousness which conventional civilization holds white folk back from enjoying—if enjoyment it can be called. That which a certain decadent section of the white American world, centered particularly in New York, longs for with fierce and unrestrained passions, it wants to see written out in black and white, saddled on the black Harlem" (Gates and McKay 759-760).

Du Bois is taking that same line as the white philosophers took during the Enlightenment. Writing is the "most salient repository of genius." Du Bois' concern is that art that deals with what he sees as the lower bowels of life will be viewed as coming from a man with a mind fit only to discuss such things. McKay responds by asserting "I want to show the world that we love and fornicate just like everyone else." In this McKay is asserting that to show oneself as human is the best defense against rhetoric that says otherwise. So even in his disagreement with Du Bois, McKay is still asserting art as propaganda. Both Langston Hughes and Alain Locke come to McKay's defense and lay the foundation for the theory of the Black Arts Movement, which though divergent from Du Bois still sees art as propaganda. Hughes goes further to address the limitations placed on African American writers under this umbrella of purpose but does not reject the notion of art as propaganda. Hughes is not rejecting art as propaganda but more affirming Achebe and Wright's notion that in order for art/literature to work in the positive for African people, African people must first have a love or positive notion of themselves, which cannot be based or built on anybody else's notion of them. This disagreement between Du Bois and McKay and Hughes is ironic because Du Bois' notion of "double consciousness" is based on African people looking at themselves with the eyes and sensibilities of others. In his essay, "The Negro Artist and the Racial Mountain," Hughes addresses the circular relationship that art has with a people's need to develop a positive sense of self.

> "...no great poet has ever been afraid of being himself. But this is the mountain standing in the way of any true Negro art in America—this urge within the race toward whiteness, the desire to pour racial individuality into the mold of American standardization, and to be a little Negro and as much American as possible. The Negro artist works against an undertow of sharp criticism and misunderstanding from his own group and unintentional bribes from the whites. 'Oh, be respectable, write about nice people, show how good we are,' say the Negroes. 'Be stereotyped, don't go too far, don't shatter our illusions about you, don't amuse us too seriously. We will pay you,' say the whites. Both would have told Jean Toomer not to write *Cane*. Most of the colored people who did not read *Cane* hate it. They are afraid of it. Yet *Cane* contains the finest prose written by a Negro in America. And like the singing of Robeson and the tom-tom joy and laughter of Jazz, it is truly racial" (Gates and McKay 1267, 1270).

Locke ties this whole debate of purpose to time and taste.

"The Sociologist, the Philanthropist, the Race-leader are not unaware of the New Negro, but they are at loss to account for him. He simply cannot be swathed in their formulae. For the younger generation is vibrant with a new psychology; the new spirit is awake in the masses, and under the very eyes of the professional observers is transforming what has been a perennial problem into the progressive phases of contemporary Negro life" (Gates and McKay 961).

Art and its purpose evolve as man evolves. Yet, its primary role has always been to inform and order. Whether I am informing you about something negative or positive is a matter of subjective taste. Whether I have some duty to put forth some positive directive is a matter of subjective taste. Yet, we can not deny the power of art to influence. So, Du Bois is right when he states that all art is propaganda. Even *The Aeneid* by Virgil is national propaganda. Virgil's chief patron was Augustus, the first Roman Emperor. Through this patronage, Virgil became a court poet in 27 BC. Aeneas, the hero of the poem, is a personification of the most respected Roman virtues. Through the beauty and power of his work, Virgil is able to align many members of Rome's educated classes behind Augustus, directly aiding in the establishment and maintenance of Rome's new government under Augustus. This act of national patronage of artists includes such names as Li Po, Tu Fu, Horace, as well as Mozart and Beethoven. The National Endowment of the Arts and the National Endowment of the Humanities are not new organizations. The act of art as national propaganda can be pre-dated and recounted from as far back as the Egyptians need to create forms in an ideal state to Akhenaton's "The Hymn to the Aton" to the *Iliad* and the *Odyssey*, which had a great influence on transforming Greek Government, to the more literal works of James Weldon Johnson and his creation of the Negro National Anthem, "Lift Every Voice and Sing," and Claude McKay's "If We Must Die." Because art creates an image in the mind of the receiver, it simultaneously informs and influences how man sees himself. The choice of whether one wants to use their art for a particular social or political motive is a matter of one's philosophical understanding of the world. I say that although the primary purpose of art is to inform, my personal inclinations cause me to decide that the primary purpose of my art is to assist man in achieving transcendentalization. Only I can decide the primary purpose of my art, and so must every individual artist choose the primary purpose of his art. A work that is enlightening is not always entertaining, and just because an artist strives to be merely entertaining does not mean that he will fall short of being enlightening. The goal of the artist is to hone his individual talent in a manner that he can be enlightening without being overbearing and entertaining without being merely frivolous. By the nature of what art is, the artist will always inform whether he seeks to or not. The ability to entertain is based on the artist's skill level as much as it is based on how the skill and the subject matter are received or interpreted by the society.

This gets at the dual nature of poetry as a form of art. Poetry, as a form of art, is ambiguous, or it has an ambiguous nature. It is to mankind as a child is to a mother. It is an off-spring of mankind's existence. In its nature of being produced by man, it is a reflection, DNA if you will, of what mankind is. Yet, it is also something else, as children are something else. Art not only reflects in the manner of a mirror, it eventually has its own life, as evident in the white response to McKay's poem "If We Must Die." McKay wrote "If We Must Die" as a battle cry for African Americans. Little did he know that it would become an inspiration for white American soldiers. My first impulse is to say that this is ironic, given the fact that this poem was initially meant to stir the rages of African Americans against the oppression of white Americans. But, art is more, much more than a mirror, although it begins there. Art is a living, breathing "thing" because it is created from the mind and soul of a living breathing thing. Though the art does take the physical shape of poetry, the notions, ideas, and concepts represented by the words and the writing are living, evolving things that transform and evolve from receiver to receiver. So although poetry shows us who we are, it also completes us and helps to evolve us. This innate or organic evolution can be either negative or positive. Yet, "negative" and "positive" are such subjective terms because one man's anarchy is another man's revolution. So, we must speak more along the lines of intent, reaction, and end result. What is the intent of the poet? And, as we see with the McKay incident, intent of the poet is not the only factor controlling how a work is received. So then, the receiver and the receiver's social, political, religious, educational, and economic make-up also influence how a work is received. Though we talk about the art of writing, there can be no true discussion of the art of writing and the technique of the writer unless we give some discussion to the training of the receiver.

By the nineteen-eighties funding for the arts was drastically cut in public schools, especially those schools where a majority of the students are people of color. We must understand this cut in funding to public education as a symbol by the white ruling class of America as a method to perpetuate African American second-class citizenship. So the art that is created is produced within the philosophical and cultural matrix of the people. Thus, art is always reacting to the socio-political condition in which it is born. In the nineteen-eighties, the two hardest hit areas were music and literature. The fact that African American children do not have regular and open access to musical and literary training in the public schools and the fact that the cost of instruments and books rose sharply during the eighties caused a decline in African American youth wanting to learn to play instruments and become writers.

There was a time when there was a music band in every African American neighborhood. Now, with the lack of education and access to instruments, musicianship is being replaced by what is commonly called sampling. Sampling is accepted because the receivers of the music are not given the basic education of musicianship or instrumentation. At first glance, this may sound like an elitist statement. The truth is, though, that education breeds respect and respectability. There was a time when every fourth grader in America had to learn some art form in either art or music appreciation class. At this early period in our children's lives we are finding and nurturing our artists. Because of the severe decrease in funding for the arts to people of color, their children are not being given the opportunity to be nurtured and evolve in the pursuit of their particular craft. Also, without this base exposure and training in the arts, the receivers grow up with no type of objective notions about art. With no fundamental or basic training in the arts, receivers are forced to accept anything as art. We must understand that the training of receivers is as vital to the maintenance and evolution of quality art as the training of the artists. Without the watchful, knowledgeable eyes and ears of the receiver, the artists will not be forced or held to any system of checks and balances when it comes to creating and maintaining a standard for quality art. Knowledgeable receivers are able to hold the artists to a higher standard.

What becomes clear is the notion that both the creators and the receivers of art have a responsibility to educate themselves as much as possible. Both must take responsibility to bridge the gap of miscommunication. Thus, both creators and receivers of art must attempt to know as many of the writing techniques and genres as they can. Although reading is, of course, essential to the poet's knowledge of culture and history, reading is so fundamentally important that it must be given a sentence or two. If the new generation of African American poets have one failing it is that, as Charlie Braxton puts it, "Hip Hop artists are having a greater influence on poetry than the traditional line of poets are having on Hip Hop" (Braxton 1998). This is because too many young poets are relying too greatly on the spoken word medium of the coffee house and the Hip Hop genre and not dedicating enough time to reading. Young poets must understand that to hear the word is something completely different than to read the word. Reading is a discourse. This is why when one reads, it is recommended that one reads with a dictionary, pen, and paper handy. Hearing has more to do with emotionalism, and reading has more to do with intellectualism. When most young poets hear Tupac, they feel him in the emotion of his delivery more than they process him in the deepest recesses of their minds. To read Tupac is a greater intellectual experience than to hear Tupac. To read him is to do a thorough dissection of his message word by word rather than phrase by phrase or sound by sound. Reading is work as writing is work. Reading is work because one is attempting to synthesize terminology and concepts into a homogeneous creature of understanding. Reading and writing work in a circular relationship where one needs the other to exist and evolve. If a young writer is not reading both his peers and those who have come before him, he is not perpetuating his evolution as a writer. The writer must be well read.

Now, after defining art and writing and discussing their purposes, the question arises *What should art discuss?* This is, again, subjective. It is up to each individual artist to decide for himself what in life moves him and is worth the time of his art. But, each artist must have the courage to discuss his own existence. Understanding everything that I have said, it leaves us with some notion that on some level the production of art is an involuntary act of humanity. Mankind creates art as an involuntary reflex to living. Only the forms of art are voluntary, and they only become voluntary once man has become cognizant of the

42

stylized manner of creation. So, the birth of the message is involuntary, manifesting the message into some physical form is voluntary. Each artist has to decide whether or not he wants to articulate every message he receives from his different existences. If we take for instance a song (which is merely poetry set to music) such as "Fuck the Police" by NWA, we know that there are two real facts. The first is a real existence by a certain group of people which produces the art. That is, the mistreatment of African Americans by the police created the response (song). The second is the reaction to that experience by the artist. The artists, in this case NWA, must decide whether or not the situation is noteworthy, important to themselves and the lives of enough people to articulate. This is the first factor in deciding what one's art should discuss. Does this particular subject matter being discussed have some importance to a group of people? The other two factors are the intent of the artist and the artist's need or desire to express himself. Whether or not a writer has gone too far, said something that is vulgar or useless or dangerous, is a matter to be decided by the audience. Yet as T. S. Eliot asserted, "Only those who will risk going too far can possibly find out how far one can go." It is the job, often, of the artist to push the envelope so that we know where the boundaries are so that we have a better understanding of our identities and our sensibilities. Also, pushing the boundaries makes the society uncomfortable, which ultimately leads to discussion and change.

I digress here for a moment from the latter two factors to discuss the creation of art, specifically poetry, on the subject of sex as it relates to the general interest of the subject to any certain group of people. Simply, *Is the subject of sex an issue to be discussed by art?* Sex and violence are flashpoints that create great debate and turmoil. There will always be art about sex because people will always have sex because it is one of the highest forms of human enjoyment on all three planes of physical, emotional, and psychological gratification. It is one of the few activities and pleasures of the human existence that can simultaneously affect all three planes. Yet, as gratifying as sex is to the human experience, we must keep in mind that the most effective poems about sex are not the ones that deal merely with the physical gratification of sex, but those that also deal with the emotional and psychological issues connected to sex. As I have commented in the "Sex" chapter of my book, *The Lyrics of Prince*, when having sex there is rarely just the physical gratification being achieved. The act of sex is often some metaphoric or symbolic act to gain or achieve higher emotional, psychological, or spiritual needs. This is because sex and sexuality are primary to defining one's identity and ideology. In America, sex and sexuality are the focal points of its racist and sexist principles. Not to comment on sex is not to comment on life. Poems about sex are no different than poems about politics, other social relationships, religion, and God. Part of the interest is the subject matter. I will admit that the subject matter of sex and sexuality has a greater interest to mass receivers than politics or God. Yet, it is the artist's handling of the subject—his imagery and mastery of vernacular—that makes the poem memorable. In the case of Sonia Sanchez and Nikki Giovanni it is their ability to weave sexual tension and gratification into the fabric of political tension and gratification that gives the work its intensity. Or in the case of Li Po or Ovid, the pure use of imagery keeps you coming back, not the sex. In fact, an effective poem about sex is like sex, itself. We are all having sex, but it is the person who does it just a bit better or gives you something that no else gives you that causes you to return for more. The same is true for poetry.

The use of profanity is the same issue. Although the academy has taught us that the use of profane language represents a lack of vocabulary, many so called "great" and important poets have and continue to use language that is deemed profane. There are several reasons why this is so.

The primary reason is that it is still used by the masses of society. With the evolution of the Greek comedy as a separate and autonomous genre during the fifth century BC and Aristophanes' use of common citizens and common language, profanity becomes a staple or a technique in art as a way to represent common people who do not have the mastery of the language unlike the so called trained writers. So, then, profanity, along with sex and violence, has been long viewed as a way to identify with common people. Secondly, profanity gives the feeling of rebelling against certain established systems and established languages that promote oppression. Sonia Sanchez has often stated that "Capitalism has always been a more profane word than muthafucker." A colleague of mine, David Brian Williams, attorney and poet, often asserts that "there are no profane words only profane people and ideas" (Williams 1998). So, then, the use of profanity for some writers becomes a way to directly throw off or rebel against certain established systems that they deem as oppressive. In this same vein, then, profanity was traditionally used for shock value. The problem is that with overuse, the shock has worn thin from far too many writers using profanity as the poem and not the seasoning or flavoring of the poem. Finally, language is, again, a tropical thing. Profanity has been arbitrarily and tropically assigned as all of these. All of this, the subject of sex and the use of profanity, is still based on how the work, the subject matter or the use of certain tools and techniques affect and relate to the public. When using profanity, one must choose wisely, which means one must have a firm understanding of one's audience.

This discussion of purpose and subject matter of art gets us, briefly, into the discussion of how art, innately, gives voice to the voiceless. The artist, as does the other leaders of the community, gives a voice to the community. This is what I mean when I say that art is a reflection of society. It speaks about, to, and for the society. Yet, unlike other leaders, artists are able to make certain statements that the general populous cannot. Under the notion or guise of "artistic license" the artist is able to say the unspeakable, thus allowing the audience to live vicariously through the works or lives of its artists. Walking that thin line of fantasy and reality, artists are able to move between these two worlds creating and expressing an experience for the audience. Columnist Stanley Crouch once stated that after reading several letters from disgruntled readers, he was overcome with joy that these people could write because it allows them to release their angers without having to resort to violence. The mere expression of art acts as an outlet for the general populous. This is the feeling of "Right on!" or "Fitly spoken!" that we get when we read a work that affirms and expresses what we were thinking or feeling. However, this is a two way street because the audience guides or governs how far is too far. Traditionally, given the certain notions of particular societies, the boundaries for artists have been almost boundless and limitless. Often, the job of the artist is seen as raising certain issues and asking certain questions which the general populous is left to ponder an answer. Yet, there is always the question of whether or not to articulate a particular idea or viewpoint to the public. Does it say something to enough people about their particular existence? Next we consider the purpose, intent, or what effect the articulation of a specific subject will have on the receiver. This, again, is in line with the artist's intent for creating. Is it to be popular? Is it to make money? Is it to affect a real change in the community? The latter is very difficult because a writer who is also a member of a group like the Klan will believe that his goal of racial purity and the elimination of all non-whites is proper. Others, people of color, will believe his work to be negative and dehumanizing to himself and others. So, even this whole notion of purpose is subjective. The artist will have a purpose. His challenge is to gain and exhibit enough skill and talent to achieve his desired duty. Thus, the mastery of language and artistic technique provides the artist the ability to mold and shape difficult or controversial ideas in a manner that will at least allow the receiver to accept the examination of the ideas. Finally, the artist's need to express himself is a driving factor. We all know of the writer or poet at the "open mic" set who refuses to sit down even when it is obvious that no one else wants to hear him besides himself. This, of course, gets us back into the discussion of self indulgence. The artist has to walk a very fine line between what he wants and what the public wants. He has to find a way to balance the two. The key is to find a balance between these three, importance or relation of the subject matter to the receivers, the intent of the artist, and the artist's desire to express.

An artist is best able to navigate the above three issues when the artist remains as a part of a particular community rather than when he separates himself from that community. The largest failure of a poet is not when his skill goes but when he begins to be perceived as being obscure or dated, when his work no longer speaks for the mass of a particular people. Here again, I am resigning myself to the notion that even the term "dated" is a subjective and complex term. The question can be asked *Is an artist dated when he no longer has the concerns of his particular group?* This gets us into the notion of an artist outgrowing his community or his base audience. Is it the responsibility of the artist to find a way to articulate his message even if he is not beginning on common ground with his audience? One of the greatest compliments paid to Martin L. King, Jr. was his ability to communicate and articulate his message to all types of people from all walks of life. The artist, then, should always keep in mind that the message, the articulation of the art, is foremost important. His job is to find a way to continue to articulate the message. So, even if an artist outgrows or evolves faster than his base readership or what he perceives as his base readership, he has a duty to reach back and pull his audience forward with him as he progresses. As man evolves, art evolves. The artist, because he is privy to more access to certain information and opportunities to be informed and educated, does have a responsibility to pass this information to his readership if he wishes for them to continue to support him. The relationship between artist and receiver is a two way street with both having a mutual effect on the other. Accepting the notion that every artist is innately a student of his particular craft, he is affected by any changes and evolutions of his craft or changes or evolutions in the environment that affect changes in his craft. Because he is involved or engaged on a daily basis with the craft, his general intelligence and knowledge of the art evolves faster than the receiver who is in a daily involvement with survival, which often causes the receiver to place his understanding and mastery of art at the bottom of his hierarchy of need. The receiver of art relies on the artist to stay abreast of his field and bring those changes to him. This is not to say that the receiver does not have some responsibility to gain and maintain some fundamental knowledge of his favorite art form. As we have discussed above, an unlearned receiver will accept anything as art which will eventually hinder or hurt the art form. But, it is the artist who has the first responsibility of evolving just as other professionals have the first responsibility of evolving. Think of what our lives would be if doctors or lawyers or scientists or mechanics refused to grow or evolve. The same is true with art. The artist has both a responsibility to grow and to educate his receiver on the growth in the medium or genre. In this manner, artists will not outgrow their audiences but help to evolve their receivers to a higher state of being which is the natural process of art. Art helps us to understand the world in which we live thus allowing us to live better.

Works Cited

Adams, Hazard, ed. *Critical Theory Since Plato*. Fort Worth: Harcourt Brace Jovanovich College Publishers, 1992.

Asante, Molefi Kete and Abu S. Abarry, eds. *African Intellectual Heritage: A Book of Sources*. Philadelphia: Temple University Press, 1996.

Baldwin, James and Margaret Mead. *A Rap on Race*. Philadelphia: Lippincott, 1971.

Braxton, Charlie. "Personal Interviews and Discussions." November and December, 1998.

Damrosch, David and David L. Pike. *The Longman Anthology of World Literature*. New York: Pearson, 2008.

Gates, Henry Louis Jr. and Nellie Y, McKay, eds. *The Norton Anthology of African American Literature*. New York: W.W. Norton & Co. 1997.

Gibson, NaTasha Ria. "..." an unpublished poem. 1997.

Hurston, Zora Neale. *Their Eyes Were Watching God*. New York: HarperCollins, 1990.

Johnson, James Weldon, ed. *The Book of American Negro Poetry*. New York: Harcourt, Brace and Co., 1989.

McInnis, C. Liegh. *Confessions: Brainstormin' from Midnight 'til Dawn*. Jackson: Psychedelic Literature, 1998.

McKay, Claude. *Home to Harlem*. Chicago: Northeastern University Press. 1987.

Olugbala, Swandi. "Lecture on Creativity and other Principles of Kwanzaa." The 1998 Jackson Community Kwanzaa Celebration. December 31, 1998.

Rosenberg, Donna, ed. *World Literature: An Anthology of Great Short Stories, Drama, and Poetry,* Lincolnwood: NTC Publishing Group, 1992.

Williams, David Brian. "Interview for Documentary." *A Nite of Poetry with C. Liegh McInnis.* Jackson: Psychedelic Literature, 1998 (VHS).

We Are our Worst Enemy

How long does it take for the freed slave to be no longer a slave? For one hundred and thirty-three years there has existed a piece of paper called the Emancipation Proclamation, which supposedly abolished slavery. Yet, it seems that far too many African Americans are still slaves, in every way. We are slaves in the physical as well as in the emotional and the mental. And, it seems that many white Americans in positions of power (economic, social, religious, legal, and educational) understand and use this to continue the perpetuation of the Negro's slavery. On November 19, 1998, the Jackson Mississippi branch of the Nation of Islam held a celebration in honor of Minister Louis Farrakhan. To honor Minister Farrakhan, the Nation of Islam extended an invitation to the Jackson State University Orchestra to perform before the showing of the documentary of Minister Farrakhan's 1993 masterful violin performance in Chicago at Christ Universal Temple. The celebration was held to show the Minister's strides and accomplishments in all areas of life to bring dignity, education, empowerment, and unity to African Americans and to the world. Music is the greatest example of this because it is the universal language and represents one of the highest forms of critical thinking. Yet, on the day of the showing of the documentary, commentators from WFMN, Supertalk 97.3 noon show held a "call in" debating whether or not the JSU Orchestra should be "allowed" to perform at the mosque. In actuality, the commentators of the noon show held a mock radio contest allowing listeners to call in to win tickets for dinner with "Louie" Farrakhan and the JSU Orchestra. Immediately following the airing of this show, the JSU Music Department began receiving complaints and alleged "threats" regarding the presence of the JSU Orchestra at a Nation of Islam Mosque. And so it happened. Master called down from the "Big House" and told the slaves not to meet with anyone unless Master so approves, and, of course, the slaves acted accordingly.

In attempting to gain some clarification on all of the issues from all of the involved parties, only Minister Frank Muhammad of the Jackson, Mississippi mosque was of any assistance, providing as much information as possible and answering as many questions as he could, given the limited response from 97.3 and JSU. The initial reaction of Minister Muhammad was that of shock, hurt, and, of course, anger. Yet, before he took any action, Minister Muhammad requested a transcript of the 97.3 radio show and attempted to contact Dr. London Branch, Director of the JSU Orchestra. At this date, Minister Muhammad has not received a copy of the transcript nor has he received any additional word from Dr. Branch or any other JSU official. I attempted to contact and gain some statement from 97.3, Dr. Branch, Dr. James Lyons—JSU President, Dr. Dora Washington—V.P. of Academic Affairs, and Dr. Dollye M. E. Robinson—Dean of the School of Liberal Arts. Staff members of the President's office and the V.P.'s office referred me to lower offices. A staff member in the School of Liberal Arts explained that since there seemed to be only a verbal agreement between Dr. Branch and the National of Islam, there was no "wrong doing" in the decision of having the orchestra not play. This raises several issues.

The excuse of a "verbal" agreement is a rather weak excuse. Any type of agreement, verbal or written, is an arrangement made in good faith. So are we to believe that breaking a verbal agreement is not as wrong as breaking a written agreement? What are we teaching our children? Secondly, it seems that none of the JSU administrators are taking this issue seriously, and I wonder if it has anything to do with the fact that the program was sponsored by the National of Islam and not the Pearl Street AME Church. JSU's refusal to honor its word cannot be due to religion given the fact that different JSU units are always performing and presenting at various religious institutions in the metro area. In fact, every JSU program in which I have been involved begins and ends with a prayer and usually includes some gospel singing. So if the issue is not religion, and the verbal agreement excuse seems to be rather weak, what could be causing the JSU administrators to look the other way when outside forces seek to strip us of our first amendment rights and our ability to meet with those who have the best interest of African American children at heart. Could it be, as some of the listeners and callers of 97.3 wish to assert, that such a program would be a waste of the taxpayers' dollars? I am a taxpayer, and I believe that the program would have been a fine use of my tax dollars. Is it a waste of my tax dollars for JSU units to perform at various Christian churches and events across the metro area? This issue is not about the waste of taxpayers' dollars or religion. This issue is about fear and control. It is about JSU administrators being afraid to do or become involved in anything that may cause Caucasian controversy, even at the risk of under-educating or mis-educating our children.

In my tirade over this issue, someone asked me about the parents. If there were threats made toward the school, should the parents of the children be contacted? (I answer this question not knowing whether or not threats were made because Dr. Branch has not returned my calls.) If threats were made, then the parents should have been notified. If threats were made, why did Dr. Branch not notify campus security or the Jackson Police Department? But more importantly, do we want threats from people who do not have our best interest at heart to decide our policy or actions? I am not advocating putting students in danger, but teachers do have a responsibility to lead students in all endeavors of their lives. Although I would not have placed any students in harm's way, I would, as an instructor, an artist, and a concerned citizen, have gone myself. As self respecting African Americans, we cannot allow fear to control or influence our ability to express ourselves, celebrate ourselves, and come together to better ourselves. Correct me if I am wrong, but neither 97.3 nor any of its listeners have done anything in the way of bettering JSU or its neighborhood. On the other hand, I see the daily work being done by members of the Nation of Islam. Many of us feel safer in the presence of members of the Nation of Islam than we do in the presence of the Jackson Police Department. So to allow fear to dictate to us with whom we can and cannot associate sets a poor example for our children. To paraphrase Huey P. Newton, "I would rather die on my feet than live on my knees."

The JSU Orchestra allowing themselves to be bullied by white power is a direct result of the philosophy of the "Willie Lynch Letter" and other Jim Crow laws that prohibited free blacks to associate with slaves. This is the problem with African American freedom. The Emancipation Proclamation is a document drafted and finalized by white Americans. So, it is the example of white Americans setting the boundaries and parameters of African American freedom. African Americans have spent the last one thirty-three years waiting on white Americans to give us our freedom, and African Americans have continuously allowed white Americans to define or greatly influence the African American strategy to gain freedom and first-class citizenship. Thus, the flaw of African American freedom and the attempts to gain African American freedom is that it is not defined by African Americans. When white Americans can tell African Americans with when and with whom to meet, and we act accordingly, this shows us to be a non-sovereign people. So, then, the truth is that we, African Americans, are our own worst enemy. To quote Minister Muhammad, "Until we have men who love freedom more than life, we will always be slaves."

The "Willie Lynch" mentality continues to keep African Americans the place of second class citizen. The African American Christian does not trust the African American Muslim. The African American professional does not trust the African American skilled laborer. The African American Southerner does not trust the African American Northerner. African American youth do not trust or respect their African American elders. Both the African American male and female are distrustful of each other. Every wall that can be erected to separate people from each other exists in the African American community. Most people attribute these walls to the Willie Lynch Syndrome, which is merely the divide and conquer strategy. I attribute the walls as ramifications of integration and a public schools system that works to systematically under-educate and mis-educate African Americans. Now, understand what I mean when I say the ramifications of integration. I do not mean the ramifications caused by merely living around and with white folk. I do mean that integration, the act of African American assimilation (melting pot) and not amalgamation (salad bowl), with white America has caused African Americans to hate and mistrust ourselves, which causes us to us to lean to the understanding and guidance of white America and not to ourselves or God. Instead of seeking first the Kingdom of Heaven, we are seeking the kingdom of white America. And in doing this we are becoming more cowardly, more perverse, more schizophrenic, and less Godly, especially when we follow the god of our oppressors, which is money and power.

How can two people who proclaim to be men of God work against each other. If the Christian loves God, he must love man. For God asks how can we love Him whom we cannot see and hate man whom we see on a daily basis. The problem is that we do not love God. We love man and man's world. That's why black people who claim to love God can forsake God for the white man's approval and riches. So instead of being like Job who waited on the

Lord, we are like Balaam who ignored God's word and carried out man's word so that he could integrate into man's world and not into God's world. And just like Balaam, instead of riding the ass, we are becoming the ass.

What Is a "Man?"

"Man" and "woman" are concepts that are assessed, named, and identified by the biological constructs of "male" and "female," but in themselves the terms "man" and "woman" have no empirical or definite identification or being because they are named, assessed, and identified by sliding, if not, arbitrary notions of what it means to be a "man" or a "woman," which changes from culture to culture and from time period to time period. There is no way of knowing or naming these concepts or "things" in any empirical manner of how we know that we know what we know. Using the model articulated by Kalamu ya Salaam in *What Is Life* and by Reginald Martin on the e-Drum listserv, a "man" is considered the active, dominate being of most societies, and a "woman" is the passive, subservient being of most societies. Accordingly, then, certain qualities, which are attributed to dominate and passive are thus attributed to "man" and "woman." Quite naturally, men have assumed the dominate roles because they were, initially, physically stronger—becoming the hunter-gathers and protectors of the species. Yet even acceptance or belief in this notion depends upon whose perspective of history you take. This is certainly true of European history, where "man" and "woman" have traditionally existed as separate and unequal beings. It is not until the Middle Ages of European history when females begin to really and regularly ascend to positions of power, which coincides with the rise of courtly love poetry, which gave woman a more divine, even if still subservient position. There are no Greek and Roman female rulers, and their female gods are subservient to the male gods. Whereas in African tradition, there was more emphasis placed on the balance brought to humanity based on the coupling of X and Y, as evidenced by the female rulers during the ancient Egyptian civilizations, the notion that Osiris, a male god, finds his salvation through Isis, a female god, and the fact that in many African tribes the lineage is dated through the female. It can be said that Africans have not assigned positions of power and dominance solely on the gender, though it would not be accurate to say that the African tradition does not have its legacy of sexism. Yet it has been the European system for naming and assigning positions for "men" and "women" solely or primarily by gender that his emerged as the dominate system for naming and assigning positions for "men" and "women." This is merely because the Europeans have been able to ascend to world/global dominance, which happens when Alexander the Great pushes into Egypt on the heels of the fall of Egypt's great empires. And during this time, females have a second-class citizenship role in European life, whereas African women had occupied a first-class citizenship role for the past 3,500 years. More than anything else, these two distinct perspectives tell us that "man" and "woman" are arbitrary concepts that were created based on what the dominate group in a society needed them to be or perceived to be the most constructive concepts to adopt. As time has progressed and Greek/Roman society became the model for global life, men have created and maintained a system that keeps them in the position as the dominate being. Though many, both "men" and "women," have worked to change this definition, it still exists today.

Again, "man" and "woman" are arbitrary concepts based on positions of power. The only way that there will ever be any concrete definitive for "man" and "woman" is if there can be an objective, empirical study of the physical and metaphysical characteristics of "man" and "woman." But for this to happen, enough men would have to be willing to release or relinquish their position of power over the study, if not over life. If not, the study will always be tainted to promote and define "man" as the more dominate being because it is a given that our physical (mortal) nature demands that we survive by any means necessary, which means working to keep in place those aspects or systems that perpetuate our survival, evolution, and dominance, therefore, attributing a certain set of qualities to "man" and "woman" as innate and/or organic. (Is this not proven to be true when we consider that literature and critical theory, the fields/battlegrounds for naming and interpretation of life, have been the battlegrounds for deciding cultural place, sovereignty, and superiority, with each group waging the continuous battle to prove their right to exist and be dominate?) So the obvious question is "Do the colors 'blue' and 'pink' represent some organic sign/signifier of 'man-ness' or 'woman-ness,' or are they merely arbitrary colors used to denote/connote, sign, or signify the state of 'man-ness' or 'woman-ness?'" If a male wears a pink signifier, is he less "man?" If a male does the dishes or paints his nails, is he less "man?" If a female does not want to have a baby or does not feel compelled to hold every baby she sees, is she less "woman?" What this proves is that all of our concepts or aspects of "man" and "woman" or "man-ness" and "woman-ness" are arbitrary, and that any concepts that we have for "man" or "woman" are political in our attempts to order a world based on dominance and subservience, which is based on the war/battle to garner the power to control life.

This final point is proven in the fact that most "men" or "male" groups that gain power in a specific culture attempt to emasculate all males not like them, i.e., white males create a system to emasculate all non-white males, thus disenfranchising them from positions of power, keeping them from becoming a threat to the dominate males or "men." "[Richard] Wright came to understand that the power to structure gender (male and female) in early twentieth-century America seemed to be an exclusive privilege of certain white males. The black boy is forever denied the achievement of manhood, so defined. The black male is to be made a permanent child and denigrated into the posture of the stereotyped female—victim, unempowered!" (Ward xvii). Thus, when one group of men can emasculate another group of men, it shows just how arbitrary this notion or concept of "man" and "woman" is. Furthermore, these very same men, who have been emasculated by the "men" of power, assert their sense of self by oppressing the women of their specific group in order to feel some sense of self and power. So "men" and "women," as concepts, are in much the same boat as words defined as parts of speech, which are truly defined in their function and not merely by their prescription. That is, a word is not an adverb in its prescription but in its function. A word, such as "home," which is prescribed as a "noun," can be best identified in its function. For instance, in the sentence, "I went home," "home" is functioning as an adverb because it is answering the question "where" and providing more information about the verb. It is functioning as an adverb when it fulfills these two roles. Thus, a "man" and a "woman" are defined by the functions they play in society. However, it must be understood that these functions or roles are closely guarded by those in power, and, therefore, the powers that be expand the roles for some and limit the roles for others, always creating a comfort zone for themselves and making everyone else uncomfortable. The fact that others are limited and uncomfortable (socially, economically, and politically) is the key example of their subservience, and the key signifier of the other group's dominance. Yet, sense none of these positions are etched in stone and have not been proven to be innate or organic to any gender group, we are back where we started. The concepts of "man" and "woman" are, at best, vague, arbitrary, and built on a sliding scale controlled by one group, which allows them to remain in power. At best, "man" and "woman" are concepts, which attempt to get at our humanity. Being male and female satisfies the physical aspect of our humanity, but we need something that satisfies our metaphysical aspects—or at least leads us toward a more thorough study of our humanity based on the manner in which our metaphysical aspects manifest themselves in our physical lives. Unfortunately, the concepts or the naming and assigning of "man" and "woman" are more tied to political ploys for human survival, which usually leads to the play of dominance, than objective science and naming, which could lead to a more constructive human evolution by learning how the X and Y satisfy and compliment each other. Until we have a definition of what it means to be a "man" how can we expect boys to grow into men. Thus, I agree with both ya Salaam and Martin, that as long as our only definition of "man" is to be the dominant and controlling being, then we cannot be surprised when our boys evolve into selfish bullies.

Work Cited

Martin, Reginald. "Response to Definition of a Man Discussion." E-Drum: Kalamu@aol.com. (Online Posting) Moderated by Kalamu ya Salaam. July 26, 2001.

Salaam, Kalamu. *What Is Life?? Reclaiming the Black Blues Self.* Chicago: Third   World Press, 1994.

Ward, Jerry. "Introduction." *Black Boy.* New York: HarperCollins, 1993.

Letter to Derrick Johnson—Attorney, Director of the Mississippi NAACP, and Co-Founder of Southern Vibes (the Saturday Night Poetry Reading)

Dear Derrick,

Before I begin, allow me to apologize for this letter. It's 12:56 a.m., and my mind, as usual, is filled with more thoughts than I can write in a reasonable time. So without trying to order them, I'll write as they come.

A time will come when our poetry group must leave Highlites. The question is, where will we go and under what terms? The answer is that I don't have a clue. Ownership is the way we should go, but there is no way I could be a part of that. My finances are in shambles and will probably stay that way until I die. The only things that I will ever own are the clothes on my back, my care, and my art. Truthfully, that is all that I've ever wanted to own. Or, I've never wanted to work hard enough to own anything else. This is something that I'm learning about myself. I'm an artist who will probably die broke. I don't have any other interest, and it doesn't seem that I'll ever sell enough books to pay for the cost of publishing them. So, I know that I would not make an effective business partner for you or anyone. If you and some of your friends find a spot to take the poetry reading, I'm there, but only as an artist. The only thing that I want from Southern Vibes is to have a spot where I can read what I felt and to have a spot that can serve as the artistic home for Jackson's black writers. Yet, I realize that I don't have the business mind to make that dream a reality.

I will always have money problems because money doesn't mean anything to me. Sometimes I want to be able to buy my wife anything she wants and needs, but poetry calls, and I am broke again. The only interest I have in money is its ability to help me create art, though I would like to have enough money to aid in the education of black children. When I'm sending my work to journals, conferences, and book clubs, I'm not thinking about a return on my investment. I'm thinking, "I hope they like it and tell somebody else." It's not so I can make money, but so I can share my work with someone else. Man, if I could, I'd just break even, earn just enough money to continue to produce my art. To be honest, I don't want a bookstore or a restaurant. I just want a place large enough to be a publishing house during the day and a poetry joint at night. That would be too cool, writing during the day and giving it away at night.

I want to do the anthology that we've been discussing. I'm there with that. 2000 is the year. Dr. Ward is still having his book club meetings every second Monday at 7:00 p.m. I'll start going so that we can get to work. Besides, I need to be more involved in a formal reading session where I can begin reading current writers outside the State.

A last note on the *Confessions* book cover— although I know that you were only trying to help, I don't want a readership that can't get pass the cover or might be turned away from an artist who wants to create literature that is as different as it is pleasing. It's not a Prince thing. I cannot lie and say that he wasn't the person who made me want to be an artist. I wanted to write poems (free from music) that made people think and feel what he made me think and feel, which includes freedom and liberation from social barriers that cause us to mistreat ourselves and others. But as much as I am influenced by Prince and others, I am just as driven to be my own person, to be true to the voices in my head. I liken it to Keats divorcing himself from the shadow of Milton. He knew he had to find his own voice. I have found mine. It is Mississippi and urban, and it doesn't care who likes it. My starting with Prince as an influence does not end my education. I have studied the literary masters as much as anyone. Yet, even after having earned a MA and twenty-four hours toward a doctorate, people still cheapen me and my work when I admit that he was my initial artistic influence. It used to bother me. It doesn't bother me anymore. The *Confession* book cover is an earnest reflection of what the work is. The book is revealing. I say shit in that book that most people take to their graves. For those who cannot get pass the picture I say about them what Prince said about the average R&B listener, "The only time they come around is when you have a hit." I don't want the type of reader or audience who only buy books because they are on somebody's bestseller list. I want to find my audience, coffee house by coffee house. I can't deal with someone who can't deal with me because of the way I may look or certain things I may say. I'll keep doing my thing, and they'll keep doing theirs. It is not one's loss. Art is subjective. My "talking book" may not speak to them.

I'm writing this because I'm tired, but I know that I still have a long way to go. The job of the artist is two-fold: create it and disseminate it. It's the dissemination that is driving me crazy. Dissemination or distribution is expensive. That's why so many want to play with the big boys, let the big boys handle the expenses. But what they don't realize is when you take somebody else's money you also take their rules. And maybe they do realize this but are willing to dance to somebody else's groove for the sake of money. And truth be told, not having to worry about the marketing and dissemination of the art leaves more time to create the art. I just have not met any body whom I'm willing to trust with my art.

You remind me of another brother whom I know, Peter Stewart. He's a lawyer also. His financial situation is solid also. He turned me on to mutual funds and term life. That's why I have two mutual funds now. Maybe, one day, I'm going to deposit money into them on a consistent and regular basis. My financial discipline pales in comparison to yours, which is why I know that you will have your bookstore and art gallery one day. And whatever goes down at Highlites, just know that I'm down with poetry. Wherever she is, that's where I'll be. If we move to another established spot, we can keep it like it is. If you and some of your friends decide to buy a spot, I can't hang, not as a business partner. But, I'll be there, every Saturday night, reading poetry. I guess I'm trying to say that I've branched out far beyond my economic means and need to close ranks to do what I do best, write. I write. I publish myself. Besides the anthology and a few other Mississippi poets, I have no desire to publish anyone else. I'm not a business man. I'm a wrier who wants complete control of my art. That's all. That's why I publish myself.

If you figure out what this letter means, please tell me. I'm tired. I'm going to bed.

The Dismantling of a Local Dream
Initially published in the *Jackson Advocate,* January 22-28 1998

January 1998 will come and go without the annual celebration of New Hope Foundation's Anniversary. The dream of Dr. William P. Lee, founder of New Hope Foundation, was to take people addicted to drugs and alcohol and turn them into leaders in the fight against those terrible diseases. Yet, because of racist and elitist policies of the Mississippi State Legislature, Dr. Lee's dream is being crushed under the heavy foot of bureaucracy. The department of Human Services has effectively weeded out all individuals and organizations that were germane to the organic development of New Hope Foundation. All that is left are uncaring, degree holding persons who are merely seeking to help in the complete annihilation of a program which was the purest example of if you teach a man to fish, he will eat forever. In its actions, the State seems to want to ensure that there will always be a certain group of people who are permanently dependent upon its service, permanently confined as second class citizens.

The catalyst for this dismantling of New Hope Foundation is 1997's Senate Bill 2100 which mandates that all state employed drug and alcohol counselors must have a four year degree in counseling. The bill itself is not the issue. No one discounts the need for properly, professionally trained counselors. The problem is that the bill is being used retroactively to terminate individuals who have been working in the field of drug and alcohol abuse for years. Both Congresswomen Alice Clark and Mary Coleman have stated that they did not support any bill that would be retroactive and cause people who were already working in the field to lose their jobs. The bill was meant to improve the knowledge base of the counselors and reduce State liability. Using the bill retroactively discounts the experience and knowledge base of those individuals who were able to conquer addiction and successfully turn around their lives. Furthermore, this bill is being used to eliminate counselors, regardless of their years of diligent and constructive service. Since the passing of this bill, New Hope Foundation has terminated several counselors who had no filed complaints, no write-ups, or negative evaluations of any kind. Among these terminated employees are Jackie Brown, Angela Groove, Terry Bennet, Shirley Bradford, Cathy S. Harris, Pam Jackson, and administrative workers Mertal Cowheard and Ernestine Harley who have been with New Hope since its inception. None of these individuals had any formal complaints levied against them or poor evaluations before being terminated by the new Director of New Hope Foundation who was appointed by the State of Mississippi.

For over fifteen years, New Hope Foundation was the flourishing dream of Dr. Lee. This foundation not only successfully combated one of the major ills of our society, alcohol and drug addiction, its goal was to rescue and intervene in the lives of those members of our society who have been locked out and forgotten. The primary patients of New Hope Foundation are poor, homeless, and mainly African American. With no where else to turn, Dr. Lee opened doors to care for these people. But, Dr. Lee did not stop there. Dr. Lee understood the value and influence that one saved life could have upon several, hundreds even. So Dr. Lee instituted a program whereby individuals who had once been patients of the program could now work to save the lives of others.

Dr. Lee understood that the best type of leadership was not one by rhetoric, but one by example. New Hope Foundation produced counselors and assistants who became living testaments of the success of the program and role models for those wanting a new life away from drugs and alcohol. Unfortunately, less than one year after Dr. Lee's death, the State of Mississippi has worked to effectively dismantle Dr. Lee's program, crushing his dream, and leaving those primary patients once again locked out of the system. In less than one year, the State of Mississippi has removed ninety percent of the counselors and assistants, who were African American, and replaced them with white counselors who do not live in or have any connection to the communities served by New Hope. The State's premise is that New Hope Foundation was operating with unqualified counselors and assistants. Yet, when they were hired, they were not unqualified. When Dr. Lee was receiving funding form the State for his program, they were not unqualified. The implementation of new counselors has only worked to reverse the progress of New Hope Foundation.

If you asked any person who has successfully worked a recovery program, they will inform you that they would prefer a sponsor or a counselor who has walked the hell that they have walked and come out on the other side, clean and sober. A degree does not make you understand the pains of addiction. A degree does not make you understand the struggle to stay clean. A degree does not make you understand the mind of an addict. And, a degree should not be the final determination for becoming a drug and alcohol counselor. Yet, regardless of this wealth of this experience and knowledge, neither DHS nor the State of Mississippi has reached out to any of the counselors of New Hope Foundation or created programs or timetables to have them meet the new requirements. As a final blow to Dr. Lee's dream, the State of Mississippi will cease all meetings held at the New Hope Foundation location on Mill Street, one of the most densely populated areas of addicts, and move the foundation to a location that only houses office space and will have not room to hold AA/NA meetings or house emergency beds for those who need somewhere to stay until the foundation can find them a bed at a recovery center. I guess the new counselors want to receive their pay checks but do not want to do the field work to earn them. It seems that the State of Mississippi and the Department of Human Services are only concerned with attempting to tap into extra funds without seriously addressing the needs of a specific group who is still being systematically locked out. That is, "We will admit you for a fee, but we are not interested in implementing any long term goals or plans for the community." The State seems only concerned with the money and the paperwork, not the lives of the patients.

It is interesting that as we celebrate the dream and legacy of Dr. Martin L. King, Jr., we are turning a blind eye to the destruction of a local dream. For years conservatives have yelled and screamed about pork programs that yield no real result. Then when we finally have a program that is teaching individuals how to help themselves and then to help others, we crush it because the lives of those of the inner city have no value. What message are we sending as a city, as a State? Are the State of Mississippi and the Department of Human Services really about the business of servicing and helping Mississippians, or do our tax dollars go to support a department of bureaucratic paper pushers who care little about healing the sick and improving the living conditions of all Mississippians.

Affirmative Action and Slavery:
What's the Relationship?

Bob "White Man" graduates from Harvard and begins to search for a job. After a diligent search, he finds that approximately eighty-six percent of the jobs are filled by white males. He then realizes that another fourteen percent of the jobs are filled by white women and other minorities. Bob believes and finds proof that the fourteen percent of the jobs filled by white women and minorities are locked out to him because of affirmative action. So Bob, feeling violated as an American citizen, cries, rages, and sues on the basis of racism. This has been a scenario repeated many times over the past ten years until we have deleted affirmative action. Yet, Bob is never asked to answer a basic question. "What about those qualified women and minorities who would have not been hired if not for affirmative action?" What about these American citizens? What about these studious minority students who graduate high schools and colleges with 3.5 - 4.0 GPAs and are still admitted to colleges and graduate schools on probation or only under affirmative action? Where is their justice? It seems that no one has an answer for these victims, especially not Bob.

Affirmative action was designed to protect the rights of qualified women and minorities. Yet Bob always says that affirmative action gives unqualified or lesser qualified applicants a leg up over him. But, Bob never wishes to deal with the reality that his white skin always gives him a leg up over every minority, and his white penis gives him a "leg" up over every woman. The only time Bob does not have an advantage is when there are eighty-six other qualified white males. All of this gets us to the heart of the matter, the relationship of slavery to job and class competition and the acknowledgement of this relationship.

71

Since the Emancipation Proclamation, white people have attempted to distance themselves from slavery. The favorite phrase is "I didn't own any slaves." By making this statement, white people feel that they are able to wash their hands of the blood of slavery. But can they? If one reaps the benefits of slavery without ever attempting to make amends, is this not as terrible as slavery? And this is, of course, the central issue. White people have all the advantages of the history or legacy of slavery without the scars or the dirty hands.

Let us revisit the forty acres and a mule debate. After the ending of slavery and the civil war, freed slaves were promised forty acres and a mule as retribution for slavery. These forty acres and a mule were not gifts. They were retribution for hundreds of years of labor and servitude without pay. African Americans were unable to develop an economic history or legacy in this country. We could not be Rockefellers. It was illegal. We must understand the importance of the forty acres and the mule. Forty acres meant you had land. The mule meant that you had the tools by which to work the land. With them both, you had the means to build a life, to invest, reap the benefits of that investment, and, most importantly, pass on those benefits to your children so that they could reinvest those benefits, thereby multiplying the family's worth. This has not been a historical pattern in the lives of African Americans. And because this has not been a historical pattern, African Americans were not able to develop themselves as central or key economic families with stock or influence on educational and economic markets. We have a history of black institutions of higher learning, but we do not have a history, a tradition, of black owned economic institutions. And without the economic autonomy, African Americans have been powerless to control their educational development. We may have single economic entities which have garnered local or regional success, but we do not have franchises and deeply

72

rooted networks that can employ the majority of our graduates. So, economically, we are still slaves. We are still slaves in the sense that we, as a majority, do not control our economic fate. One controls his economic fate when he is able to decide for himself who works, where they work, and how much they earn. All of this is directly tied to slavery and the fact that we have never made amends for it.

Now Bob will look glassy eyed and ask, "But what does this have to do with me?" The answer is quite simple. By being white, he has reaped all of the benefits of a society centered on skin color, culture, and gender. White communities have the better equipped educational institutions because they have higher paying jobs. They have higher paying jobs because they received an education from better equipped educational institutions. The relationship to education to economic status is circular. This is a chain of events put into motion by slavery. With slavery, there was no overhead. This is what made it so appealing. Think about the raises in minimum wage. Employers are irate because this raises their overhead. As a small (very small, tiny even) publisher, I understand the cost of labor. That is why I do not have any. But this means that I have to do everything myself. In big business, this is impossible. During slavery, plantation life was big business. Without having to pay their laborers, slave owners were able to take that income and reinvest it, save it, or use it for emergencies or lulls in business. So, not only were slaves denied to right to use their wages to put themselves in a position to control their destiny, slave owners were able to use earnings which should have gone to slaves to further increase their empires. Thus, the rich got richer and the slaves become further entrenched in their slavery. When America finally ends slavery, freed slaves, with no money or land, had to continue in their past conditions as slaves. Although the knowledge may have been there, the freed slaves did not have the capital or

73

resources to invest into their dreams or goals, at least not on the level as whites. So without the forty acres and a mule, slaves, as a mass, were never able to construct the community of equal capitol and resources of their white counterparts, even thought the slaves were directly responsible for the economic status of their white counterparts. So, white Americans, traditionally and historically begin in a better position than African Americans. And this better position is due to of a lack of moral fiber. Affirmative action was supposed to be used to elevate or level the playing grounds if not the starting positions. It is not to be used to stop or break the positive chain of education and employment in white communities. It was to be used to construct positive chains or circular relationships of education and employment in African American communities. What Bob must understand is that by being white, he traditionally and historically begins in a better educational and economic position that African Americans. And where Bob will say that this is not his fault, he certainly is not making steps to change this situation.

As I have often said, this is not Bob's job. (Check my essay "The Ending of Affirmative Action, the Beginning of Opportunity for African Americans.") This is the job of African Americans. The truth is that Bob does understand the legacy of slavery. James Baldwin often alluded to the convenient naiveté of white people. That is, they are able to have amnesia or become suddenly mis-educated on the plight of African Americans when it best benefits them, which allows them to ask, "What do Black people want?" and "Why are Black people so angry?" So, I do understand that what Bob does is a calculated attempt to ensure that he continues to have his "leg" up over minorities. Now, of course, this all smacks of "conspiracy" theories. That is, there is a government conspiracy to "keep Black people down." Well, not in the sense that there is this board of white males sitting somewhere masterminding

74

the fate of America, though these types of organizations did exist at one time. It was called the White Citizens Council, and let us know forget about the Mississippi Sovereignty Commission. But Bob understands and, to some degree (it varies from individual to individual), believes that America is the white man's country and that white people being in better positions than minorities is ingrained into the American fabric of how things should be. So it is more likely for Bob to ask how many unqualified or lesser qualified African Americans were hired when he did not get the job than for him to ask how many more qualified African Americans were not hired when he did get the job. Now let's be clear. Bob is not unlike most individuals. Bob is not a member of the Klan, and he does not spend his every waking moment thinking of ways to rid the Earth of Negroes. Racism is only a problem when it affects him. Truly, most of today's African Americans do not experience racism in the manner that our forefathers did, so we also perceive it differently. And in fact, most employed African Americans are reluctant to say much if anything about institutional racism. And this is why the ending of affirmative action is not Bob's problem; it is the problem of African Americans as is the ending of the legacy of slavery.

The reason that the continuance of affirmative action and the ending of the legacy, i.e., the cultural, social, political, and economic ramifications of slavery is a problem and a responsibility of African Americans is because the legacy of slavery has been so beneficial to whites. History and human nature tell us that no man is relinquishing his advantage over another man, at least not willingly. So it is up to African Americans to pry themselves from beneath this perpetual, systematic force which causes far too many of us to exist as second class citizens. There is either one or two ways of erasing the legacy of slavery. The first is to use a private legislation of affirmative action. No self respecting African American should patronize any business where as least fourteen percent of its employees are not African American. The second way is to employ the theory or concept of economic nationalism. That is, shop only at African American owned stores. Or before one purchases a good or a service from a white owned business, make sure that no African American owned business offers this good or service.

Understand, the legacy of slavery and achieving first class citizenship is based on who had the power, and power comes from capital and other resources. If we do not have capital and other resources, then we have no citizenship. Bob knows this. Bob uses this to continue to keep his leg up on African Americans. We do not have to lie there and allow Bob to stand on us. Let Bob work for his white owned company. Just do not patronize the company. Eventually one of two things will happen. African Americans will gain more opportunity for self-control and determination within white owned corporate America, or we will construct a separate, healthy, prospering existence which will include schools and jobs that allow us to perpetuate the good of our own.

This is why I say that the problem of race and the situation of us in America can not be solved by whites or by government action. Only two tactics were successful in the 1960s fight for civil rights: economic boycott and the use of the media to embarrass America, mainly the South. Since the sixties, white folks have learned not to make a habit of committing open violence or racist acts. Along with this, white people have learned that African Americans will continue to buy crappy products from them merely because we now have the opportunity to do so. So, the only course of action for African Americans is to build a strong economic base by spending our money with African Americans. Only then will we be able to force white economic leaders to take action on our behalf. But, having our own economic base will allow us to take action for ourselves? Working as an instructor of English at

Jackson State University I notice that we have the worst city transportation plan or service in America. Yet, the city has found a way to transport JSU students to the Northpark Mall and the Metrocenter mall. With approximately eight thousand students, each pumping about two dollars a day into the city income, JSU students account for close to sixteen thousand dollars of daily city revenue. Much of this is spent at the Metrocenter and Northpark malls. Sixteen thousand dollars a day equals eighty thousand dollars per a five day week period. If these students merely stop going to the mall for two weeks, all of the board members of the mall would make a bee line to JSU to rectify whatever the problem that is keeping the students from shopping at the mall. Then we would have some bargaining power to put pressure on the economic leaders to do our bidding.

As Tavis Smiley often says, this is not rocket science. The Affirmative Action debate exists only because we, African Americans, have failed to do our job. Major companies know that Affirmative Action is an excellent idea. It builds creativity through diversity and allows you to tap into an infinite amount of markets. For example, JSU's copier account is with Xerox. Even though I know that Xerox's employees are overwhelmingly white, for the past four years I have only seen one white Xerox employee at JSU. All other Xerox employees from the sales representative to the technician have been African American. This says to me and JSU that Xerox will not only take our business, but they will hire our people. Recently, we had to open the contract to bids as mandated by State law. A rival copier company came to the various departments with questionnaires to ascertain the university's needs. All of their employees were Thad, Muffy, and Bobbie Sue. As a paying customer, if I am faced with two equal companies with one providing opportunities to African Americans and the other not providing opportunities to African Americans, with whom do you suppose I will do business? Needless to say, Xerox is still our copier carrier. We must understand that spending our dollars wisely offers us the opportunity to affect the employment market. If companies know that most African Americans will not do business with companies that will not hire and promote African Americans at all levels of its company, then surely this will improve the job opportunities of African Americans.

Now of course the question is *How much impact can Affirmative Action have on America's race problem?* Well, we must understand two points. First, people socialize within their own economic class. Secondly, racial disharmony grows from economic and legal disharmony. Mr. Charles Groden stated that we can begin to solve the race problem through white people and black people getting to know each other. Yet, the truth is that we can not get to know each other if we do not live with or around each other. Economics determine where and with whom we live. In a short story "A Drink in the Passage" by Allen Paton, a white South African man is moved to meet a black South African man after viewing his art work. The white South African is so moved with the work of art that he invites the black South African to his house for drinks. Well, herein lies our problem. First, during apartheid, it was illegal for black South Africans to consume alcohol. Secondly, black South Africans were not permitted in white townships after dark. So, you have two men unable to be friends because of a social condition created and maintained by an economic condition. If two men can not meet on equal terms, then they can not be friends in a true sense of the word. If Mr. Groden invites me to dinner, where will we eat? If I cannot afford the food, can I go as an equal? If I can not afford the house, can I live next to him as an equal? Until two men or two women have equal opportunities to take care of their families and fully achieve their roles as men and women within a society, they can not be equals; they can not be friends. So until African

Americans are able to create a system or a base that allows the majority of African Americans equal opportunity to achieve adulthood in the American system, we will continue to be second class citizens, unable to meet whites at the American table as equals.

Affirmative Action attempts to level the playing field that was made uneven because of slavery. It is a direct attack on the injustice of slavery which is still being perpetuated. For those who believe in integration, affirmative action is the only protection against Jim Crow. If we are going to have assimilation through integration, African Americans need some tool which guards and protects their rights in a society where they give up control of their lives by assimilating into a culture that has a history of fragmenting, marginalizing, and oppressing them. Affirmative action is but a small step to acknowledging the continued ramifications of slavery and attempting to do something about those continued ramifications of slavery. It is not that Bob "White Man" does not understand all of this. He is just hoping to muddy the waters by scaring and enraging his other white friends and by shaming African Americans through his use of pseudo-logic and misrepresentation of history.

Letter to Cal Thomas, Columnist for
The Los Angeles Times Syndicate

Dear Mr. Thomas:

What I fear is an assault by all Republicans on my rights and citizenship as an African American. As an African American, when I vote, it is usually for the lesser of the two evils. Even with everything that President Clinton has done, it still does not equate to the Reagan/Bush Administrations and their war against African Americans. What is interesting is that it seems that the republicans have alienated more then just African Americans; Clinton's approval is still high.

Why am I for big government? Big government took African Americans from the back of the bus to the front of the bus. Big government allows African Americans to live, play, and work where they choose and where their abilities take them. Remember, it was federal troopers not state troopers that protected the integration of America. (I will admit that I am no big fan of integration. African Americans lost their tax base by losing many of their businesses due to integration.) With strong regulations, big government keeps planes from falling from the sky. Big government attempts to give equal access and opportunity in education to all children and not just white children. Therefore, I know why you do not like big government, Mr. Thomas.

Finally, I could never be proud of Ronald Reagan. Ronald Reagan was many white Americans' attempt to roll back the clock to 1864. Whenever a white person says that they are proud of Ronald Reagan, they are stating that they believe in second class citizenship for some, which allows others to live off the blood and labor of the oppressed. Any man who says that he is proud of Reagan will say that he is proud of our legacy of slavery.

The Ayers Case: The True Evil of the
New College Admission Standards

With the new admission standards for the State supported institutions of higher learning, we are being either evil and vindictive or lamely and mindlessly hypocritical. In either case, the educators of the State are turning a blind eye to their responsibility to offer equal opportunity and access to all of its children of the State and not merely the white or affluent children. In reaction to the charges of discriminatory funding practices and academic policies, the State of Mississippi has decided to raise the admission standards across the board for all of its colleges, including the Historically Black Colleges and Universities (HBCUs) without first attempting to address the inadequacies that exist in its public elementary and high schools.   For years, the State's HBCUs administered programs and policies that served as bridges to address the needs of African American children who had attended elementary and high school in lower income areas that lacked the needed funds to offer advanced, college prep courses.   Forcing the HBCUs to adhere to the new standards before addressing the inadequacies that cause African Americans to fall behind is a clear sign that the State of Mississippi continues not to be serious about educating African Americans.

We must first consider and remember what the Ayers case was and is as far as its purpose. The primary concern of Jake Ayers was for equal opportunities and access to education for African American students. The only way that one has equal opportunities and access in State education is to distribute the funds to the State institutions on an equal basis.   The decision of fund distribution should be based solely on each school's current enrollment, but also their potential student population. But instead of doing this, the State has chosen to limit funds to specific schools based on the inadequate education that their potential students receive in the State's secondary and elementary public school system. Regardless of the documented fact that these schools, Mississippi Valley State University (MVSU), Alcorn State University (ASU), and Jackson State University (JSU), have a successful history of taking the responsibility of meeting the needs of these students who received inadequate education in the State's public school system, the State now sees fit to terminate the programs and opportunities provided to these less fortunate students by these schools. Thus, it seems that nothing in the State of Mississippi ever changes. Every time concerned, responsible African Americans create ways to address the lacking education of their children, the State is right there to terminate the program, which herein shows that Governor Fordice and the Mississippi Congress are not concerned with the education of the African American children in this State. And not only are they not concerned, their primary concern is to deny any access of African American children to a higher education, or, at least deny African American children the opportunity to be properly educated by African American educators. And to deny African American children the right to be properly educated is to continue their perpetual second-class citizenship.

We must understand that the Ayers case is not just about equal funding in a vacuum. It is about the reason behind the inadequate funding, which is racism. The HBCUs in this State were under-funded because of who their leaders and students were. They were and are under-funded because they are Historically Black Colleges and Universities that attempt to meet the needs of higher education of African American children. They are not under-funded because of where they are located. They are not under-funded because they are producing students who can not compete with the students of the so-called "Big Three." They are the under-funded because the State of Mississippi has never and does not take seriously the position of equal and adequate education for its African American students. Thus, the State's attempt to educate their African American students is a farce. Look at the hypocrisy of the admission standards. African Americans are not exposed to certain courses due to a lack of funding caused by the State Legislature, and then the State College Board, an agent or the legislature, denies the children access to college because they cannot perform well on a test based on the courses that have been denied to the students. How do you justify raising the admission standards to the State's Colleges and Universities when you have not begun to rectify the problem of mis-education and under-education of the students in the public school system? The two are not separate. Governor Fordice and the Mississippi Congress know this. This is just their way of denying African American children the opportunity to empower themselves with knowledge and the documentation of that knowledge which is also needed.

Yet much of this we, African Americans, know. And this is not any more evil than the State of Mississippi has acted toward us and our children in the past. But what is more deceptively evil is the clause written into the new admission standards governing the enrollment of athletes. It seems that the State of Mississippi does not want hard working, analytical, independent African American scholars enrolled in their institutions of higher learning. But the State of Mississippi will make large and gross exceptions for the African American athletes who fall tremendously below the standards achieved by many none African American athletes. So, I am led to believe that while there is not room for African American scholars who have worked the best that they can with the materials and resources that the State has given them, there is always room for African Americans who can run fast, shoot baskets, run or catch touchdowns, or even hit home runs regardless of their academic achievements or potential. Here again, the State is saying, "We don't want you thinking yourself equal to us as scholars, but you are welcome to serve our institutions of higher learning as slave labor." And that is what it is. Come to our school, play a sport, make us money, and be turned out into the streets after three or four years. They get no pay check or no education. When a head coach tells a child that I brought you here to make touchdowns not make rockets, that child is prone to neglect his studies to stay on the team with fatal dreams of being a professional athlete. And this is why so many college juniors and seniors continue to major in Undergraduate Studies, with several hours of electives in basket-weaving. Now, do not get me wrong, it adds culture to a society to be able to weave a good basket. But I do not believe that these young men and women will be able to sustain a good job with this type of curriculum.

This is the true evil of the new admission standards. Not only does it lock out young, hard working African American scholars, but we then reward those students who have achieved less academically, merely because of their ability to play a sport. This action by the State's adults, this gross misconduct adversely affects the children of the State. We create a class and even a generation of children who begin to believe and internalize that sports not academics are the key to success. And so, it is clear what we must do to protect our children's future. We must either stop sending our young athletes to these white schools that care nothing about cultivating their minds for a world beyond sports, or we must demand that under whatever standards that you want our athletes these are the standards under which you must accept and enroll all of our students. We must not forget that sports are extracurricular activities, and less than one percent of all college athletes go on to play professional ball. So, in reality, an African American has a better opportunity making it in academics than in athletes. Unfortunately, the only public schools in that State that believe this is MVSU, ASU, JSU, and Coahoma Community College. All the other State supported institutions have traditionally believed and still believe that the only young African American of value to them is one who can handle a ball. And through the new State admissions policy our children are not being given an opportunity to receive an education from those institution that have proven history of caring for them outside and beyond the realm of athletics. This is truly evil. The whites of the State have declared, "We don't care about you or your future, and we don't want you to be given an equal opportunity through someone who cares about you!" These words are directly spoken through the new legislation of the State. The question is, "Now that we, African Americans, know, what are we going to do about it!?!"

Jackson Mississippi's Reaction to Louis Farrakhan:
I Am Sick of the Hypocrisy

If I hear "racial healing," "bringing communities together," and "promoting racial harmony through Christianity" one more time, I am going to explode. As it is, I have a severe headache from the hypocrisy and ignorance. Now, let us be honest. The major problem with racism is the economic issue, not the social issue. Racism, itself, is primarily an economic theory whereby one group creates a system of domination and control over another group to gain certain benefits, usually economic. The problem, of course, is when racism is discussed as prejudice, which is a belief or a notion held by one race that another race is innately inferior to them. As an African American, this notion, in itself, does not bother me or the majority of people whom I know. Most people truly do not care if someone does not like them. So the issue is when racism is the foundation of policy which governs job hiring and college admission rules. Yet, for all of their "Let's forgive and love each other rhetoric," I never see these Christians, especially white, republican Christians, discussing policies which will create equal access in education and employment opportunities for African Americans. (And by the way, I was raised in the Mississippi Delta as a "fire and brimstone" Baptist.) Many of them (white Christians) support programs which give a man a fish, but few support policies which allow a man to learn how to fish. So, if you are not for educational and economic development for all minorities, you can not be for racial healing, which makes your brand of Christianity a farce.

Understand, social healing is centered on forgiveness, education, and a nurturing of mutual respect. African Americans have to learn to forgive and forget and get pass the event and legacy of slavery which continue to have a major impact on our society. Now, I would say that

86

white people need to learn to forgive African American, but I do not know for what, except maybe petitioning for our rights in this society. Of course, someone will say for crime, but ninety percent of all crime committed by African Americans is committed on African Americans. Yet, for all of the anger and mistrust, education is primary to removing the negative stigma that both races have about each other. That is, the American public education system and its system of colleges and universities are the key perpetuators of our current negative stigma. White kids do not know of the contribution made to civilization by ancient Africans and of the contributions made to the development of America by African Americans. Without this knowledge, white kids mature into adults believing that African Americans have never been anyone of value and have never done anything of value except be slaves. Thus, white adults believe that African Americans innately lack the skills to become leaders. A nurturing of mutual respect can only come when both races view each other as equals, not before. This is what creates an atmosphere for two people to become friends. Now the Christians will argue, "What about a person's value from being a human being, a creation of Christ?" When is the last time you have called that friend who always borrows money from you? In fact, he probably owes you money now. Think about it. How many of us have former friends or associates whom we do not respect or in whom we find no value because they can never contribute anything to the relationship? Constructing mutual respect between different groups means constructing an atmosphere which allows the two groups to thrive as adults. This is racial healing and bridge building.

So with all of the above said, assimilation (in theory) and integration (in practice) have failed. They failed because too much emphasis was placed on people liking each other and getting along rather that placing the emphasis on educational and economic development. They also failed because integration caused African Americans to lose ninety percent of their businesses, stable communities, and educational control. Now, this is not the fault of white people, but the fault of African Americans who suffer from an inferiority complex because of the legacy of slavery as perpetuated through the American public school system. That is, too many African Americans believe that white is right and better. So then, the white school is better. The white grocery store is better. The white restaurant is better. The ice cream at the white parlor is colder and sweeter. With integration, African Americans abandoned their economic institutions which debilitated their tax base which debilitated their ability to control their communities and its institutions.

And yes, I am making a case for black nationalism. But I have noticed that nationalism is only a bad theory when discussed by African Americans. Brandon, Ridgeland, Richland, Clinton, and Pearl are all examples and successes of social and economic nationalism of white Mississippians. I remember when Northpark Mall was the only entity off County Line Road, just outside the Jackson city limits. I hated to be out there after dark. Coming back to Jackson was a long, dark ride of narrow road and trees. Pearl was nothing more than a gas station on Highway 80. And the majority of the population of Clinton was Mississippi College. But with white flight from the inner cities, white citizens have honed their capitol and created thriving communities away from African Americans. And to use a slang phrase of the kids, "I ain't mad at 'em." In fact, I think that African Americans need to reexamine assimilation and integration and take a look at nationalism. Unfortunately, nationalism, in theory, has negative emotions attached to it for people in the mainstream. White folks hear "black nationalism," they see young, militant brothers wearing red, black, and green, speaking a mixture of African and American dialect, carrying M16s, and rioting and looting the streets in the name of revolution. African Americans see middle age white men on camping trips playing war games, preparing for the inevitable race war. (Hey, this sounds like my National Guard weekends.) But throughout the years, nationalism has been as liquid as any other term in constant usage and debate. Nationalism centers on separation from the oppressive forces, pride in one's culture, and self-reliance.

African Americans need to become more economically self-reliant. We need to invest and reinvest in our communities to build a tax base which allows us to create and control institutions. If African Americans have a strong economic base, we are able to improve the inner city schools such as Lanier, Provine, and Jim Hill. If we have a strong economic base, we have safe and progressive parks and other recreational centers. If we have a strong economic base, we have less crime in our neighborhoods. African Americans need to ask one question every time they are about to spend money, "Is there an African American business that offers the same good or service?" Jackson, Mississippi can be like Atlanta, New Orleans, or Memphis, which all thrived despite white flight. And once you have African Americans who have the same educational and economic opportunity, stability, and prosperity as whites, then you will find your social healing.

So, I have gone on at length to this notion of social healing without one reference to Farrakhan. What bother's me about this issue or controversy over Minister Louis Farrakhan speaking at Anderson Methodist Church here in Jackson is that white people only hear him when he blasts them. White people never hear Farrakhan when he blasts African Americans. With Farrakhan, Americans seem to be more concerned with how he says something than what he says. His message is simple. Integration has failed black America. You do not have to be a Muslim to see that. (Now white people will rush to mention Oprah, Prince, Cosby, Jordan, and our own Frank Melton, C.E.O. of WLBT. But these people are not the rule, they are the exception. Further, most of these African American are in the world of entertainment. African American academicians and professionals do not have the same opportunity to success as those in entertainment. And the majority of those African American entrepreneurs who have made it outside of entertainment have done so with a primarily black customer base.) I do not agree with name calling. Yet Farrakhan has never made me want to hate white people. To paraphrase Frederick Douglas, the more a man knows about his oppressive situation, the more he begins to hate his oppressor. Yet, Farrakhan has never said that African Americans should expect white America to right the wrongs of slavery. That is like asking the Bulls to give up Jordan. It is not going to happen. What Farrakhan and a growing number of African Americans advocate is for African Americans to begin coming out of the halls of white corporate America and its public school system that has never believed in or lived up to the notion of equal access of education for all children. And what is so wrong with advocating a separation from white America when white America does not want the responsibility of educating us, hiring us, and paying us on equal levels after they are forced to hire us? This question is particularly poignant since affirmative action and government set-asides are on the way out. Without these instruments, it will become almost impossible to regulate equal opportunity for African Americans. Whether white Americans will admit to it or not, the American public school system perpetuates this atmosphere and attitude as articulated by a white professor at the University of Texas when he stated, "Blacks just can't compete." And again, there will be no racial healing until African Americans begin to take on the responsibility of cleaning its own house, building stable communities, and a stable and strong economic base. Then, and only then, will there be racial harmony. And then, and only then, will white people be rid of Farrakhan. For Farrakhan is like Baldwin, he is the conscious of America. Every time that you do wrong, your conscious is there to inform you of your iniquities. He is that one black finger pointed into the face of America, calling both white and black Americans to task on their failings. If you are doing right, you never hear from your conscious. If American does right by African Americans, they will not hear from Minister Farrakhan.

Wait 'til Next Year

Originally published in the *Clarion Ledger*, January 24, 1999 as "Reaction to Vikings Loss Tempered by Greater Reality."

The true evil of racism is how it keeps people from realizing and celebrating the humanity in each other. For years I watched Morten Andersen maintain his excellence as one of the league's best kickers for one of the league's worst teams. I, as most Mississippians, hated being forced to watch the Saints lose because of regional coverage. The only time that I would watch the Saints was to see Andersen live up to his name of "Mr. Automatic." Yet, even before the Andersen era, my father, a hard core Jackson State University alumnus and supporter who was also protesting on the JSU campus during the infamous 1970 shooting by the State National Guard, the State Highway Patrol, and the Jackson Police Department, cheered for Archie Manning. In shock about this I once stated to him and my other Vietnam Vet uncles, "Man, y'all taught me about this State's evil and racist history and tradition. How can you now cheer for that white boy from Ole Miss?" At that moment, a house of six no none sense African American men became densely silent. My father spoke in his authoritative voice, "Archie gives you four quarters every Sunday." He added, "He's the only person in the league who works as hard as Walter Payton."

It was then that I understood the power and influence of sports. It has a way of cutting through our cultural notions of who we are and getting at the core of humanity, our desire to put forth the effort of being the best or doing out best. And yet, this is the complexity of racism. My father can hate Ole Miss and everything that he feels that it represents, and, with that same heart, respect Archie Manning. This is the beauty of sports.

Today, the day after the Vikings' loss to the Falcons, I must remind myself of this. I can not lie. When

I watch professional football, I cheer for the African American quarterback, especially the black college quarterback, or the African American head coach. So, Sunday, I had double reason to cheer for the Vikings. In fact, I had three. Had the Vikings won, Coach Green would have been the first African American head coach in the Super Bowl. When Andersen kicked that field goal, my initial reaction was anger fueled by disappointment. "Damn white boy!" Yet, I am reminded that this is the same white boy for whom I would cheer during his years of excellence with the Saints. This is the same white boy to whom I would point to tell young children that being a winner or a loser is not only about winning and losing. It is about your personal commitment to excellence.

To Morten Andersen I say, "Congratulations. It could not have happened to a more deserving athlete." To all of my fellow African Americans I say, "Green and Cunningham did us proud this entire year." They both overcame their own personal hells to play in the NFC Championship game. Besides, one of the saving graces of sports is the ability to say, " Wait 'til next year."

The Ethics of Art Versus Commerce: A Discussion of the Rights of Artists Versus the Rights of the Companies

The debate between the Artist Formerly Know as Prince and Warner Bros Records brings to light the notion of ethics in the question of any artist's natural right to control the direction or volume of his work. It is essential that we begin to reanalyze and determine the relationship of artist-art-company for the sake of saving the creativity of the artist as well as maintaining the manner in which art is created to aid in the evolution of humanity rather than merely as a way to pick the pockets of the consumers. We much understand that the primary goal of a music company is to make money, not to create art. Thus, music companies are not in the business or habit of creating, patronizing, or marketing art that seeks to challenge how its customers conceive of art as something for more than leisure. In fact, to market art that demands that its customers become critical thinkers is a risky move because most companies are hoping that the customers are not thinking critically because a lack of critical thinking allows the company to pass off almost anything as well-crafted art. Thus, the problem with the music business or any business of art is that it begins to follow the trends and theories of business, which is to water down or mold or shape the art into something bland, mundane, or unoriginal so that it becomes palatable to a mass of people. And by owing the art, accountants are given more power as to what type of art is created and distributed to society. And these accountants are not thinking about how the art affects or helps the audience but how it sells.

The only place an agency, such as a recording company or a publishing company, should have in the creation of art is with the marketing and distribution. They should not, in any manner, be able to influence or determine, in any hands-on participation, the direction or quantity of a work. Further, these agencies should not be

94

entitled to any royalties or monetary payment other than return on investment. They should be compensated only for their services provided, such as marketing, distribution, and any production cost that provide. They should not be entitled to any sense of ownership or copyright, insomuch as the art is a production of the artist. The art, innately, belongs to the artist, and it is unethical to think or to put forth otherwise. Any means that an agency provides, be it studio equipment and time, packaging, handling, and shipping, are merely mediums to be used by the artists. They are materials that the artist used to produce the art, but the art or the creation, itself, existed innately within the artist. Thus, agencies should be compensated for the use of these materials as tools used in the trade. But the providing of these tools or materials should not be viewed as the agency playing any role in the creation of the art. The services provided only assist the artist in the production of the art for public consumption. Thus, agencies should be compensated accordingly, for the services that they provide, not for the entire life of the art. Therefore, agencies should receive a percentage of the sales, possibly anywhere from twenty to fifty percent depending on the amount of investment the company has made. But a company should never receive over fifty percent for an artist's work. At best, it is a fifty-fifty relationship. The royalties as well as the right to shop or lend a particular work to other venues or artists should be held/owned solely by the artist.

All of the above is the core of the battle by the Artist Formerly Known as Prince to gain creative and economic control over his art. His situation with Warner Bros Records has powerful ramifications for future artists as to the way we think of an artist's right to his work. Not only did the Artist find that he had limited control over his art, but that his image, his very self, was controlled/owned by Warner Bros Records. Thus, in being dissatisfied with his artistic relationship with Warner Bros he is unable or quite limited to shop or market even the works of art that Warner Bros will not release to the public. It is my assertion that a work of art innately belongs to the artist no matter what services are provided by the company to help bring the art to the public. And with these rights is the artist's right to have the final vote as to how much and in what form a work of art is to be released for public consumption. When a company invests into a work of art, it invests into the artist. In the company's obligation to itself to support what it feels as the most commercial work, it has only the right to choose to support/market a particular work or not to support/market a particular work. And, in their decision not to support/market a particular work of art, the company's decision should innately release that artist to shop that particular art to another company or outlet. A multi-year deal means that an agency has bought into the concept that the artist represents, but the company also assumes the risk that the artist will evolve and mature at his own rate and in his own direction. However, as it stands recording and publishing companies not only own the artist's work but have sole authority to control or dictate an artist's direction and growth. Take the issues of singers/songwriters John Fogerty and Neil Young. Fogerty was sued by a former label for plagiarizing himself. The company claimed that Fogerty's 1985 song "The Old Man down the Road" shares the same chorus as "Run through the Jungle," which is a song from Fogerty's days with Creedence Clearwater Revival. Young was sued by his record company for making "unrepresentative" music - i.e. music that did not sound like Neil Young. So, an artist can be sued for sounding too much like himself, and an artist can be sued for sounding not enough like himself. And they wonder why Prince wrote "slave" on his face. Companies should not be in the business of creating art but marketing and distributing art. And even if a company is in the business of creating art for public consumption without regard for the artist's conception of the project, then the company should release an artist whose work goes against their concept or ideal of the type of music that best sells rather than continuing to enslave the artist. If the company does not want or think highly of the art, the artist should be allowed to seek avenues that do want the art.

"Central to artistic freedom is the freedom to fail on your own terms" (Baumgold 103). This is the risk that companies take when they invest in an artist. To compromise this arrangement is to compromise the product delivered to the public. In most cases a company such as Warner Bros Records will promote only what they deem as saleable. If they do not like a particular work, it will sit on the shelf without any opportunity of being delivered to the masses. This is the power that exclusive contracts give to recording and publishing companies. Thus, when an agency has the final decision as to how or if to promote and market a work and the artist is unable to retain control over the life of that work, then the artist has become a slave to the system, or has been reduced to a farm animal that lays eggs or produces milk on demand. An exclusive contract makes an artist a slave to the system. Of course, artists do not have to sign exclusive contracts, but we must understand that exclusive contracts are the standard contract. And for a beginning artist in any field, this contract becomes what they see as the most effective way to get their art to a mass audience. And so I will accept that as a society, especially for those who are parents of artists, we must do a better job of educating artist on the business of artistry. But, just because someone can or has the ability to mistreat or take advantage of someone does not give them the right to do so. Even if an artist signs a multi-year or multi-work deal with a company, the artist should still have the ability to release or market a work that is not accepted by the company. For instance, if a writer signs a three book deal with a publisher, and the publisher does not like the second book submitted and chooses not to publish it, then writer should have the right to market that book on his own or through another company who chooses to invest in the work. Since there is an agreement for three books, the writer still owes the publisher two more books. In this manner, publishers are protected by having the first opportunity to publish a work by a writer signed to their company. This also protects writers because it allows them a sense of artistic freedom to create and release work as their creativity dictates and not as some accountant dictates.

In all of this, ownership is the key term. Who owns the art? As I have stated, the artist owns the art. It is his creation. A master recording or manuscript is the property of the creator. Companies may be given limited rights to market the work and should be compensated for their services, but one cannot own what he does not create. Art is an organic creation of the artist. It springs from the very fibers of his being. For some company to have more say over when and how a work of art is released than the artist is contradictory to the creative process.

Work Cited

Baumgold, Julie. "Glitter Slave." *Esquire Gentleman.*
    Vol. 3, No. 2. Fall 1995: 100-106.

When Fear Becomes Rage

"...Officer Bell's eyes were as blank as George Washington's eyes. But I was beginning to learn something about the blankness of those eyes. What I was learning was beginning to frighten me to death. If you look steadily into that unblinking blue, into that pinpoint at the center of the eye, you discover a bottomless cruelty, a viciousness cold and icy. In that eye, you do not exist: if you are lucky. If that eye, from its height, has been forced to notice you, if you do exist in the unbelievably frozen winter which lives behind that eye, you are marked like a man in a black overcoat, crawling, fleeing, across the snow. The eye resents your presence in the landscape, cluttering up the view. Presently, the black overcoat will be still, turning red with blood, and the snow will be red, and the eye resents this too, blinks once, and causes more snow to fall, covering it all."

from *If Beale Street Could Talk*
by James Baldwin

If you read the *Clarion Liar* or listen to any State politician in the pocket of some lobbyist, Mississippi is a new place. However, the vote on the State's Rebel Flag along with the comments of Trent Lott affirm that Mississippi is still the same "Ole Miss." This past weekend, this realization became more real to me and my family as my wife was physically and verbally assaulted by Jones County Sheriff Deputy Kevin Flynn. Before you conclude that I may be overly personalizing the issue because my wife was involved in this incident, allow me to inform you that the City of Laurel and Jones County has one of the highest suspension and expulsion rates for Black children in the State of Mississippi, and the Black community has lived under a reign of white terror since the bombing of the home of Susan B. Ruffins who was a Civil Rights Activist in the sixties and seventies. Therefore,

Deputy Flynn's actions are more of the same. In previous articles, I have discussed that the new movement in perpetuating Black second-class citizenship is by combining education and crime legislation, such as the so-called School Safety Act, which was designed and authored by white teachers as a way to target Black children and quickly route them to juvenile and adult criminal facilities. Accordingly, the two places where this can be seen clearly are Jefferson Davis and Jones County. Both counties have found ways to criminalize the behavior of children as a means to route them from the schoolhouse to the jailhouse. So, it does not surprise me that Deputy Flynn and his cohorts feel free to treat black people with the utmost contempt and disrespect because that is par for the course in the City of Laurel and Jones County. However, it is not just that Deputy Flynn's actions are illegal, but that he felt so free to act in such a heinous manner in such a public place without any regard or concern for retribution. Unfortunately, this type of lawlessness by city police and county deputies is supported and affirmed by the State's judges. Therefore, when the judge of your case announces from the bench, "I'm just a 'Good Ole Boy'...a country judge," you know that you are in trouble—that the fix is in.

Judge Rushing's finding of my wife as guilty of Disorderly Conduct, even after witnesses and Deputy Kevin Flynn contradicted themselves, goes to prove that white supremacy is alive and well in America and wears a Jones County badge and a judge's robe. So after my wife is assaulted by Deputy Flynn and then Judge Rushing finds her guilty of being a second-class citizen, one cannot be surprised that I see integration as nothing more than another check marked with insignificant funds. I have often wondered if icons such as King and Du Bois came to the logical conclusion that integration was not an effective plan of action by which African people could gain first-class citizenship, then why do the vast majority of Africans dislocated in America continue to embrace this failed strategy. The answer is fear and self-doubt.

I have spent most of my life asserting that anger is a secondary emotion, created by a primary emotion, such as fear or embarrassment. That is—anger is the mutation of something else. In the case of King and Du Bois anger was the result of years of frustration that caused King to realize that African people were being integrated "out of power" as they were being integrated into "a burning house"—a house that Du Bois had to escape. However, when you see every effective leader that you have ever had killed at the hands of your oppressors, then fear begins to trump anger, especially when we begin to realize that the white power structure will give us a few token seats at their table as long as we behave like crabs in a barrel to get them. And, it is the stripping of self-worth that allows us to act like crabs in a barrel or stars in a minstrel show. No matter what you think of a man begging on a corner, you must understand the human tragedy of the loss of self-worth that has to happen before begging can occur.

A very important mentor once asked me if I actually believed that white America would allow African people to create their own institutions on American soil. My first answer, without much thought, was yes…why not? Then immediately, my mind was bombarded with thoughts of the U. S. sanctioned bombing of African people in Philadelphia, PA, the sanctioning of the criminalizing of African children through suspensions and expulsions, and the national sanctioning of police brutality all across this hellish country. There, then, is no wonder that the two driving arguments against Black Nationalism are "Black folks ain't gon' act right," and "White folks ain't gon' let Black people have nothing." More specifically, white terror is not a theory; it is a historical and current reality—a reality from which Africans living on this soil have done every thing, moral and immoral, to escape.

As Carter G. Woodson proves in *The Mis-education of the Negro*, by the eleventh grade African people are taught to love everyone else but themselves. Thus, the notion of a sovereign African people is, at best, a far-fetched idea and, at worst, insanity. The only option becomes integration—grin, bare it, and scramble for crumbs that hopefully fall from white America's table. (Somebody tell Hughes that they never did become ashamed.) And as we grin and bare it, we lie to ourselves that grinning and baring it is a tactical behavior, which buys us more time to construct freedom for our children. How long will we continue to wear that mask that Dunbar both laments and celebrates? It will probably be forever since every African leader who attempted real structural change that would lead to African first-class citizenship has been killed. Since 1975 African people, as a collective, have been too afraid to take off the mask and show that they are "sick and tired of being sick and tired." Or if we do, our anger is often misguided or misdirected at other Africans. It is easier to mistreat and kill somebody without power than someone with power. This is not to say that African people do not make the types of mistakes that perpetuate our second-class citizenship. However, when your leadership consists of Negroes who think that the opportunity to sing, dance, and be patted on the heads by white folks is progress, then can we really be surprised that our inner city children hate us because they know that the only thing that separates the Rockefellers and Kennedys from the common crack dealer is American policy and Negro fear that keeps them from calling a spade a spade? The only good or decent thing about America was the Civil Rights Movement, but now the CRM is housed in a museum protected/controlled by a white guard while pseudo-Negro leadership wipes its muddy feet on current policy, such as the Ayers case, like it is a doormat to mainstream acceptance. According to Farrakhan, only when we have men who love freedom more than life itself will African people gain first-class citizenship. Rulings such as the Ayers settlement and our continuance to turn a blind eye to police brutality and the character assassination of African lawyers, such as Chokwe Lumumba, tells me that we still love this crummy existence of a life over freedom and sovereignty. Of course, someone will assert that I try living somewhere else. My response is I do not have to do so. What very few rights that I enjoy come from the African liberation movement, which was later co-opted into the CRM by the Johnson Dixie-crates. Every freedom or liberty that is enjoyed in this land, including women's rights, children's rights, and rights for the disabled, all grew from the Africans in America liberation movement. But, that movement was stopped by Nixon and crushed by Reagan and far too many Negroes willing "to kneel and suck again" and again, exchanging sovereignty for shinny things.

Ultimately, Africans in America are afraid and have been convinced that life can get worse. Most African people try to live their lives under the white radar. We must understand that being "cool" has two historical meanings. One is, of course, associated with style and attitude—the notion of being so "in step" with the times that nothing can bother you or make you loose your sense of calm. The other has to do with not making a scene, especially one that will warrant the attention of white people. Thus, we try to get good paying jobs, wear nice clothes, and walk and talk in a "non-threatening" manner. Yet, what we do not realize is that suit and tie Negroes are considered more dangerous than so-called "ghetto" Negroes. The ghetto Negro is what white America expects us to be, and the suit and tie Negro represents the inability of whites to completely suppress the African, unless the suit and tie Negro earns his gains by cutting deals with his white masters to work as a gatekeeper against the masses of African people. This is why we have more civil rights historians than civil rights activists. White people will pay you to be on a panel and talk about past accomplishments, such as Brown vs. the Board, but there is no money paid to address the current policies of poor funding for schools populated by the African underclass.

I have often wondered what would happen if all of the drug dealers, pimps, and gang members put all of their monies and guns together for a revolution, like the American revolution? The American colonists are heroes despite the fact that they stole and sold land, money, and human beings. So I often wonder, for what are the ghetto revolutionaries waiting? "Nigger/ Can you kill?/ Can a nigger kill the man?/ A nigger can die/ We ain't got to prove that/ Can you kill a white man?/ Can you kill your nigger mind/ and free your hands to/ struggle?" The truth is that the drug dealers, pimps, and gang members are not waiting for anything because "Niggers are scared of revolution." They are just as afraid of the white power structure as the suit and tie Negro. In fact, they understand that they exist at the whim and fancy of white power in the same manner as the suit and tie Negro. Drug dealers, pimps, and gang members all work with the permission of white political leadership and law enforcement. So, they are not going to bite the hand that feeds them. We all "wear the mask that grins and lies/ It hides our cheeks and shades our eyes,--/ This debt we pay to human guile;/ With torn and bleeding hearts we smile,/ And mouth with myriad subtleties." We all are a part of the minstrel show of integration.

Yet, there is a seed in me that continues to grow. Every time I am a witness to another unjust ruling in a courtroom regarding my wife's case against Jones County Deputy Kevin Flynn and I just sit there and take it, I must ask myself, "Which do I love more—life or freedom???" What truly happens to a dream deferred? When does it explode?

Brief Comments on
the *Without Sanctuary* Lynching Exhibit

In his disagreement with Plato on the nature of Reality, Aristotle asserted that things are only real when they have meaning. So it was for me that racism became real the moment that I saw the Emmett Till photograph when I was fourteen, and his distorted face etched for me, in no uncertain terms, what my life's struggle was to be. In this same manner, *Without Sanctuary* is a perpetual post card from the past, a lingering voice of conscience-ness that demands that we perpetually revisit ourselves in a manner that we are always analyzing and measuring the humanity that we are becoming. Just as a traveler on a long journey constantly checking his map, so must we check the map of our history to ensure that we are headed in the right direction.

As Margaret Walker does in *Jubilee*, *Without Sanctuary* affirms the beauty and worth of a people who have been treated as the worst of humanity but have managed to love and live like the best of humanity. While we remember these horrific events, we should also remember that we—all of humanity—survived these events, which gives us the hope that we can become better. This exhibit is not one of failure but one of victory for the human spirit. And as we celebrate the victory of Black survival and the ability of Black people to live with honor and dignity in the worst of times, we must also use this exhibit to question and measure our current times. *Without Sanctuary* provides context as to how we all have gotten to this moment in time of renewed racial polarization because we continue not to address what W. E. B. Du Bois deemed as the most important issue of America, the issue of the color line. The pain of *Without Sanctuary* is not that lynching is a part of our history, but that lynching, in one fashion or another, continues to be a part of our fabric. Houston Baker has coined the phrase, "critical memory," which means that African Americans must use their history to remember who they are and to develop proper and effective responses to the present as well as to make plans for the future. As a cultural and political tool, lynching was used to terrorize blacks from asserting their rights as human beings and to affirm black inferiority to whiteness. Thus, the struggle against lynching is the struggle to assert one's humanity—that one human life is equal to all human life. It was this very struggle that the Ayers case attempted to assert by ensuring that all children are treated equally, especially in the funding of their education. However, because we view lynching as a past activity and fail to contextualize lynching as a continuous act of disenfranchisement, we fail to properly analyze all forms and aspects of lynching, which causes us, especially in the Ayers case, not to understand the importance of ensuring that the funding of the education of black children be equal to the funding of the education of white children. When my eyes fall upon the photographs, my mind does not wonder backward to a vague and mysterious past. My mind automatically asks the question, "Are we addressing the lynching of today, when black minds are hanged by the State's policies of 'schoolhouse to jailhouse' and improper funding of educational and cultural programs?" When I study the document that this exhibit is, I wonder who will document the unfair manner in which black children are suspended and expelled from school? When I understand that these victims were not only victims of heinous murders but victims of an unjust legal system, I wonder about the millions of black inmates who have more severe sentences than their white counter-parts who have equal or greater charges against them. The faces on these photographs are the same faces that represent sixty percent of America's prison population. *Without Sanctuary* does not make me think of how bad things used to be. It reminds me of how much work is left to be done. The blood, scars, and broken bodies flapping like rag dolls are no different than the young black men and women who, today, are pulled over for driving while black, or are not hired because they are black, or are paid less because they are black, or are incarcerated because they are black. *Without Sanctuary*, as does all good art, forces us to address the difficult issues of today, which are the issues that will upset and unnerve the people in power—the people who continue to profit from the oppression—social, educational, cultural, and economic lynching—of others. When we turn away from *Without Sanctuary*, we are turning away from the struggle of all humanity to become better than what we are.

Funk's Jes Grew Quality:
The Struggle of Black Art to Find Its Way
Presented at the 2007 Funkativity in African American
Culture Conference at the University of Alabama

"My name is the One; some people call me the Funk." For Parliament/Funkadelic, Funk is the Alpha and the Omega of life, the thing/entity/spirit that orders the universe and makes life worth living. It is, ultimately, the essence of life (the living part), the thing that makes life beautiful. Along with Earth, Wind, and Fire, Parliament/Funkadelic has spent its lifetime looking to find, reconnect with, and deliver the funk to humanity in the same manner that Papa LaBas does with Jes Grew in Ishmael Reed's *Mumbo Jumbo*. "P Funk," "Mothership Connection," and "Give Up the Funk" all seem to follow the logic of Reed's Jes Grew theory that Jes Grew or Funk lies dormant until the right people who understand both its physical and metaphysical powers are able to raise it and use it properly. What separates Parliament/Funkadelic from its Funk Colleagues, such as the Ohio Players, Bar Kays, Lakeside, the Commodores, Cameo, Zapp, ConFunkShun, and the Gap Band, is that there seems to be a purpose to Parliament's Funk, which is equaled only mildly by the Commodores. "Citizens of the Universe, we have returned to claim the pyramids..." where the Funk/Jes Grew has lain dormant, waiting for someone to find it and use it to bring life/living into full reality (completion). If we examine the spiritual quality of Parliament/Funkadelic's work, the specific theme of "Chocolate City," and the Jes Grew phenomenon of Hip Hop, we will see that there is a deeper, more metaphysical aspect to African creativity that continues to struggle against white perversion and oppression to survive and lead African people to their proper place in the universe. Additionally, as Bootsy Collins asserts that Prince made the funk legal, Prince becomes the dominate force of the 1980s to take up the metaphysical quest of Parliament/Funkadelic and in doing so affirms that the Jes Grew quality of Funk is the ability of black culture to seed and grow anywhere, especially in regards to the inspiring and healing qualities of black music to sprout when black people need it most.

It is Parliament who takes James Brown's Funk and reclaims its spiritual nature. Brown knew the power of his music to create social change as evident in "Say It Loud (I'm Black and I'm Proud)," "I Don't Want Nobody to Give Me Nothing (Open up the Door I'll Get It Myself)," and "Soul Power." However, Brown chose to concentrate primarily on the physical aspect of Funk's powers because that was the height of the struggle for himself and his audience. A product of Southern poverty, Brown's music seeks to address, heal, and overcome the pains of that reality. Yet, "Soul Power" is interesting in that it is ambiguous in its definition of what "soul power" is. As Brown asserts, "I want to get under your skin," there is a notion that he is discussing something that is more than or not limited to just the physical. And throughout the song, there is the notion that whatever "soul power" is we seem to be falling just short of grasping and obtaining it. "I gotta have it...gotta reach it...though we need it...what we want, what we missin', what we need..." If nothing else, "Soul Power" can be seen as a bridge or a first step in the evolution from the physical to the metaphysical. After Brown lays the foundation of Funk's healing possibilities, Parliament reopens the gate for the Loa to re-impregnate black music with their powers. David Hill, author of *Prince: A Pop Life*, asserts that "Funk was about The Body: how it looked, what it did, all the hot, nasty, lovely smelly things about it. God would have to shake His ass or just stay home. What Prince did with funk was remind it, curiously, of the sacredness it had left behind. He reintroduced the libido to the Holy Ghost" (96). Traditionally, black music has always navigated the line of the sacred and the secular. As Ray Charles asserts, "The only difference between gospel and blues is they say

'Lawd, Lawd' and we say "Baby, Baby.'" From the spirituals and shouts of slavery to the songs of the Civil Rights Movement, African people have always appropriated art for their particular needs, as evidence by songs, such as "We Shall Overcome," "Oh Freedom," and "We Shall not Be Moved," all of which began as or were based on purely spiritual songs. This is why the blues must be seen as secularized spirituals, not because the blues is sinful but because the blues is designed to attack physical demons and oppression and the spirituals are used to address the metaphysical world. Yet, even with this dual or two-pronged approach or solution, African people have never completely drawn a line in the sand, separating spiritual things from secular things. This is why artists such as the Ray Charles, Sam Cooke, Aretha Franklin, and the Staple Singers could mix and match sounds/phonemes as a way to transfer imagery and meaning from the sacred to the secular and back to the sacred, allowing the intense emotions of spirituality to be substituted for and replaced by sexuality as well as political concern as evidenced by the work of Curtis Mayfield, Marvin Gaye, and Stevie Wonder. If Jesus could go to the whorehouse to save souls quite surely the Staple Singers could go to the café. And if we understand the sermon and miracle on the mountain, we realize that at the core of Jesus' message was that man cannot fulfill his destiny if he separates his body from his soul. Unlike the European understanding of the body, Africans have always understood that God wants the body to be a part of the praise. As Reed asserts in *Mumbo Jumbo*, "…people were allowed to go out of their minds so that spirits could enter their heads; all under the watchful eyes of trained priests who knew the knowledge that Dionysus brought from Egypt" (213). Reed's scene is the affirmation of "Free your mind and your ass will follow."

The current problem is that today's black artist, especially the musician and the "spoken word" artist, are following a flawed or false blueprint of the black aesthetic.

In 1976 with *Songs in the Key of Life*, Stevie Wonder becomes the fulfillment of the Black Arts Movement by creating a work of art that is a social, political, and commercial juggernaut. Though *Songs in the Key of Life* makes a lot of money for the industry, Wonder sees himself as an artist first and an entertainer second. And more specifically, Wonder sees himself as a member of the Black Arts Movement with the responsibility to create art that improves life, especially the lives of African people. However, the strength of the American Empire is its ability to co-opt the creations of its underclass to perpetuate its own structure and power. This is why Edwin Star's "War" can be used to market the NFL and rap music can be used to sell cereal and liquor. The music industry, fearing the power of Wonder's ideology, wanted to find black artists who were as talented as Wonder but saw themselves as entertainers first and black people, second or third. This is what gives rise to Michael Jackson and Prince. This is not to say that Jackson and Prince were not the most talented of their era, but this is to say that cultural sensibilities play as large a role in the success of an artist as does the talent level. Why do you think that Elvis Presley and Pat Boone were so popular? Thus, Jackson and Prince become the first black faces on MTV for the same reason that novels that feature mulatto characters are the first novels by African people to be published and gain success in America. So in stripping certain aesthetics from black music to make it more palatable for white listeners and more controllable for white companies, black music was being stripped of its primary sensibility that linked it to the Continent—the utilitarian nature of art. So today, black art is able to move people, but the movements are often empty because they have no real direction other than to entertain. The spoken word movement is filled with artists who are trying to mimic the performance/entertainment quality of the "writers" of the Black Arts movement, but far too many of these spoken word performers have not read the texts, which include the criticism/theory produced by the writers of the Black Arts Movement, which leaves the spoken word movement empty and without direction.

White controlled media and institutions of learning have purposely marginalized or minimized the intellectual aspects of the writers of the Black Arts Movement and purposely celebrated the performance aspect of these writers. Therefore, the spoken word artists of today are being mis-educated, mislead, and co-opted to become entertainers and not intellectuals or activists. Those who do not have the text or a complete understanding of the totality of Jes Grew will use Jes Grew (Funk or the black aesthetic) merely for entertainment purposes; therefore, the other bands, such as the Ohio Players, Bar Kays, Lakeside, ConFunkShun, and the Gap Band, were funking merely for entertainment, even though the Commodores did choose to interject some spirituality and social conscienceness into their work. But, for the most part, Funk was never taken as seriously by the other bands as by Parliament/Funkadelic who sought to find the metaphysical purpose in their art, in the same manner that Africans injected much of their spiritual/emotional sensibilities into the white man's stoic Christianity. Today, however, the shouting and other emotive qualities in today's Christian praise are misguided and work mostly for entertainment/personal relief purposes and are unable to manifest itself in any real, tangible form because Westernized Africans have accepted the "pie in the sky" theology, which African religion was never about. Unlike the European take on Jesus' teachings, Africans, whose Text on the metaphysical was before Jesus and the Torah, understood, as Jesus understood, that the true goal is to reconnect the physical with the spiritual and not separate the two as Europeanized Christianity does in its separation of the body from the soul, which is clearly not what Jesus had in mind. Jesus performs miracles because he understands that the body must be dealt with before you can get to the soul, or to put it another way, a soul cannot grow in a decaying body. Therefore, Jes Grew or Black

113

Art causes so much chaos because humanity, especially African people, has allowed itself to be separated from the root, the history, and the Text, which is why Parliament/Funkadelic is always talking about "reclaimin'" the Funk. To affirm both Reed's *Mumbo Jumbo* and Kalamu ya Salaam's book *What Is Life?* black people, as evidence of Jes Grew, are the soul of America. As Salaam asserts, there was no decency, democracy, or Christianity in America until black people forced America to parallel its behavior to its ignored ideology. Or as Gil Scot-Heron asserted, black people wanted to be free, then the whole world wanted to be free. The problem is that since the 1970s black people have given up or suppressed their Jes Grew quality to get jobs. And by rejecting the metaphysical for the physical, African people have become as perverted as the people who oppress them. Thus America struggles to have a moral center because its moral compass, which is black people, is broken. This is why Wonder asserts that "Love is in need of Love today." African people, the moral compass of civilization, are engaged in an internal battle for their souls which is being waged between Jes Grew and the lust for all things material.

Thus, "Chocolate City," especially the reoccurring line, "Gainin' on ya'," is in line with Jes Grew coming back to reclaim its place within humanity. In "Chocolate City" Jes Grew is making the rounds the same way that Reed has it making the rounds in *Mumbo Jumbo* to reclaim humanity. George Clinton asserts, "We got Atlanta, Newark, DC. And I'm told we jus' got LA." Given the fact that LA is predominately white but with a large minority population, it seems that LA and New York are Chocolate Cities more in spirit than in physical reality. That is, the notion of the white Negro seems to manifest itself not only in Detroit and Chicago, but also in New York and LA, where it seems that a white person becomes infected with Blackness (acting Black), which is a symptom of Reed's Jes Grew. Accordingly, some of the most horrific documented incidents of police violence over the past ten years have been in New York and LA. The NYPD and LAPD have been acting in the same violent, reactionary manner as Hinckle Von Vampton, Biff Musclewhite, and the Wallflower Order in Reed's *Mumbo Jumbo*. The violent manner of the NYPD and LAPD should be read as the dominant order flexing its muscle at the threat of becoming overrun by minorities and Jes Grew. Thus, Parliament's Sir Nose who seeks to stop the Funk from spreading should be seen as and equated to the leader of Reed's Atonist Group who is trying to stop Jes Grew from infecting the population with Blackness. And both of these incidents represent the struggle of Black Art—the struggle to infect the people with righteousness—to be useful to the people while it is being co-opted by white hands for its own perverse enjoyment and profit. This conflict of how one's work should be used is at the heart of the black struggle for expression and fulfillment through the arts, which is a foreign concept for the European. African art has always been utilitarian, which means it was always used for ritual, for something higher than merely entertainment. On the other hand, European art was art for entertainment, which is why their art has always been open to the spectacle. Entertainment without purpose will always become spectacle, which is why Jerry Springer/Reality Television is the leading form of entertainment in America because the white leaders have been able to wrestle purpose from Art in their attempts to ensure that Art is never used in a rebellion against them. African Art, even the government/tribal sanctioned art, was always used for religious/ritual purposes to ensure that the gods blessed the community. The first time that art was sanctioned by a European State/Government was when the Greeks began to realize that art could be used as a tool of propaganda, which the Africans had realized 3500 years earlier. Thus, European leaders have always used art to either control the masses or create an elite class of leaders

115

whereas African art has a history of both religious and political propaganda designed for the benefit of the people. Today, art, especially Black Art, has been colonized as a tool to pervert the masses, sedate the masses, or gain their loyalty. It will be unlikely that humanity will ever again produce another Curtis Mayfield, Stevie Wonder, or a Black Arts Movement whose sole purpose is to liberate African people and ultimately all people from the control and oppression of the money changers. (Quite frankly, Tupac never had a chance because the white money changers saw him coming since 1920.) As Langston Hughes asserts in his essay "The Negro Artist and the Racial Mountain," the Black artist is either seduced, forced to conform, or is silenced. However, this conformity does not delete or negate Jes Grew, which is always there, fighting to be heard even if it is perverted or misheard, which is why Prince can sing "The Cross" and "Sexy Muthafucker" at the same show.

In fact, this whole battle of black musicians/ griots/artists who see their work as much more than merely entertainment has created the phenomenon of black artists and their civil warfare of music for God versus music for man. Little Richard, Marvin Gaye, Al Green, Prince, Mase, and Lauryn Hill are all generational indexes of black people struggling with the purpose of art because they are at war with how Jes Grew should manifest itself and be manifested by them. All of these artists, at one point in their careers, struggled with the choice of serving the secular or the divine. And in affirmation with Reed's notion, Stevie Wonder and George Clinton have had the least trouble dealing with the schism of the sacred and the secular because they, moreso than the others mentioned, have embraced their African selves, which allows them not to be confused or confined by white notions of what is proper to discuss in "popular" music. Black art will always be powerful because it innately contains the remnants of Jes Grew (the African Juju), but due to a calculated disconnect orchestrated by the white money changers, the people who create the art do not fully understand how or why they create the art, and this is dangerous. Instead of inspiring black people to evolve to our highest point where the metaphysical and the physical converge on utopia, we are being inspired to fornicate ourselves into oblivion. However, the fight is not over because Jes Grew will not go away. The latest example of Jes Grew is Hip Hop as a culture and DJing as an artifact of that culture. The Reagan Administration, which should be seen as the administrative arm of Reed's Atonists, sought to control African people by cutting the arts in public schools. The Atonists were hoping to produce a "Maggot Brain" effect where the society turns to nihilism and the money changers run wild, i.e. President Bush and Halliburton. But, what the following generations heard in "Maggot Brain" was not just that "America eats its young," but it also heard the hope that if we turn to Nature and treat her right, she will fulfill all our needs. As George Clinton declares, "I believe in God, and I know that law and order must prevail. But, if and when the laws of man are not just, equal, and fair, then the law of nature will come and do her thang....Free your mind and your ass will follow."

African peoples' belief in the power of the metaphysical over the physical is what has allowed them to survive the most heinous conditions of humankind. It is this hope that allows Jes Grew to reform in the midst of Reagan's attack on black people. Even without access to musical instruments, Africans dislocated in America's Ghettos have been able to continue the creation of the most powerful music on the planet by co-opting the oppressor's technology. This ability to turn the turntable into a musical instrument is evidence of Jes Grew. The problem is that the generation before Hip Hop saw Hip Hop as a threat because Hip Hop was seen as rebuking the integrationist sensibilities of the artists of the eighties. Because of this, another gap is created, which continues the disconnect or fragmentation of Jes Grew and its ability to manifest itself for its rightful purpose. But this does not mean that Jes Grew was not there, struggling to be heard. With his releases of *The Rainbow Children* (2001), *The Slaughterhouse* and *The Chocolate Invasion* (2003), *Musicology* (2004), and *3121* (2006), Prince's goal has been to reclaim musicians and musicianship for their rightful purpose, which is to uplift man, and, to be more clear, to reconnect man to God. As he asserts "Technology is cool, but you got to use technology and not allow it to use you…we need musicians not computer programmers." To this Prince adds, "Without real spiritual mentoring, too much freedom can lead to the soul's decay." And the theme of the importance of connecting the physical to the metaphysical is nothing new to Prince if we correctly remember *Around the World in a Day*, *Sign 'O' the Times*, and *Lovesexy*. So Prince, like Dizzy Gillespie, Charlie Parker, Thelonious Monk, Sun Ra, Miles Davis, and Parliament/Funkadelic, is trying to move beyond the physical qualities of music and find its metaphysical qualities—that thing that reconnects us to our higher purpose and being. The problem is that Prince was one of the people who openly waged war on Hip Hop with his song "Dead on It," so reconnecting to the Hip Hop generation and acting as a griot for them may be difficult if not impossible. But, if Amiri Baraka and Maulana Karenga can "reconcile," then anything is possible. Artists, such as Chuck D, ?Love, Doug E. Fresh, OutKast, and Alicia Keys, have long stated their respect for Prince. Yet, it remains to be seen if anyone has the ability, knowledge, and heart to lead current artists back to the root and Text of Jes Grew. Until this happens, Black Art will continue to be used against black people rather than for black people. Thus, our artists will continue to be "talkin' loud and sayin' nothin'," as we continue to wander in this wilderness with no hope of making it to the promised land.

Works Cited

Brown, James. *Star Time: Box Set*. Polydor, 1991.

Charles, Ray and David Ritz. *Brother Ray: Ray Charles' Own Story*. New York: Da Capo Press, 1978, 2004.

Funkadelic. *Maggot Brain*. Westbound Records, 1971.

Funkadelic. *One Nation Under a Groove*. Priority Records, 1978, 1993.

Hill, Dave. *Prince: A Pop Life*. New York: Harmony Books, 1989.

Parliament. *Tear the Roof Off: 1974 – 1980*. Casablanca: PolyGram Records, 1993.

P-Funk All Stars. *Live at the Beverly Theater in Hollywood*. Westbound Records, 1990.

Porter, Eric. *What Is this Thing Called Jazz?: African American Musicians as Artists, Critics, and Activists*. Berkeley: University of California Press, 2002.

Reed, Ishmael. *Mumbo Jumbo*. New York: Scribner Paperback Fiction, 1972.

Salaam, Kalamu ya. *What Is Life?: Reclaiming the Black Blues Self*. Chicago: Third World Press, 1994.

"Until today, talking with you, I was under the impression that the Jackson State students were assaulting and firing on the highway patrol. But you tell me that there is no evidence of that. That's just always the way that it was told to me, that the students were rioting."
Former Jackson Police Officer Perry Martin

The Jackson State University Assassination: What Does it Continue to Mean in the Annals of Time?

What are the facts of the Jackson State University Shooting? In May of 1970, the Mississippi State Highway Patrol, in full riot gear, along with the Jackson Police Department and the Mississippi National Guard, marched onto the JSU campus and fired upon students, leaving two dead, several injured, buildings severely damaged by bullets, and classes closed for the remainder of the semester. These are the facts. These are the only documented facts that we have. There are no other documents or facts that tell us why this horrible event happened. Yet, remembering and analyzing an event that occurred thirty years ago, it is logical to understand that many in this Jackson, Mississippi, metro community have differing opinions as to what happened, why it happened, and what it means. The real problem is that thirty years ago there was no consensus as to what happened, why it happened, and what it meant then. This horrible crime has seemed to go the way of slavery for African Americans, out of sight, out of mind, reduced to less than a sentence in newspapers and history books. Nevertheless, the questions thirty years later remain the same. Why did it happen, and what does it mean? This sliding scale of truth remains because history is androgynous for it is both concrete and relative as memory is always randomly selective since it is the child of experience and perception all housed in the matrix of politics. The truth is that white officers of the City of Jackson and the State of Mississippi murdered

African American students who were not committing any crimes. Anyone who does not understand this massacre as an act of colonization probably still believes that Jefferson did not rape Sally Hemings and that the Civil War was not about the perpetuation of cheap labor through the continuation of slavery. At any rate, after questioning both white and African American citizens, it seems that the true legacy of this shooting is that America is still a country divided, one white and one black, separate and unequal, still struggling to reconcile itself to its past, often through the process of selective amnesia. Dr. Ivory Phillips, JSU graduate and now social science professor at JSU, asserts that people must begin to perceive the JSU shooting of May 14, 1970, not as a singular event, but as a significant point fixed within a larger event. In his paper, "The Historical Process: The Local Community and the Gibbs-Green Experience Then and Now," Phillips writes, "Just as any other significant event in history, the barrage of gunfire that killed Phillip Gibbs and James Earl Green did not occur in isolation. It was not its own root. It grew out of a historical process...The shootings were an adjunct to or grew out of the national Civil Rights Movement which had begun sixteen years earlier in Montgomery, Alabama." The JSU shooting, then, evolved from the desire of liberty by African Americans and the desire of white Americans to keep African Americans as second class citizens. As such, one must understand the issues regarding J. R. Lynch Street, white concern over JSC developing as a vanguard of intellectual and socio-political leadership, and the need to seize JSU as a satellite for the University of Mississippi to contextualize this event as a major aspect of the Civil Rights Movement so that future generations are able contextualize and protect themselves from current decisions made by Mississippi's elected officials and so that JSU students can be cleared of any culpability of this event.

Like all watershed or monumental events in history, the cause is often dual, being both literal and symbolic, much like the crafting of a poem. The literal, specific issue was that Lynch Street was a major city throughway going right through the heart of Jackson State College. Bill Minor, award-winning journalist/columnist who worked with the *New Orleans Times Picayune* as its Mississippi correspondent and with the *New York Times* and *Newsweek*, states that "the 1967 Ben Brown murder by a Jackson police officer mobilized JSC students, but Lynch Street is the flashpoint to the 1970 shooting." Lynch Street meant constant danger for JSC students attempting to navigate the campus, having to cross the major lane of traffic. In his book *To Survive and Thrive*, Dr. John A Peoples, JSU President during the time of the 1970 shooting, summarizes the danger. "Three times a day, four thousand students crossed Lynch Street…" (176). Because there was no interstate circling the city, Lynch Street was the only way to get from one side of the city to the other. For the JSC students, crossing Lynch Street to get to class was akin to crossing an interstate highway where white motorists normally reached speeds as high as sixty miles an hour. This enhanced the tension between JSC students and white motorists who feared and resented having to drive through the JSC campus, during a time of high tension and activity in America. Additionally, Lynch Street represented more than just a traffic hazard. It symbolized the disregard for African American life, well-being, and education. On several occasions Peoples pleaded with the state college board to construct an over-path so that the students could commute from their dorms to their classes safely, but the state board refused, showing an obvious disregard for the students' safety. Jackson State College was never expected to become a major institution of higher learning in the eyes of the state's white power structure. In fact, Jackson State, because of its growth, had become a thorn in the side of white oppression, and Lynch Street was the last remaining symbol of the state's control and dominance of the institution. Dr. Peoples recounts how Lynch Street became the point or apex of conflict. The day before the shooting, Jackson's Chief of Police, M. P. Pierce, states to Dr. Peoples, "Well Doctor, your people better keep those students out of the streets, because we are going to keep Lynch Street clear. There are a lot of people who drive up and down that street to get to their jobs, and they have to be protected" (Peoples 175). Lynch Street was the line drawn in the sand. As it was the major intersection and throughway for the metropolitan area, it would become a major intersection for the battle over black education in the state. Over a period of two years, two JSC students were struck by motorists, and countless other students were assaulted by white motorists who would shout obscenities at the students and even threw items at the students. After years of being denied protection from the city, the county, or the state, the JSC students decided to take matters into their own hands.

Pierce's attitude shows not only a disregard for African American life, but for African American sovereignty and autonomy. Never did the Jackson Police Department, the Mississippi National Guard, or the State Highway Patrol ever once try to coordinate some solution or compromise to the Lynch Street problem. In fact the night of the shooting, the police department, the national guard, and the highway patrol all refused to talk directly to Dr. Peoples or his head of security, Sergeant M. R. Stringer. Peoples recounts, "...I was never in direct communication with the mayor or police department. The decision to mobilize the national guard and the highway patrol was done without consulting or even informing me until they were on the scene...I was not able to communicate with the Jackson police, the highway patrol or the national guard. Thus, I was unaware that around 11:00 p.m. the national guard had been moved within blocks of the campus at each end of the Lynch Street entrances. Presumably, Major General Johnson, of the national guard, made this decision after monitoring the Jackson Police Department's radios" (Peoples 173, 178).

The police were on a different radio frequency, keeping Peoples and Sergeant Stringer from being able to monitor their actions. This gets back to the sovereignty issue. Although Lynch Street ran directly through the heart of JSC, it was considered by the city as under its jurisdiction, putting the coming and going of the students under the city's jurisdiction and not the university's. "Lynch Street, always the focal point of action, was in the domain of the City of Jackson. It has been made very clear that Jackson State College security police had no authority on Lynch Street. For the City of Jackson to grant such authority to the Jackson State security police would have given them the authority to arrest white motorists who traveled the streets. Such was verboten at the time" (Peoples 165). So, President Peoples had very little control over Lynch Street or its security. His hands were tied, and the Jackson Police Department, the Mississippi National Guard, and the State Highway Patrol could take whatever action that they saw fit.

Current Chancery Clerk and former Mrs. Jackson State College (1970-1971) Eddie Jean Carr asserts that Jackson State was, for the most part, a conservative college, which raises more questions about the ire and actions of the government against the institution. "There was a balance of political activists and serious scholars, but as a student body we were mainly concerned with grades and being good students." She marvels at the diversity of African Americans that were enrolled at the college. "I was the daughter of a preacher, and most of my family worked on the plantation in McGee. My grandfather used to tell us that we could get a good education to that we would have opportunities like becoming a bank teller or a secretary. Then, I get to Jackson State, and I was amazed at the number of black kids who aspired to be doctors or lawyers or scientists. I asked myself 'where did they get these ideas?'" Carr admits that she was sheltered by living in the country. "We knew about racism, but it was subtle to me and my siblings even back then. You knew when you went to a restaurant in town that you had to a hole in the back to order. But we mostly stayed on the farm. We knew about John F. Kennedy whom I thought was awesome and of course Martin Luther King, Jr., but it was all on television. I was not particularly political even in college. I joined the normal college organizations, such as the Health and Physical Education Club, the Baptist Training Union, and I was Mrs. Sophomore Class. However, the students that lived in the Jackson area like Carl Griffin whose parents were art professors at the college were a bit more radical than me. These were also the students who had participated in summer programs such as Upward Bound. But even these kids were ultimately about getting their education. The most political group on the campus was the Vet Club, which was a group of older students who had recently finished military duty, including just returning from Vietnam. And yet, their activism was more of community protection from the white motorist who refused to obey the speed limit of J. R. Lynch Street. The Vet Club would escort the students, especially the females, across Lynch Street. Of course this would anger some of the white motorist, but we were left to protect ourselves. Now, I did see some students throw rocks at motorists, but that was only in response to the white motorists refusing to obey the traffic laws."

Porter, now the owner and president of Porter's Insurance Agency, affirms Carr's notion that the JSC campus was not as politically radical as other campuses. "As a student from a small town like Monticello, I was scared to death when I first arrived on Jackson State's campus. My older brother had come to Jackson State and was on the baseball team, but it was like a whole new world. If it had not been for meeting Bergie Jones who worked in Financial Aid, I probably would have gone back home. What helped me most was that I was in a controlled situation. As a cheerleader and as a scholarship recipient of the Thirteen College Curriculum Program, I was monitored a great deal. As such, I did not have much leisure or extra time for political activism. In fact, the campus was a quite conservative campus. Most of the students were focused on changing the world by getting their degrees." Porter continues, "Lynch Street could be an adventure. It was very busy, especially at night. But it was consistently busy during the morning, noon, and evening rush hours. People forget that there was no I-220, so Lynch was a major avenue. There was a difference in the speeds of the drivers because whites just wanted to get through the campus as quickly as possible while black motorists drove slowly because many wanted to view the campus. But, yes, white motorists tended not to obey the speed limit, would often blow their horns or mouth something to express their frustration with the situation."

Realizing that they were not going to be protected, the JSC students took matters into their own hands and decided that it was time for the street to close. My father, Claude McInnis, Sr., JSC graduate and current Hinds County Youth Court Counselor, states, "We [students] decided that it was time to close the street. We were tired, fed-up with the careless disregard for our lives, our institution and our education." Phillips affirms this sentiment. "The Black Power Movement was also recognition that there were limitations to simply marching and lobbying…These black and proud students [would not just stand before national guardsmen] as if they were toy soldiers. The Black Power Movement created a new type of student for which the so-called peace officers were not prepared, but it also thrust students into roles for which they were not fully prepared" (Phillips 2000). Lynch Street was the catalyst and the fuse for this standoff. Peoples adds, "One thing I felt for sure of was that Lynch Street must remained closed…" (Peoples 173). Lynch Street represented the battle for power between the races, a battle that like all battles for power often end in bloodshed.

Hollis Watkins, activist and President of Southern Echo, believes that in order to truly understand why the shooting happened and what the shooting means, we must look at the shooting as an integral and inextricable part of the Civil Rights Movement. "One of my major concerns has been the fact that there has never really been an effort to connect the Jackson State University shooting to the Civil Rights Movement as an attempt by the State of Mississippi to crush the student movement arm of the Civil Rights Movement. We must go back a couple of years earlier to the Ben Brown shooting of 1967, which was just up the street from the campus of JSU. Ben was intimately involved in the Civil Rights Movement, working for the COFO (Council of Federated Organizations) office on Lynch Street. Ben and others had the duty of guarding the COFO office from the insensitive and thuggish white folks who would attack Civil Rights Workers. Ben was not only a protector of the COFO office, he and his colleagues were protectors of the community that housed JSU, making them protectors of JSU. The community had a bond with Ben and his colleagues who were working in their best interest to protect them. So, Lynch Street, the COFO office, and Jackson State were not strangers to white terrorism. And this is what people need to know, that the JSU shooting was not an isolated event. That shooting was only a manifestation of the terror inflicted upon African Americans all over the country, all up and down the black Farish Street District and all up and down Lynch Street. Ben's assassination by Jackson Police officers inspired, motivated, and mobilized the young people at JSU because Ben was working in the JSU community. The protesting of the JSC students caused white people to become afraid to pass through the campus, which they had to do because Lynch Street was still the major throughway of the city connecting one half of the city to the other half. Yet the irony is that the students were always peacefully protesting. What this white fear did was perpetuate a fraud of the

127

dangerous students at JSU, putting the students, not the white motorists, in danger of retaliation from the city and the state. In perpetuating a fraud, the state and the city decided to make a mass move on young Black people. The white power structure was determined, willing, ready and prepared to shut down young black people" (Watkins 2000).

Dr. Peoples affirms this testament of the importance of the Ben Brown murder which added to the increased mobilization of JSC students into the student movement. "This May 1967 disturbance was the one in which Benjamin Brown, a non-student, was killed at Lynch and Rose Streets...the students straightway took their struggle beyond the bounds of the campus in the May 1967 riot against the Jackson Police. It was in this initial disturbance that I first perceived the deep seated anger in the students who had suffered racial discrimination and suppression. When white policemen invaded the campus and fired shotguns and tear gas at students who were doing no more than peacefully protesting, all the repressed anger, rage and aggression came forth. The students stoned the cars of any white persons who drove down Lynch Street" (Peoples 163).

Although Watkins acknowledges the pressure put on by the state, he also questions the leadership and decision making of the local black leadership. "There were some so-called leaders who always played between the cracks, doing just enough to pacify whites while staying in the good graces of blacks. The reaction of the JSC shooting was par for the course for the so-called black leadership. Their division left them inept." Watkins also feels that the JSU administrators must share some burden of the incident. "One must have a game plan before the game. This was JSC's biggest problem. An institution should be a body that has, for the most part, its own autonomy and authority. The JSC administration should have been the body deciding who could and who could not come on campus, but that was not the case. And even in the case where their decisions and desires were not achieved, the administration still had the power to disseminate an all-points bulletin to the community at large, informing the students and the community that the state is monitoring us and will eventually move on us, using physical force. I just have a difficult time believing that some of the JSC administrators did not fully understand the situation and the atmosphere. If the master is displeased, the slaves on the plantation always know it. Someone could have alerted the students and the community. So, then, this explains the lack of reaction from the administrators. They were just not in a position to do much or say much."

In addition to Watkins' comments, Dr. Glen Watts, author of the book *The Sovereignty Files: The Real Story*, alludes to the fact that all of the black institutions in the state had "plants" or "spies" who worked for the State Sovereignty Commission. Further, John Dittmer, in his book *Local People*, points out that because JSC was a public institution, it could be counted on by the state to take a conservative, accommodationist stance. Moreover, former JSC President and Peoples predecessor, Jacob L. Reddix, as Dittmer shows, "had accommodated to this reality and had previously made it clear to students that he would not tolerate civil rights activity on his campus" (Dittmer 88). In response to the JSC students attempting to show allegiance to Tougaloo and the "Tougaloo Nine," Reddix took direct action to stop any type of civil rights activity on JSC's campus. During a JSC prayer vigil in support of the "Tougaloo Nine," Reddix, accompanied by members of the Jackson police force, angrily demanded that the students go to their rooms, but only after he threatened to expel them if the meeting did not break up" (Dittmer 88). However, Reddix's actions in no way embodied the student's sentiments or determination. "The next day Jackson State students boycotted classes and staged an illegal rally on campus, after which a group of fifty began to march to the city jail, where the Tougaloo students, still in custody, were meeting with their president, Daniel Beittel, who came to demonstrate his support…when the students refused to disperse, police charged into the group with clubs, tear gas, and police dogs." (Dittmer 88). So, we have as far back as 1961 examples of the city's and state's willingness to use terror and physical force on African American students, all the while employing the adults and educational administrators as pawns to perpetuate white supremacy.

As always with race issues, there is no clear-cut way of completely perceiving and understanding Reddix's actions. Attorney and poet David Brian Williams, former JSU student under Peoples and former Director of Housing and Public Access Network for the City of Jackson, has always contended that Reddix was acting more out of concern for JSU and its students than as a pawn of the state. "Reddix saw his job as being an educator first and foremost. His job was to ensure the education of JSU students. He felt that he could not properly or adequately educate JSC students if they were not in school or living under the terror of white threat." Minor adds to this discussion of the differing philosophies between Reddix and Peoples and sheds even more light on the complexity of this event and the complexity of the struggle of African Americans for Civil rights. "Reddix would be called an Uncle Tom, but he was a decent guy. (Laughter) He was an accommodationist. He tried to work within the framework of segregation. He was fighting for the life of the university. Peoples, on the other hand, was not a radical, but more of an intellect than Reddix. It is his intellectualism and his desire to see JSC evolve as a highly regarded institution of higher learning that would cause him to take carefully calculated stands on academic issues."

130

At best the relationship between President Reddix and his students was adversarial. So when Peoples, a former JSC student, becomes the school's president in 1967, the students and the community embraced him with open arms. Although his tenure is marred by those in his administration who remained connected to the legacy of Reddix's tenure, Peoples, for the most part, is viewed as the greatest and most progressive president that the university has ever had. So it is both typical and ironic that it is under Peoples' tenure that the 1970 shooting occurred. Again, for the most part, Peoples was not an accommodationist. He believed that JSC could be developed into the urban and possibly metropolitan university of the state and took steps to develop it as such. It is under his tenure that both the academic programs and the campus facilities almost triple. Peoples was insightful enough to wage public fights against the state's increases in college admission standards, such as the raising of the ACT score, but he also used the ACT as a way to recruit some of the nation's top academic performers by granting scholarships to students earning an ACT score of 17 or better. However, all of this progress was viewed with very close scrutiny by the state college board, who wanted a JSC president in their pocket and not as a thorn in their side. Most importantly, under Peoples' tenure, JSC students felt free to associate with Tougaloo students who had a history and a tradition of civil rights activity. There was no Reddix there to stop the students' political activity, so the state was forced to take direct action.

In his book Peoples discusses that his first major hurdle was to bridge the gap between the administration, the faculty, and the students. "Jackson State students were in double jeopardy whenever they engaged in civil rights activities, on or off campus. They were subject to arrest by the civil authorities, and they were subject to suspension or expulsion by college authorities...The college board had also put into operation a 'speakers ban' policy to bar speakers with liberal or civil rights viewpoints from speaking on state college campuses" (Peoples 161). By banishing several "antiquated regulations" on the campus, Peoples noticed a "great reduction in hostility between students and the administration…With students and the administration freed from internal feuding, Jackson State could now get on with the real fight for education…" (Peoples 162,163). Peoples' plan of action was working. "The spring quarter of 1970…Jackson State had more than doubled its enrollment. I could hardly wait until commencement, scheduled for May 24, 1970. We were going to have the largest graduating class in the college's history. Six hundred fifty-five students were to receive the Baccalaureate degree and thirty-four were to receive the Masters degree" (Peoples 168). Peoples was a new type of leader for black colleges in Mississippi. His three boldest moves show this. Peoples not only supported the students' right to editorialize the social-political events of the day in the student newspaper, *Blue and White Flash*, he even assisted in the founding of a more radical underground newspaper, *The Gadfly*. Secondly, Peoples founded the Faculty Senate, an adversarial group and mouth piece to address the concerns and issues that faculty may have with him. This was a move toward shared governance, a policy with which the all-white and racist college board would fight. Peoples was attempting to create a university where he and his co-workers would have some collective say in policy. Yet, his boldest move had to be that he had a habit of not allowing the media to attend JSC meetings. This sent a direct message to the college board through the white controlled media that he was going to run Jackson State and control what information was disseminated about the school.

Watkins asserts that the shooting was a direct reaction to the changes that were occurring at JSC. "What had long been a plantation type administration under Reddix was now starting to have some rumblings. The state had to move on JSC. The shooting was intended to and had a serious impact on the local movement as a whole. It illustrated to young black people that they were not protected anywhere. Even if you are on a college campus, you do not have the support of your administrators as a whole. They will allow the foxes to enter the house to capture and destroy anyone talking about constitutional rights. Then to have everyone, the state, the city, even some schools officials to attempt to justify the actions that were taken by the State Highway Patrol Troopers and the Jackson Police Department further puts a chill on the effect, like putting snow on an ice bed. This deterred many of the young black people in the community from becoming involved in the Civil Rights Movement and created a further divide in the community, which negatively impacted and continues to impact the activism of local residents. Think about it. Many of the college students of that time are now somewhere between the ages of forty-eight and fifty-one. Most saw integration, assimilation, and accommodation as the only way to protect themselves and their family. This is the message that the shooting sent and etched into the hearts of the JSU community." Phillips readily agrees with Watkins that "Jackson State has been an integral part of the local community. An attack on Jackson State is an attack on the black community." It was an attempt by the state to tighten the reins on the black community by putting its hands around the throat of its institution of higher learning.

Watkins also draws a distinct and contrasting correlation between the JSC shooting and the Kent State shooting. "Deep in the guts and hearts of most white people, especially at that time, many did not see black people as human. That is what drove their naiveté. That is why they could ask, 'What do black people want?' 'Why do they want civil rights?' So when you are slaughtering animals for the good of the community, there is really no need to publicize it. It happens all of the time. It should happen. But when we inadvertently kill white children at a white institution, we must publicize that so that people will see and understand the loss of human life in order to lead people to the conclusion that it was a serious mistake. The same holds true for Pearl and Columbine. There is no media and social outreach when little black babies die, only when little white babies die. The only reason the country looked for James Chaney is because Michael Schwerner and Andrew Goodman were also missing. That is the nature of the beast, which is America. That is why you have an apology or an admitted mistake when we are discussing the Kent State issue and not for the JSU shooting. In fact, the action or reaction of Mississippi to the shooting was to justify the actions of the troopers and the police officers." This is in fact true. When I interviewed Officer Perry Martin, an African American police officer on the force since 1968, he told me that he was always under the impression that JSC students were firing on state troopers. Both Peoples and Watkins further elaborate that there were two of three reasons, justification, given to cover up the shootings but none of the accusations against the students were ever proven. First, it was that JSC students were firing upon state troopers. Next, it was that a bottle and other objects were thrown at the troopers, and the troopers mistakenly took the breaking of a bottle for gun fire. Thirdly, it was that the sound of someone breaking glass in a JSC dormitory caused the troopers to believe that students were about to begin firing upon them. There have been many explanations of the troopers' and police officers' actions, but not one apology issued forth from the State of Mississippi nor the City of Jackson. Derrick Johnson, attorney and Mississippi NAACP Director, adds, "…and there will never be an apology because of the Ayers Case. The State is fighting for its life not to adequately fund JSU and its other Historically Black Colleges and Universities because of the Ayers Case. An apology for the shooting issue will mean more momentum for the Ayers Cause, supporting that JSU, as well as all of the state's black colleges and universities, has been forced to exist in a hostile environment in which it has been harassed, terrorized, and under-funded." Statements like these do much to cast the JSC shooting directly into the light of the Civil Rights Movement. There is a notion that the State of Mississippi saw JSC as a threat to its plantation system of education and needed to do whatever necessary to stop the slaves on the plantation from rising. The connection between the Ayers Case and the JSC shooting again prompts us to raise more critical questions regarding the shooting and its meaning.

Watkins also believes that there should be an apology made. "JSU deserves an apology from the state, and JSU should also give an apology to the community. In both cases an apology is not enough, but an apology takes us into the steps of atonement. You must clearly accept the wrong of your actions, and then you must compensate for your wrong actions. A naked apology is useless." When asked why JSU must apologize, Watkins states, "For not being good stewards, keepers, and protectors of the university and the young people who were entrusted in their care, for not telling the truth, and for not building bridges with the community and with the other black institutions in the state. JSU was and still is the lead African American public institution in the state. They were the first African American public institution in the state to gain the status of university. They were the first African American state institutions to grant masters and doctorate degrees. This type of status breeds responsibility to your own community, the community that has patronized you and allowed you to achieve. Instead, the university has bought into the city's and state's rhetoric and plan which has allowed the state the scale back the number of African American students who enroll in four year public institutions. Thus, those who were responsible for the shooting are now reaping the benefits of the current chaos surrounding JSU. Because JSU has walled itself from its community, both physically and emotionally, it is divorcing itself from the community that created it. JSU's separation from the surrounding African American community makes it more vulnerable to be colonized and completely controlled by white citizens to create the University of Mississippi at Jackson. White leadership has long since realized that it has made a major mistake by not putting a historically white university in the capital city. As early as 1927 then Governor Theodore G. Bilbo presented a plan to the State legislature to move the University of Mississippi from Oxford to Jackson. So, Jackson State, as a symbol of black progress, has long been seen as a hurdle to white progress. And we can add to this history and struggle, the fact that Jackson State, which relocated to Jackson from Natchez in 1882 on the land now housed by Millsaps College, was forced to leave the city limits of Jackson in 1894 by Major Reuben Millsaps who served in the confederate army.

> "Dr. Ayers received many letters protesting the presence of Jackson College in that part of the city. He was approached by whites who asked him to sell the Jackson College property to Major Reuben Webster Millsaps...[These protests worsened when Dr. Barrett becomes the Jackson College President.] When threats began to be made on his life, Dr. Barrett—after consultation with his family— appealed to the Board of Trustees of the American Baptist Home Mission Society to consider relocating the school" (Rhodes 28-35).

As documents show, since 1894, Jackson State has been under relentless attack from the State of Mississippi, which came to a boiling point in 1970.

McInnis Sr. also sees the shooting as an attempt by the state of Mississippi to squash the student movement and roll back the hands of time. "I entered the halls of JSU in

'67, but I first came into contact with JSU around '61 or
'62. It was the community's school. I had family who had
attended JSU. It was very visible in my community as the
community's school. We all felt a part of the institution.
During my junior and senior high school years, I would sit-
in on several JSU classes. This was before any type of
"official" bridge program between JSU and the surrounding
public schools. It's just always been that way. JSU was
our, the surrounding community's, school, even though it
was never as politically involved as Tougaloo. In fact,
given my own social-political involvement before college,
Tougaloo should have been my first choice. I was very
active with COFO and SNCC during my high school years.
In fact, I was run into the army because both the local
police and sheriff officers threatened my parents of bodily
harm to me. When I returned from Vietnam, I wanted to go
right back into the movement. Although Tougaloo was the
more active college, JSU was my home. It was the school
of my community, and I wanted to be there, making a
difference. Finally, JSU had the best social work
curriculum in the state. I did the research. JSU's
curriculum was far superior to Millsaps', Mississippi
College's, or Belhaven's. Not only were there more
extensive classes, the JSU social work program allowed
you to do extensive field work. It also required you to
complete and defend a senior paper which the others did
not require. So, I knew that JSU would prepare me to be
able to make a difference in my community. The state
wanted to stop JSU's influence over the community."

McInnis Sr. suggests that the time was right for
political action on the JSU campus. "Peoples brought a
fresh atmosphere and attitude to the campus. We used to
call him president of the student body. There was
electricity in the air, political electricity. My first political
involvement on the JSC campus came through the aid and
organization of the Vet club. A group of us wanted to take
care of vets and encourage yets to get degrees. We felt that

this would help society. As a vet, I was older and had a more complete view of the world and how it works as it relates to the perception of seventeen year old freshman. I saw myself and the other vets as an invaluable source of information and guidance for these young minds surrounding us. We felt that it would be a great marriage. Vets are trained to protect and serve. What is a better way to protect and serve than by getting college degrees and helping to mold the minds of younger college students through social and political interaction? What's more is that Peoples somewhat worked with us. He would solicit our involvement in various activities. We even worked doing minor security around the campus. During a couple of earlier demonstrations in '69, the national guard was called out, and it was then that we, the Vet Club, decided that the university needed some protection, the type of protection that was not being afforded by the state. So we began monitoring the campus as much as we could."

McInnis Sr. also asserts that all political activity was directly related to the improvement of the academic atmosphere. "My first political stand as President of the Vet Club was on the price of books. Man, books were overly expensive because our bookstore only sold hard back books which are usually double the cost of paperback books. We had to go to Millsaps to purchase paperback books. So we began to petition for the sale of paperback books only. Of course, the minute we graduated, they started back to selling hardback books. Now, why is this a political issue? Education is political. It has always been the arm of white supremacy in this country. That's why there has always been a price tag on education, to price it out of the range of the working class. What sense does it make to price books out of the range of students? You cannot get a proper education without books. We understood that if you are able to decrease the cost of books, the students would be more inclined to purchase all types of books in the bookstore, not just textbooks. For a

138

people to be a thinking people, they must be a reading people, and this all starts with the cost of books. Then we moved on to the accessibility of teachers to students. There were some excellent teachers at JSU, but the Reddix administration had produced a generation gap as wide as the Grand Canyon. Teachers did not interact well with the students. So, we began to petition for venues, specifically, informal venues where students could be free to ask professors about anything pertaining to the subject matter, questions like 'How do I get a job in this area?' 'How does this subject matter relate to the present condition of black people in America?' We did not have the freedom to ask these types of questions in class. And if you did, you were often ostracized, scolded, or labeled a trouble maker. These forums created a place known as the 'Knowledge Tree,' which is where I received my best instruction. It was a tree outside the social sciences building which I now think is the Charles F. Moore Building which sits between the academic tower and the library. This is the type of forward, progressive atmosphere that Peoples brought to the campus."

That atmosphere of electricity was spreading. Both Peoples and McInnis Sr. attest that "Jackson State was becoming known for its annual spring riots in protest of some issue or another." From 1967 to 1970, there were four straight major protests in each spring quarter. McInnis Sr. states that "they were generally peaceful but loud. The campus was always tense because Lynch Street came right through the center of the campus. It was a major throughway for the city. No other college or university campus in the state has or had a major metropolitan throughway running right down its center. The existence of Lynch Street running right through our campus spoke volumes about the state's perception of JSC. We were meant to be nothing more than a little nigga college to raise cheap labor. But we fooled the state and began producing some of the best intellectual talent that this state had ever seen. And there was animosity about that. We were not supposed to have 4,500 students at that time. We were not supposed to have a thriving graduate school. We were not supposed to be moving toward having a certified and respected school of business. We were not supposed to be producing students able to compete in law and medical schools. Every year there was some debate over cutting the funding to JSU. Having Lynch Street run directly down the center of campus was a symbol and constant reminder of what the state thought of JSU. We were an afterthought that, unfortunately for the State of Mississippi, grew into an integral part of the state's college education system. So, there was animosity from the whites who would ride through the campus, mooning the students and propositioning the female students. We, the students, wanted that street closed. And the street became a way for the state to disrupt the school. It was reported to us that the highway patrol was on the campus in full riot gear because of threats and other incidents toward white motorists. Yet, there was never any formal charges brought against any JSC student for the harm, assault, or harassment of any white motorists." McInnis Sr. falls in line with others who cite the ongoing Lynch Street situation as the "agent provocateur" for the JSC shooting. "The Vet Club was worried about the incidents on Lynch Street more than anything else. So, we began watches to aid with security. I had duty the night of the shooting. My shift ended at 9:00 p.m. Until that point, the campus was quiet, quite different from the previous night. There was literally nothing happening. At 9:30 p.m. I left for home. That's when all hell broke loose."

Thirty years later, Carr seems as surprised by the shooting as if it happened yesterday. As she begins to discuss the day of the shooting, memories come flooding to her face like a tidal wave, and her eyes become red and wet, mirroring the blood and sweat of the event. Yet though her face shows the obvious pain and agony, Carr continues to recount the event, needing to share the horror of the story, not for anger or revenge but so that the truth will be told. "It was a typical day. There was no riot or marching or campus activism or anything. We were just normal college kids living life, trying to become the best that we could be. Of course, the girls' dormitory was the major gathering spot. After you finished your homework, we girls would hang out the windows being nosey, talking and teasing people passing by, trying to see who was with whom. I was on the fourth floor of the A wing, which is the base of the U of the dorm that faces the main campus areas. My roommate Mary Gibbs, my friend from Tchula Bernice Hayes, and Patricia Patterson, and I were watching the campus. Phillip [Gibbs] came walking by the dorm, and we were teasing him about his female company because we all knew that he was married and had a child. Then, someone said that something is on fire, and we all ran to the other side of the dorm with the hopes of seeing it from the other window. We could see the smoke and the fire, but not what was burning, but we concluded that there was not enough smoke or fire for it to be a building. Then someone yelled, "The police are coming up Lynch Street!" We went back to our original room to see the commotion. We were all a bit puzzled about the police presence because nothing was happening. Then, there was the sound of a bottle crashing to the ground, and the police began firing. At first we thought that they were firing blanks because there had been no incident to warrant police presence or response. Then when I saw people running and trying to hide, I knew this was for real. The gunfire may have only lasted a minute, but it seemed like hours. I saw Phillip hit the ground, and then I heard countless others exclaim that they were hit. Then, I passed out...I didn't awake until the next day."

Porter tells an equally horrifying story. "It was a warm spring day, just an average Thursday school day. I went to class and noticed nothing unusual that day. Once I came from class, I washed and rolled my hair. After I finished my hair, someone yelled 'The police are coming up Lynch Street.' Gloria Mayhorn and I went to the exit of the dorm to see what was happening, but we were headed that way anyway as most of us girls would sit on the hill in front of Alexander Dormitory to chat and past the time, simply fellowshipping with classmates. Of course, we noticed the police marching down Lynch Street, but none of use was worried because nothing had happened or was happening. We were more curious or puzzled than anything. As the police marched up the street, there was a spreading rumor that a car had been set afire and turned over, but that was at the corner off the campus. We continued to chat and watch with curiosity as the police marched right in front of the dorm and stopped. Then, they did a left face and opened fire. There was no warning. No anything..." Ms. Porter stops for a moment, and I can see her retreating deep inside herself. Her eyes are open, but she is no longer facing me. She is once again face to face with the horror of that day. I ask her about a bottle crashing, and she replies. "I didn't hear anything...I don't remember anything but the police turning and firing. Then I heard the glass behind me shattering. I...we...were between the officers and the shattering glass. There were so many students standing at point blank range. There was screaming and running and chaos. Harold Stewart grabbed me around the waist and Gloria by the shoulder, pulling us from the direct line of the fire. As he is moving us, the glass right behind where we were standing begins to shatter, and Harold pushed me through the shattering glass away from the firing. Gloria pulls away from Harold, runs into the building, and is hit by the gunfire. With all of this happening, all I could think is 'Why is this happening? What did we do?'" Porter stops for a moment and collects her thoughts, her eyes finally refocusing on me. "Getting up from the floor, I could see that all of the rollers in my hair were now on the floor. My roommate asked me if she was shot, and quite bluntly and still in a daze a responded,

142

'Yeah, you are.' Harold was visibly upset and could see that I was bleeding. He could see the pellets and glass in my arms and legs. Blood and glass were everywhere. People were screaming, crying, yelling. I just started walking. I had to get away from there. I had to leave. I walked down Dalton Street to Bergie Jones' apartment...When my parents arrived at Bergie's apartment, they did not want me to go to a hospital in Jackson. They were adamant about it. They were no longer willing to trust that I would be safe. They took me to King Daughter Hospital in Brookhaven. I found out later that the baseball team was playing a game in Livingston, Alabama. The Jackson State team was winning, and the white Livingston fans began to yell 'They are killing you niggers in Jackson, and we are going to kill you niggers if you win this game.' To my brother and the rest of the team's credit, they used the threats as fuel and won the game. It made them stronger."

McInnis, Sr., continues his story from here. "An hour or two after I was home, someone called me and told me that the troopers were on the campus shooting. I went back to the campus, but it was like walking into a tornado. By midnight it was pure chaos. I still remember the smell of blood and gunpowder. I had not smelled that since Vietnam. There was a continuous sea of whaling, blood on the stairways, carnage, people fleeing in panic. Then, by 8:30 a.m. cars were lined from Lynch Street to Terry Road with parents from all over the state and nation coming to gather their children. Children were running to their parents. Students left clothes and books. Personal items were scattered all over the campus. I distinctly remember a trinity of blood, bullet holes, and flies everywhere. I had given a paper to a young lady to have typed. I find my paper in the debris, stained in blood. All could think is, 'This is education at Jackson State? What are they teaching us?'" Carr's emotions are similar. Now noticeably holding back her tears, Carr's face deepens with a pain that seems to stretch for forever. "When I awoke at the hospital, my father and Dean Haskell Bingham were at my bedside. I just knew I was dying because my father told me he loved me. That was not my father's style. He was not a man of those kinds of words. He showed love by supporting the household...When I was released from the hospital, I was escorted by Dean Bingham to gather my belongings to leave. The campus was quiet. There were papers and people's things everywhere, but there was this heavy quite that seemed to hover over the campus. The air was thick with the lingering smell of smoke and blood, and the dorm was covered with gunshot holes. I kept thinking, 'Why did they do this?'"

The same images still haunt McInnis Sr. "That night I kept asking myself, 'why did they try to kill us all?' As naive as it sounds, I still had faith in a college campus. It was the seat of knowledge. And there were no activities on this campus that warranted this type of action. Then, as I later reflected, I realized and understood the state's action. We were demanding to be free and equal. When black people demand to be free and equal, that is an act of treason to the state because the State of Mississippi and America lives off the back of African slave labor. And this is the irony of the shooting. Jackson State has never been as politically charged as Tougaloo. The students themselves were very conservative. We were not nearly as active as Tougaloo. Students like me were the exception, not the rule. We were harassed by the administrators who were holdovers from Reddix's tenure. Although Peoples never asked students not to be politically involved, it was a very quiet, conservative campus. And this shows the heinousness of the state, that it would attempt mass murder on *this* school...We were a direct affront to the state's white power structure. They expected Tougaloo students to protest but not us. So after four years of uprisings, the State of Mississippi decided it was time to lynch Nat Turner. It was purely evil and almost debilitating. Man,

144

the school didn't cancel classes. The students closed the campus by leaving. Three or four days after the shooting, JSU was a ghost town."

Former Assistant Secretary of State, Attorney Constance Slaughter-Harvey recounts this same horrible scene. "I lived on Eastview, which is just up the street from JSU, lest than a mile. While listening to Bobby 'Blue' Bland and B.B. King with a friend, I heard this roaring, rolling, exploding sound like a combination of thunder and a train wreck. I got up to run to the campus, but my friend would not let me. After a few minutes of chaos, my friend and I started up the street in his car to the JSC campus. When we arrived at the campus, the National Guard and the Jackson Police Department had the streets barricaded and blocked. When we attempted to find out what was happening, we were told to get back and that we could not go onto the campus. I became incensed because my sisters were students at JSC, and they both lived in Alexander Hall. Things were so crazy that I just go blank from there. All I knew was that there was madness all around me; JSC looked like a war zone, and I could not see my sisters."

Yet even with his pain and haunting memories, this massacre holds a place of moral and historical significance for McInnis Sr. "The Civil Rights Movement is a physical manifestation of the notion, 'I want to be as free and as equal as any other citizen.' If you elevate the servants, who does the labor? What happens to the pigeons that refuse to pay the extortionist interest and finance charges? The shooting was a statement by the state that 'We will do whatever it takes to suppress you. We will kill the best of your best people, even those willing to accommodate themselves to us to ensure your servitude. We will destroy an institution of higher learning to make sure that you stay in your place.'" This event also has an equally significant effect on Attorney slaughter-Harvey. "The verdict redirected my energies from law and into politics. I knew that we had to change the political system which is the matrix for the judicial system. My goal in the area of politics was to change the lives of black Mississippians. This is the only possible tribute to the struggle, change the rules that create and permit the injustices and inequities. After working eleven years for 'mail-in voter registration,' the signing of this bill and the significant number of black elected officials are the best tribute that we can give to Medgar. The best tribute to the lives lost in the Jackson State massacre is to change the system which allows its agents of death to march on black students. This was my goal in the civil suit of Burton vs. Williams."

As Carr Stops to gather herself and reflect, I ask her about returning to campus for her senior year. "I did not return for summer school as I normally did." But she had no thoughts of not returning. "This was my school. This was my senior year. I was Mrs. Jackson State. I had no thoughts of not returning...They could not stop me. When I returned to school, I met friends who had survived being shot, and the story was that same for each. They all spent the summer recovering from their physical and emotional wounds." During those days, the average black college student worked during the summer to earn money for school. According the Carr, most of the students caught in the crossfire spent that summer trying to recuperate, trying to put their lives back together. Even today, Carr marvels and wonders about the event. "We were used to the police bringing Thompson's Tank to the campus to scare us, to remind the niggers to stay in their place. But we hadn't done anything. If we had been rioting, if we had hurt somebody, but we hadn't done anything to anybody accept try and become the best people we could become." Unfortunately for Carr and her classmates, the development of the African American mind was a threat and a crime in Mississippi. Carr continues, "This is Mississippi history, good or bad, and we must never forget it. We must learn from the past. Now, as an elected official, I have a responsibility to tell the truth and to help people. Jackson State is a great university. I am here because of my parents, my faith, and Jackson State. And that dreadful day in May 1970 could not stop us from becoming what we are."

Porter affirms Carr's notions of not being deterred. "I did not attend summer school as I usually did. My parents sent me to Joliet, Illinois, on vacation, but not returning was not an option for me. Where was I going to go? I had invested too much time, energy, and money into Jackson State. It was my school. It was my home. And of course, when we returned in the fall there was an air of concern, of being cautious, of being preventative. But mostly, we tried to identify what we had done to warrant the attack on us. James Baldwin once stated that a white police officer cannot tell the difference between a black student and a black thug. This incident causes me to believe this point. Even if there was a problem or an incident off campus, why bring that problem to us, a group of students just trying to mold ourselves into positive contributors to society. And to shoot up a girls' dormitory, a bunch of girls just out sitting on a hill, that is almost inconceivable. We will never know the hidden agenda, but I believe that the police and the government were looking for a reason to scare us if not kill us. King talked about being a drum major for justice, and I think that the whites in the state wanted to be the only drum major or intellectual leader, and Jackson State was seen as getting out of its place. As far as the state was concerned, there was room for only one intellectual drum major." Porter continues, "As far as the aftermath, my two issues have to do with how we were treated or the lack of our treatment and that the community and the school has not done more to memorialize the event. As a victim, no one ever asked me how I felt or what my thoughts were until just recently. So many of us have been emotionally scarred if not physically scarred, and the emotional scarring can be more difficult to overcome. Secondly, we have not done enough to remember this event. I know that African American history is filled with pain and struggle, but if we don't ever address and study that pain and struggle, we can never move forward, we can never grow, and we can never celebrate what a powerful and beautiful people we are. If we look at our children today, they act the way that they do partly because they have no conception of who they are, of from where they come, and the wonderful history of survival and creativity that produced them. Remembering this murder is not about blaming others, but it is about saying to our children that this is your legacy, your accomplishment, and your strength."

However, along with his pride of the school's survival, McInnis Sr. is also dismayed that more is not being done to perpetuate the event's significance. "JSU has failed to mandate the teaching of this incident to its students. Every Jewish person knows about and understands the significance of the Holocaust. Not every African American truly understands the significance of slavery. In order for an event to become significant in this country, it must be put into print and taught in the halls of academia. That is just the nature of this country. Until JSU takes up the responsibility of teaching this event and its significance, all generations to follow will not understand the significance of the event. Even the State of Mississippi understands the importance of this event. Immediately after the shooting, the state, itself, wanted to remove the damage and the evidence of the shooting as soon as possible to hide their heinous deed. A few days later, the state had people in place to remove and repair the physical damage. This move by the state caused the only real protest that was had after the shooting. The students, while still packing to leave, had enough wits about themselves to keep the repairs from happening before the local and national media could get there. These are the real heroes, the students. Call us anything that you want to call us at JSU, but JSU students are survivors. We keep surviving."

Minor affirms McInnis' concerns by asking, "Where are the panels which were destroyed by gunfire? There was a big showdown four days after the shooting when a guy in charge of the state building commission wanted to take down the panels from Alexander Hall to remove the scars of their chicanery, but the students barricaded themselves in the building and refused to

148

give up the panels. This created another showdown because this building commissioner was a real red-neck clod who had no compassion for the situation. President Nixon sent Jerris Leonard of the Justice Department over night to negotiate this confrontation. He promised the students that the FBI would take charge of the panels and give them back to the university." Peoples tells the same story with different players. "I contacted an official in Nixon's administration...a Mississippian from Jackson who was a White House staffer, Mr. Fred La Rue. I don't know exactly what he did, but the Department of Justice became actively involved. U.S. Attorney General John Mitchell was dispatched to Jackson....Significantly, an agreement was made with the students and black community leaders that no effort would be made to remove them or to repair the building until the joint funeral of Phillip Gibbs and James Green was held..." (195). No matter the players involved, Minor's question still stands. "Where are the panels? JSU should have those panels framed and displayed as symbols of this tragic event. Every JSU student should know the price of education." To Minor's question, Attorney Slaughter-Harvey seems to point to a state and federal conspiracy at work. "The Committee of Concerned Citizens demanded that the state not remove the panels. That was the day I was detained. Jerris Leonard who was working with the U.S. Justice Department assured us that the panels would not be destroyed and would be handed back to the school. The panels disappeared, and Leonard started working for the State of Mississippi."

Former JSU student and current JSU professor, Dr. Gene "Jughead" Young agrees with Minor that there is a need to teach new generations about the shooting. "That's why I'm talking about it to students and everybody else. "People need to know what happened that night." (Young is given a great amount of credit by Peoples for securing order and providing direction the night of the shooting.) Even former JSU student Demetrius Gibbs, son of Phillip Gibbs who was one of the two students killed in the shooting, states that "before I started attending college the shooting was never given or presented to me in any real historical or contextualized manner. I just knew that my father was killed at JSU, but I never really knew why. I never saw it as part of the Civil Rights Movement before going to college. It wasn't until I got to know Dr. Young as one of my professors that I began to fully understand the significance of the event....Now, I just want people to understand that my father's death is an opportunity for us to make the world better through education. I don't want any money or anything else. I just want the truth to be told that my father's death is a symbol of our people's struggle for education. My daddy and many others never had the chance to fulfill their dreams of a better life through an education. We, all generations that follow the shooting, have that responsibility to walk through the doors opened for us and create more doors for the generations to follow us." Minor shares the disappointment about the handling of the legacy of the shooting. "The event needs to be reviewed periodically to discuss what happened, why it happened, and what it means. I am disappointed that too few of the JSU students and the black and white community have allowed the doors to be closed on this issue. They act like it is antiquated history that no one needs to know. We need to be made to realize that the whole community is responsible for this event." McInnis Sr. affirms Minor and adds another reason why this event has not been remembered as it should. "Secondly, like slavery this is an event that is too painful for some African Americans. No one likes to admit that they were somebody else's fool or concubine. How many black men are stopped and slapped around by highway patrolmen on a nightly basis, and it goes unreported? What is a man gonna say? What is he gonna admit? 'He slapped me around?'" Attorney Slaughter-Harvey supports McInnis Sr. and Minor's assertions when she states "A final problem is that those who know are not telling the truth. Although truth is a measuring stick and a catalyst for freedom, it is also very painful. We need to tell the truth about black people who acted as gatekeepers and by doing so helped to destroy young black minds wanting and needing guidance and knowledge. And even today, the students do not know the significance of this event because the system does not want them to know the truth." Here, Attorney Slaughter-Harvey seems to be echoing the Carter G. Woodson's statement, "When you control a man's thinking you do not have to worry about his actions. You do not have to tell him not to stand here or go yonder. He will find his 'proper place' and will stay in it. You do not need to send him to the back door. He will go without being told. In fact, if there is no back door, he will cut one for his special benefit. His education makes it necessary."

Along with discovering the truth of the specific events of the shooting, former Attorney Slaughter-Harvey demands that we must also understand and address the truth of the reaction of the black establishment to the shooting. Attorney Slaughter-Harvey represented the families of the murdered students as well as the other victims in the civil suit filed against the State of Mississippi, styled Myrtle Green Burton, et. al. versus the State of Mississippi, et. al. She insists that we need to know and study the black reaction to this crime if we are to ever make sense of it, learn from it, and grow from it. "The greatest and most lingering question is 'why was there a negative response from the black elite to the search for justice?' The truth is that I had to fight the Jackson State College administration and the black elitist hierarchy of the Jackson community in our fight to gain justice for the family of the victims as well as for the school. We must be both careful and critical with a case this complex. There was division all the way around, even in the local media. Two newsmen working for channel 12 were present on the scene. One said he did not see a sniper, and the other one said he did. Bert Case indicated that he did not see a sniper. Jack Hobbs indicated that he did. There was confusion, and the confusion still remains." The sniper in question relates to the fact that some officers stated that their fire was in response to a sniper who was shooting from the window of the JSU dormitory, but there has never been any evidence to support this claim. In fact, former Jackson State student Eddie Jean Carr who was there the night of the shooting firmly states that the last sound heard before the officers started firing was a crashing bottle, not shoots from students. And former student Gailya Porter who was outside in the direct line of fire states that the last sound that she heard before the shooting was the chatter and laughter of the students.

For Attorney Slaughter-Harvey, understanding the truth is the first step to creating a proper understanding and reaction to the shooting. "Moreover," attorney Slaughter-Harvey continues, "what still concerns me is that there was no anger (apparent) from the black community. There were too many comfortable black folks who did not want to make waves. I was big-eyed and on a cause—fighting for the principle of this issue. There should have been some respect for individual rights, and the power struck system should not have been permitted to come in and shoot up a girls' dormitory or any other dormitory for that matter. That situation would never have happened on a predominately white campus. Instead of the black community getting upset with the power structure, they appeared to take their frustrations out on me. They said I was moving too fast and that I was jeopardizing all of the progress that we had made. What type of progress do you have when you can shoot up a college campus? It was the combination of the obstacles from the black community and the losing of the case that caused me to take a sabbatical from the practice of Civil Rights Law. When I heard those 1972 'not guilty verdicts' and those rebel yells from those white police officers, I knew I was finished with this approach to problem-solving. Inside my soul, I went berserk even though I knew I had to hold a strong exterior for the young students and my clients. My soul was bleeding. For the past thirty years nobody has taken a stand on this case. The community has been virtually silent since that one day. Thirty years ago, the Jackson State administration had its chief of security put me in the back of a Jackson State College patrol car when I tried to talk to my client who was a Jackson State student. I can not to this day respect the position of the Jackson State administration following the shooting. Because of this type of action/inaction and the general atmosphere set by the other black community leaders, I spent most of my time fighting black people to get justice for these young children and their families. I spent too much of my time justifying the need to pursue criminal and civil action on behalf of black people."

Slaughter-Harvey continues, "Now, why is this important? It is important because we cannot heal properly, grow, and evolve if we do not use the truth as our measuring stick. We know that the shooting was orchestrated by the white power structure. This is not a point of debate. If you know that fire is hot, get out of its way. But what we need to know and understand is how some black people worked as pawns and gatekeepers for the white power structure. We do not need to know this to merely condemn individuals. But if we do not know the roots and all of the complications and complexities of the illness, we will never get well. Yes, the shooting was a terrible, hideous crime, but the lack of action from the black leadership has been just as hideous and just as criminal. Furthermore, we no longer have any excuses for our lingering inaction. We cannot say that we are not equipped to deal with this issue. We are professors and writers and lawyers and politicians. With all of this we still have not done anything to right this wrong. This is not about blaming and jailing individuals. This is about the continued perpetuation of the entire system that feeds off racism, hatred, and black fear and greed, which causes inaction in the black community. We must realize that one man did not kill Medgar Evers, and one man did not kill those college students. A system killed those students just like a system killed Medgar Evers. The question is 'what have we done to change the system?' If we do not tell the whole truth and lay blame just on white racism, we will still be perpetuating the system by not showing the far reaching and smothering arm of white supremacy. This has been my greatest disappointment, the lack of an explanation of the pitiful actions of the so-called black leaders in not getting justice for this crime."

Even with the testimony of Dr. Peoples, Watkins, Minor, and Slaughter-Harvey, the complexity of this event is ongoing and never ending. Officer Martin seems to have a bit of a different perception on the shooting and its meaning. When asked about becoming a police officer at such a time, Martin answers, "I needed the money. I was actually a student at JSC from 1963 to 1965 when I decided to join the police department, not the force but the department. I was married. I had to support a family. So I joined the department as a porter. I did jobs such as keeping the building and grounds clean, cutting the grass, and delivering parts. After noticing other black police officers, I wanted to become an officer. It was a unique job and an opportunity to work in the community. When I told my mother that I wanted to become a police officer, she said that it wasn't the job for me (laughter). But it paid good, one hundred dollars a week. Martin is a bit more matter-of-fact when it comes to discussing the JSC shooting, "I was off, and I heard it on the news. My first response was 'Why?'…Could this have been avoided?' I didn't have any facts. I had to get the facts. That's what a police officer does. But I did keep asking myself, 'Could this have been avoided?' My first assignment was patrolling and securing a rally at the Jackson State College Park Swimming pool. I remembered how we handled that incident. There was no problem there. But I had to get the facts. Until today, talking with you, I was under the impression that the Jackson State students were assaulting and firing on the highway patrol. But you tell me that there is no evidence of that. That's just always the way that it was told to me, that the students were rioting."

It is interesting to note that there have always been rumors that rioting JSC students provoked the state troopers by throwing bottles and other items. There was also a rumor that JSC students were shooting, but there is no documentation of the event. Col. Tim Powell who works in public relations for the Mississippi National Guard could not provide me with any information on the incident. He stated that "there are no members of the guard still around who were in the guard then, and the guard, itself, has no press release or media information on the incident." Cal Adams, former local Jackson television reporter who now works in public relations for the Mississippi State Highway patrol, stated to me in a phone interview that they have absolutely no information whatsoever on the incident. "In fact," Mr. Adams added, "the records are in a shambles, almost like they were tampered with." This is only important information because it is odd that there is no official documentation of JSC students assaulting any of the state officers, yet so many people believe that they did. Furthermore, no student or anyone for that matter has ever been arrested or charged for assaulting troopers, guardsmen, or police officers in connection with the JSC shooting. Minor states that "there were several investigations, one by the U.S. Congress, which was conducted by Minnesota Senator, Fritz Mondale, and one by a Hinds County Grand Jury, and neither investigation showed any attack by the students on any of the lawmen there. In fact, what it proved was that both the state troopers and the Jackson police officers fired at students with no conclusive evidence of being attacked first."

Despite the evidence of the unprovoked attack by the officers, Martin does not believe that the shooting was a planned act. "Well, the State Highway patrol and not the Jackson Police Department was involved in the shooting. But based on what I know about the shooting, there was no conspiracy against the school or the students. Poor training, more than anything else, seems to be the cause of the shooting. Even if JSC students were shooting at the troopers, the troopers could have taken another course of action than shooting at students. But I don't think that it was in malice. It was just a case of poor training." Minor refutes Martin's assertion that JPD was not involved. "Both investigations proved that Jackson police Officers fired shots as well as State Highway Troopers." Minor's statements also refute Martin's assumptions that the shooting was a training error. "Kent State was a mistake. JSC was going to happen, if not that night at some other point. Look at the actions taken, the callous disregard for life, to riddle a girls dormitory with machine gun fire. Why not use tear gas? Look at the length and the direction of the shooting. The officers did not just fire in one direction as if returning fire on a sniper or an attacker. Remember now, Lynch is a major throughway and intersection, but people are killed on both sides of the street. Why were they shooting in two different directions? This particular night's shooting may not have been planned, but the scene was set for this kind of action. John Bell Williams, the state's Governor at that time, was a racist. He had no sympathy for black students or blacks period. He had a history of racism directed at the state's black colleges. For instance, he refused to place blacks on the draft board or the state college board. Williams had a documented get tough attitude toward blacks in general, and a desire to stamp out black student protests and other political actions." Phillips affirms Minor's position, citing that the Nixon administration was laying the foundation for getting tough on African Americans throughout the country. "The Nixon administration took a very reactionary turn, being led by the rhetoric of Vice President Spiro Agnew and the repression of FBI Director J. Edgar Hoover. They egged on blue collar racists and conservatives. Hoover's FBI began a program of identifying and moving to discredit, silence, or destroy radicals." So, the Nixon-Hoover attitude permeated the entire country, manifesting itself at South Carolina State, Kent State and Jackson State.

Martin defends his position by discussing the action taken by the state and the city after the shooting. "Just after the JSC shooting black police officers from all over the State of Mississippi were selected to go to Mississippi Valley State University and bring order to their campus. That's the job of police, to restore peace by restoring order. I believe the fact that we were a cadre of black officers helped us to reach those kids. They recognized many of us from their communities, and it helped us to be able to talk to them. Right after we arrived there, the students were willing to talk to the administrators. So because of us black police officers, we saved lives, physical

156

destruction, and restored order. Then, right after all of the chaos of 1970, in 1971 the City of Jackson started an outreach plan to build roots in the community. I was chosen to aid in the establishing of community sponsored recreational facilities. I was chosen because my family was well rooted in the Washington Addition neighborhood which is the neighborhood which houses JSU. We created community outreach programs, softball, and bingo where we gave away household prizes. We set them up all over Jackson, on Medgar Evers Boulevard, on the JSU campus, and out by Tougaloo." Johnson does not see the centers as being that helpful toward the black community. "Those so-called 'community centers' remind me of a Frederick Douglass essay when he talked about how the masters of the plantation would use Christmas time as a time to give the slaves all the free food and liquor that they wanted as a way to appease them into believing that slavery wasn't all that bad." "Secondly," Phillips adds, "the centers also remind me of the old COINTELPRO (a FBI program called Counter Intelligence Program) way of establishing units to spy on and monitor black activity. It seems to me that these centers were strategically placed by JSC, Tougaloo, and other black areas and housed not with social workers but with Police officers so that black problems did not get solutions but were criminalized." Johnson reiterates that "it does seem to be a bit like old FBI tactics to monitor so-called threats." In his defense, Martin rebukes this statement. "The people who say those types of things are the ones with the plantation mentality. We were providing the community with resources that they needed. At bingo they would win things like washing powder and skillets. But the centers provide more than this. To this day I still have kids who have grown up and gone on to lead productive lives come back to me and tell me how much the centers helped them." Johnson questions the importance or impact of the centers. "Washing powder and skillets equates to food and liquor for slaves. None of it really answers the questions or provides solutions to the issues that bring about protesting students. The students were shot down in cold blood, and the city's solution is bingo games and washing powder?" Martin, however, defends his work with the centers. "It was more than bingo. JSU Professors Jimmy Bell and Dr. Bass would allow JSU majors to intern at the centers so that they could get some hands on training. The centers were a big help to the black community, and they represented our understanding of a need for outreach to the black community."

Both Peoples and Minor agree that Jackson mayor Russell Davis worked and did what he could to assist JSC in building bridges with the Jackson Community. Peoples states that "Davis was very cooperative in placing traffic lights on the street." When Peoples was not able to get the state to lend support for new sewer lines for the growing JSC campus, Davis gave Peoples his support. "Mayor Davis did not agree that a sewer line for a state college was the city's responsibility, but he wanted to help. He told me he would unobtrusively insert the funding to replace the six-inch sewer line with a twelve-inch line into the pending city street repair bond. We both agreed not to publicize his decision." This shows Davis' desire to help or work with Peoples, but it also shows the complexity of the issue. Davis who would often help Peoples also understood the times, his limited role, and the attitude of the Governor. Minor even tells of how Davis was distressed to find that Jackson Police Department officers had fired shots. "It crushed him to learn that Jackson Police Department officers had fired shots." All of this goes to show the complexity of the JSC shooting and the complexity of the Civil Rights Movement. The JSC shooting, then, is a perfect microcosm of the complexity of the Civil Rights Movement. It would be Mayor Davis who would work with Peoples in getting Lynch Street, between Dalton and Prentiss, deeded over to JSU. Having Lynch Street deeded to JSC was Peoples' solution to the riots. With JSC owning that stretch of Lynch Street, it gave Peoples more autonomy to have a direct impact on the tensions and security of the campus. Since the closing of Lynch Street, there has not been one campus riot. Nevertheless, JSU continues to do battle with both the city and the state for funding, area improvements, and their general dispositions toward the university. Additionally, attorney

Slaughter-Harvey does not agree that closing Lynch Street was the best or proper action for the school or the community. "We also need to understand that the closing of Lynch Street was not a solution to the murders, but it worked in accordance with the shooting for the further devaluing of the institution and the neighborhood. Once the street was closed, it meant certain death for the black owned business as well as lowering the property values of the black owned homes in the area. Some people feel that the Gibbs-Green Plaza is a tribute, but it is not. Brick and mortar will never take the place of justice. A tribute to the lives lost is to make JSU what it should be as the flagship university of the state."

Thirty years later, Jackson State University and the Jackson Metro area is still grappling with the shooting, in one way or another. The current proposed Metro parkway which will run from I-55 directly to and around the campus is the exact same plan that was tabled thirty years ago in an attempt to accommodate for the closing of Lynch Street. The debilitating houses in the JSU area is a direct effect of the JSU shooting. The cloud of fear and crime that lingers over the reputation of JSU like stank, spoiled fish is an effect of the shooting. The mistrust and lack of communication between JSU and the college board and the JSU faculty and the JSU administrators is another lingering effect of the shooting. The shooting is a deep and lingering scar, but it is a hidden scar, hidden because of the pain and embarrassment of African Americans for not being able to prevent the shooting, hidden because of the need by African Americans to get on with their lives, in a speedy and timely manner, hidden by the fear of African Americans that big brother is still and always will be watching, so walk and speak lightly. On the surface, it seems that the state has won another one. The state lynched JSC students with automatic weapons and got away clean. Yet if you look deeper, you will see that JSU is actually up one, for it continues to survive. JSU is still here, still educating African American children. It may be hobbling, limping, at times even crawling, but it is a door for African American children to gain a higher education. Yes, JSU as well

159

as the state is infected with a plague much like Thebes. And yes, until Oedipus comes to answer the riddle of the injustice, they will continue to be plagued. But under the plague of white supremacy and the acid rain of racism, JSU continues. So by right, every JSU student has the right to look the State of Mississippi in the eyes and say, "You missed." Demetrius Gibbs and Mary Green-McCray, sister of James Earl Green, both graduated from JSU and are now constructive citizens in their respective communities, are evidence that the state missed.

Attorney Slaughter-Harvey summarizes the course of history this way. "The shooting and the verdict of the civil suit affirmed four truths. One, I found that even if you thoroughly prepare for a case and have the law on your side, you will still lose if you are a black person fighting to make a white person pay for a wrong committed against a black person. Two, I realize that it is difficult for whites to look at themselves and be critical, and the legal system cannot force this. That's why I dedicated myself to the election of fair judges. Three, justice is relative. And four, the life of a black person is tantamount to zero." Even with these realizations back then, Attorney Slaughter-Harvey still finds some hope. "This will be corrected. I do not have the same pessimism that I have had in the past. I don't have the same attitude now that I had in 1970. I have seen change, watching my father elected as the first black Alderman in Forest in 1977. We have the ability to right this wrong. We can learn and make sure that this never happens again. I did not suffer for it to happen to my child who is now a college senior at Tougaloo. If other parents take this same approach, we can right this wrong and make a better system for our children."

Bibliography

Adams, Cal. "Personal Interview." January, 2000.

Carr, Eddie Jean. "Personal Interview." July, 2007.

Dittmer, John. *Local People: The Struggle for Civil Rights in Mississippi*. Champaign: University of Illinois Press, 1995.

Gibbs, Demetrius. "Personal Interview." January, 2000.

Johnson, Derrick. "Personal Interview." January, 2000.

Martin, Percy. "Personal Interview." January, 2000.

McInnis (Sr.), Claude. "Personal Interview." January, 2000.

Peoples, John A. *To Survive and Thrive: The Quest for a True University*. Jackson: Town Square Books, Inc. 1995.

Phillips, Ivory. "The Historical Process: The Local Community and the Gibbs-Green Experience Then and Now." Commissioned by the Jackson State University Library for the Thirty Year Anniversary of the 1970 JSC Shooting. Housed at the Jackson State University Library.

Phillips, Ivory. "Personal Interview." January, 2000.

Porter, Gailya. "Personal Interview." August, 2007.

Powell, Tim. "Personal Interview." January, 2000.

Rhodes, Lelia Gaston. *Jackson State University: The First Hundred Years, 1877 – 1977*. Jackson: University Press of Mississippi.

Slaughter-Harvey, Constance. "Personal Interview." January, 2000.

161

Spofford, Tim. *Lynch Street: The May 1970 Slayings at Jackson State College*. Kent: Kent State University Press, 1988.

Watkins, Hollis. "Personal Interview." January, 2000.

Watts, Glen. *The Sovereignty Files. The Real Story*. Jackson: Town Square Books, Inc., 1999.

Williams, David Brian. "Personal Interview." January, 2000.

Woodson, Carter G. *The Mis-Education of the Negro*. Trenton: Africa World Press, 1998.

Young, Gene. "Personal Interview." January, 2000.

JSU's Alexander Hall and Black History

Since his appointment as Jackson State President, Ronald Mason, aided with the funds provided by the botched Ayers settlement, has coordinated the most ambitious and massive campus/building development since the tenure of Dr. John A. Peoples. Though most view the progress as a positive, many worry that the renovations have not adequately taken into consideration the historical legacy of the JSU campus. For instance, their has been the demolition of the Green Building, which was part of the historic Campbell College that allowed Lanier High School students to enroll in college after the State College Board attempted to prohibit the students from attending college because of their senior year protest. And now it is rumored that JSU has plans to either renovate or demolish Alexander Hall. I have spent four days trying to get clarity of JSU's intentions, having contacted the Office of the President, the Director of Housing, and the Office of Public Relations, but as of yet I have received no answer. Most, including Peoples, agree that Alexander Hall was poorly constructed and needs immediate attention, but the concern is that often renovation of HBCUs means an erasing of history. In 1970 the Jackson Police Department and the Mississippi Highway Patrol fired hundreds of shots at and into Alexander Hall, killing two and wounding seventeen. The miracle is that more were not killed. Since its creation as the main female dormitory, it continues to be a major meeting hub for the JSU students. And such was the case on that May evening, when for no reason at all, other than white leaders deciding that the education of African Americans is a crime, officers of the City of Jackson and the State of Mississippi fired upon unarmed students whose only crime was being black and intelligent.

Even today, when my students write papers about the incident, I send them to view the holes that are still embedded in the building. This generation needs to be anchored to their history to know that JSU exists not because whites wanted them to be educated but because African Americans refused to be denied their proper place in this society. However, another reminder of African American struggle, endurance, and survival may be demolished, erased, and marginalized. Dr. Preselfannie W. McDaniels Professor of English at JSU asserts that "historically black colleges and universities, in their push forward toward improvements on campuses across the states, are also diminishing the mission of our institutions to preserve black pride, history, and purposefulness. If we forget from whence we've come, we shall never reach our intended destinations." Today, we love to assert that the children have changed, that they are worse today than yesterday. But, that is a mistruth. It is not the children who have changed but the adults, who are a generation of pseudo-integrated Negroes who have sold our souls for class status, cars, and chump-change. So, if we as African American elders do not respect our past, archive our past, and teach it to the next generation, how will they know who they are? But, of course, progress for African Americans is always driven by what Langston Hughes calls an "urge…toward whiteness…to be as little Negro and as much American as possible" (Hughes 1267). In short, a complete demolition of Alexander Hall will be a whitewashing of black history? According to Dr. Jacquelyn C. Franklin, former Curriculum Coordinator for the Center for Urban Affairs and the editor of the JSU *Academician*, "Alexander Hall is important because of the professional work of the professional for whom it is named, but more importantly Alexander Hall is significant to the history of Jackson State University because of the actions of students who were critical thinkers and effective citizens. Our students through a series of positive decisions challenged *de jure* segregation and unfair practices and treatment of black people in America, especially Mississippi and the South in the early 1970s." So to delete

Alexander Hall is to delete a large amount of Mississippi's black history.

I have not voted since the Ayers case settlement, and did not think that I could feel anything as deeply as the pain of watching African Americans being betrayed by their own elected officials. So, I have been pretty numb about what can be done to achieve first-class citizenship for African people. And yet somehow the notion of demolishing Alexander Hall cuts even deeper, to a place where I thought there was no more feeling. It may be the stinging realization that African Americans relinquish so much for the rewards of integration and get so very little in return. And we wonder why our children are vile and wild. There must be a way that African Americans can move forward in a manner that does not demand that they relinquish the essence of themselves. Without the roots of the past, we become a blind branch flapping indiscriminately in the wind. Gailya Porter who was wounded during the 1970 shooting asserts, "I understand the need to renovate properties, especially one as old as Alexander Hall, but there is a way that we can renovate the building and preserve the identity and integrity of the building. It is done with antebellum homes and government buildings all the time. The face or the front of Alexander Hall should remain intact, bullet holes and all, so that the next generation will know what happened there." Former JSU President John A. Peoples affirms Porter's statements and provides historical and economic clarity. "There was a history of the State of Mississippi poorly funding HBCUs in the area of campus development." In his book *To Survive and Thrive: the Quest for a True University*, Peoples details and documents his battles with the College Board to gain proper funding for building projects. He continues, "Former President Reddix did the best he could to maintain Alexander Hall, but due to poor funding the building was poorly constructed. Not only does it leak, but its design makes it difficult to monitor or control traffic, which creates a major safety issue. If I were still president, I would not want to burden the university budget with trying to repair or maintain it. However, we must preserve and maintain the memory of what happened there so that those who come after us will know our history of triumph. Since the building is in such disrepair, a good idea would be to take the façade or the front of the building that faces toward Lynch Street and place it within a new building with the proper markings to commemorate the event." Reflectively, Peoples continues, "President Mason is in a difficult place of balancing budgetary issues with the need to preserve history."

The question arises "Why is it important to preserve monuments like Alexander Hall?" According to the Director of the JSU Margaret Walker Alexander National Research Center Dr. Alfredteen Harrison, "All societies need examples of their past, and Alexander Hall does have historical merit because it marks the spot of an historical event." Let us not forget that there are those who deny that Africans had a civilization before Caucasians arrived in Africa, and there are those who deny that slavery was an evil institution—just check *Gone with the Wind*. And, there are even white scholars who argue that slavery was a justifiable means to a beneficial end of Christianizing and civilizing the savages of the Dark Continent. Accordingly, there are still officers of the law who claim that there was a sniper inside Alexander Hall when no one has ever been able to prove or find this alleged sniper. And if JSU demolishes Alexander Hall, there will be those who will attempt to deny that the incident happened, or they will be able to minimize the seriousness of the event because there will remain no physical, tangible evidence. Some things, like a lynching exhibition, need to be seen and touched so that liars cannot deny what happened, so that our children will understand from whence they come. Dr. Franklin declares "The crack in the 'Liberty bell' has meaning for

Americans because it represents the work of people toward freedom, and the bullet holes in the bricks of Alexander Hall have meaning to every Jackson State University student and professional because we believe in the mission of Jackson State University. How long will it take for us, black people in America, to maintain our past? Why do we allow others to erase and change the facts about our past? We cannot embrace 'right reasoning' and 'the tenets of a participatory democracy' if we allow 'select' historical symbols to define us and our past. We are action oriented Mississippians and Americans. We must control our lives, and we must produce leaders who are committed to assisting us improve our social conditions. Effective leadership does not mean changing history for an honor of a select few; effective leadership means 'knowing who you are and from where you come.' It also means correcting the present for a brighter future. The history of JSU has meaning, and we must teach the meanings of our complete historic past to our children's children. Maintaining Alexander Hall helps us to know who we are, and to never allow similar mistakes in the present or future." So if we do have young people on college campuses masquerading as students, it is because we have elders masquerading as scholars and educators. Failing to protect and maintain Alexander Hall is a failure to protect the history and legacy of African American struggle. If you would like to express your concerns or gains answers about the plans for Alexander Hall, call the Office of the President at (601) 979-2323 or the Director of Housing at (601) 979-2316.

Works Cited

Harrison, Alfredteen. "Personal Interview." August, 2007.

Hughes, Langston. "The Negro Artist and the Racial Mountain." *Norton Anthology of African American Literature*. Henry Louis Gates, Ed. New York: W. W. Norton and Company, 1997.

Franklin, Jacquelyn C. "Personal Interview." August, 2007.

Peoples, John A. "Personal Interview." August, 2007.

Porter, Gailya. "Personal Interview." July, 2007.

The Pros and Cons of Mainstream and Self-Publishing

There are two basic routes to getting published, mainstream and self-publishing. Mainstream is when one submits one's work to journals/magazines and publishing companies to be published. Self-publishing is when one decides to publish one's own books. They both can be equally effective although the mainstream manner is the most respected because it allows one to reach a larger audience more quickly and it has an aura or illusion of validation. Although self-publishing does not offer the validation from the establishment, it offers a satisfaction of artistic and economic control of one's work. Yet, the most effective manner of publishing is to use various aspects of mainstream and self-publishing simultaneously.

Mainstream:

Again, the mainstream route is when one is hoping to obtain a book deal with an established publisher. The cons of publishing using the mainstream route are: 1) most larger publishers do not accept unsolicited manuscripts from writers without an agent, 2) the larger publishers usually require writers to surrender their rights to the material for some period of time, usually anywhere from two to five years, 3) even though one may have a deal with a major publisher, it is still required of that author to schedule readings and signings across the country, and 4) most first time authors earn only ten - fifteen percent of the profits of the book. The pros of publishing using the mainstream route are: 1) because they are established (ingrained into the minds of the reading and buying public) there is an innate sense of acceptability and validation of the writer and the work and 2) one has the mega-machine behind one, which allows one's books to be placed in bookstores across the country as well as gain entrance into "so-considered" prestigious organizations and societies.

Most writers embrace the mainstream route because it frees them to be creative, or so they think. Although one is always responsible for promoting one's own books, publishing with an established publisher accesses one to roads, connections, and certain avenues, such as book clubs and other literary societies and organizations which wish to only deal with authors who have been validated by the establishment. Self-published authors are often left outside or are locked from these organizations or societies. Again, the established publisher represents, ideally, immediate access to mass markets and elite persons and organizations. In reality, most writers, even after acquiring these mainstream deals, still find themselves having to pound the pavement to sell their books. So, validation is the major pro for publishing with an established publisher.

This validation is important if one plans to make a career as a college or university professor. If this is one's pursuit, then the importance of accredited and validated research must be realized. One of my mentors, Dr. Reginald Martin, professor of English at the University of Memphis and editor of the best-selling anthology *Dark Eros*, puts it this way.

> "If you're in the scholarly writing game, it is not only validation that you receive by being published by a commercial publisher; it is also job perks and being allowed to keep the job. This is very important for younger black scholars to understand. Walt Whitman's self-publishing of *Leaves of Grass* (1843) would still be the great book it is, but, if Whitman were a professor, he'd get kicked out of his job because only peer review and publishing by a large house matters to a university. This is wrong, and you can easily see how this will only re-create the same boring material and ideas, but that's the way it is" (Martin 1999).

Most established publishers like Random House, St. Martin's Press, etc., will not accept unsolicited manuscripts from writers who do not have agents. Often, one will find oneself submitting to agents in the very same manner that one will submit to a publisher. Finding the appropriate agent for one' book is a hit and miss process. *The Writer's Guide* as well as other publications has a list of agents as well as the types of books and writers they sign. You can also locate their websites for more information as to what types of writers they sign. Before any writer submits to a publisher or an agent, it would be a good idea for a writer to subscribe to and submit to local, regional, national, and international journals. Journals are a way by which a writer is able to gain a feel for what is being published in the field or a particular genre, hone one's skills, and submit, hoping that even in rejection one will gain some type of feedback. A writer should also submit one's work to various emerging and established writers. They, of course, will have very demanding schedules, which will not allow them to respond to every inquiry, but I have found that most will take the time to send some comments about one's work if one includes a SASE. Also, attempt to identify persons working in the filed as critics or scholars. One will usually find these individuals through journals and university presses. That is, identify certain colleges, universities, or writing programs and send work to them. The feedback one receives from journals and other writers will allow one to measure one's talent and growth as a writer and will also act as marketing tools when one approaches an agent or a publisher. It is always an added plus to be able to say that "you should publish me because my work has been hailed by this renowned scholar, critic, or artist". This makes journals and publishers "sit up" and "take notice". In fact, I would suggest that a beginning writer work the journal circuit for about two years before submitting work to an agent or a publisher. Along with submitting to journals, join a writer's group that is well connected to people who publish. Before joining a group, ask the members questions regarding their aesthetic, writing/publishing successes and failures, and their publishing desires. It is one thing to participate in a creative writing group where one is able to grow, but it is more effective to participate in a creative writing group that has the connections to get one's work considered for publication in journals, anthologies, and by publishing houses. Ultimately, writers should join writing groups that have the same focus, drive, and direction as one has so that one can be nurtured and educated by similar and more mature writers. Cave' Canem, for example, is an excellent example of this, and there are other writer's groups whose goal is to develop writers and provide access to publishing. The goal is to connect to groups, conferences, and organizations, especially the ones that sponsor writing contests. These seminars, retreats, and contests often lead to publishing opportunities.

Another interesting trend is the manner in which established publishers are looking to independent or self-published writers. That is, once a writer has proven that one can sell a certain amount of books by pounding the pavement, often larger publishing houses "come-a-calling". So, self-publishing is no longer just an avenue for writers who want to own and control their work and ideas. Self-publishing is now a very viable vehicle, which allows writers to gain the attention of larger publishers. Depending on one's knowledge of contracts and the publishing business, one may need an agent. Agents often create query/proposal letters for their writer's books. It is a good idea for the writer to know how the construct a query/proposal letter so that one can retain some amount of control as to how one or one's work is marketed. One can obtain a copy of a query/proposal letter online or from any college textbook that is used for a professional or technical writing course. If all else fails, check to see if there is a grant/proposal writer in your area. They usually work for ten percent of the proposed amount. Some will only charge if the grant/proposal is accepted, and others want their fee upfront. Check the local small business or community business development centers/institutions to see if they can refer a grant/proposal writer. However, the core of the query/proposal letter should include an abstract/overview of the work, a table of contents, data showing how these types of books generally sell, and data of the target audience's buying habits—especially as it relates to this type of book. The query letter must clearly present the theme/central issue/focus of the book and that there is an audience for the work. But, do not waste time "telling" them how great your work is; allow the work's message, craftsmanship, and potential audience to "show" the work's potential.

Self-Publishing:

The pros of self-publishing are: 1) Not having to wait to be validated, which is important if one is a doing something that is not being regularly marketed, 2) controlling what one writes and publishes, when one writes and publishes, and how often one writes and publishes, and 3) being able to directly reap the artistic and economic benefits of one's hard work of pounding the pavement. The cons of self-publishing are: 1) publishing work when, as an artist, one may not be ready or well-crafted and 2) the money that one must invest. People who decide to self-publish must understand that, often, one only gets one chance to make a good impression, and poorly-crafted work will follow a writer for one's entire life. As poet Kisha Brown, co-founder of Runagate Press and a member of NOMMO Literary Society, stated: "I would rather take my time and publish one good poem than publish ten poorly-crafted poems."

Self-publishing is a good idea if the writer has a balanced and level head, which is driven by a desire to produce well-crated work and not driven by the desire just to publish or to gain stardom. A person who self-publishes must create a system of checks and balances so that one's work is not guided by a self-absorbed ego. This, I submit, is the most difficult task of self-publishing, being objective, if such a thing is possible, about one's own work. Thus, the self-published writer must continuously identify and engage writers and critics whom one respects. So, every writer is always submitting work to someone other than oneself. Even when self-publishing, every writer needs an editor. An effective editor is not just correcting grammar and spelling; the editor is also helping to make the work more powerful by honing the writer's technique and delivery because sometimes writers are at a loss as when to add or subtract. For instance, I can add imagery, dialogue, action, setting, etc to enhance or improve a work, but I am too emotionally tied to my work to delete any of it. This does not mean that I think that everything that I write is well-crafted, but my writing comes from such an emotional place that to delete something is akin to removing a part of me: my body or my emotions. An editor is not as connected to my work and can read it objectively and, dare I say it, rationally, and can make objective decisions about what parts and techniques are being effective and which are not. Of course, professional editors are expensive, often being paid by the word or the page. But, if one can identify an English teacher with whom one has a good relationship or any English teacher who may be interested in the experience of editing or just willing to provide a favor or act of kindness, one can save some money. It also helps if one has friends who read a great deal. They may also be able to help. But, one needs someone to put a second, third, or even fourth pair of eyes on one's work to ensure that it is readable and well-crafted.

Again, self-publishing is expensive. It is expensive to publish one's books, and it is expensive to continue to re-print older books while simultaneously publishing new work. And the expenses do not stop there. Once a book is published, one has the responsibility for delivering complimentary copies all across the planet, which can be anywhere from thirty to one hundred and fifty complimentary copies, and this must be included in one's budget, not to mention postage for all of this. To distribute thirty complimentary copies at three dollars a pop is ninety dollars. Bulk mail helps, but it is not as helpful as one may assume. Yet, the complimentary copies list is a must for the self-published writer. While one's book is in the editing process, start compiling a list of writers, magazines, newspapers, book clubs, and organizations. Once one has a thorough list, send a complimentary copy of the manuscript to the people on the list for reviews. Some of the reviews (the most enthusiastic) can be used for the back of the book. The goal is to inform as many people as possible that one has a book that will be released soon. Then, once the manuscript is in final book form, send the finished version of the book to the people on the list. Every writer's list will have some of the same names and some different names. It depends on one's style and subject matter. When I was first started, I simply created a wish list of folk I wanted to know about my work and sent them a copy. Some people did not reply, some people replied favorably, and some replied not so favorably. No matter the response or reply, it is all part of the process of informing the public that one has a book for sale. Additionally, one still must be willing to submit work (poems, short stories, and chapters from books) to various magazines and newspapers to be published. Again, it does not make sense to have a book for sale when nobody knows that it is available. By publishing work in various newspapers and magazines, people can read excerpts of one's work and then decide to purchase a copy of one's book.

An added issue is when authors wish to have illustrations within the text of the book. Photos, of course, do increase the cost of printing. Ordinarily, printers charge somewhere in the area of seven and thirty-five cents per page, depending on the quality of the paper and the quantity of the copies. (A high volume order of books decreases the price.) Color copies can increase the cost of copying a page to the range of one dollar to one dollar and fifty cents per page, again depending upon the quality of the paper and the quantity of the copies. Black and white copies are a bit different. If one is attempting to get a high quality gloss looking black and white, then the printer will shoot it with a laser printer or copier (the same method as color) and will charge the same amount as a color. If one is able to reproduce those black and white illustrations by way of a standard copier, then it should not increase the cost at all, since the printer is not required to do any additional work. Of course, always ask. Here is the general rule of thumb. No matter what one needs done to one's books, always try to pay no more than three to four dollars per book. This, of course, keeps your price for the book low. Three dollars should really be the limit, and one will probably purchase about 500 copies minimum to get a cost of three dollars or lower. Of course, on-demand printers and publishers are now more feasible than traditional printers, and I would recommend going online to review what they offer. Some writers prefer on-demand publishers while others prefer on-demand printers. As always, I suggest that one researches to secure what works best for each writer. I personally prefer on-demand printers, such as Lulu.com or CreateSpace.com because of the quality of their work, I can control as much of the book-crafting/layout process as I desire or allow them to do it, and they allow me to keep my books digitally archived at no costs until someone desires to purchase copies of my books. Others prefer on-demand publishers, such as Xlibris, because along with the other services they also offer marketing services for an additional fee.

Even though I was not ready, not as well-crafted as I needed to be, self-publishing allowed me to gain the attention of some folk who would say, "Most of this stinks, but there are some moments here that let me know that you seem to have talent." With hindsight being twenty-twenty, I should have worked the journal circuit more, even if I was going to self-publish. Even if one plans or desires to self-publish, one must gain feedback from journals, university scholars, and critics as well as established creative writers. Feedback can come in the form of writers' groups, such as Cave' Cannon listed above. Even if one does not desire to be published by a major company, a writers group can connect one to schools sponsoring conferences, book clubs, editors of anthologies, and magazines, which can all help promote one's self-published work. This is important because a self-published writer will need some validation from somewhere else since one will not be validated by the larger publishers.

What is this validation of which I keep speaking, those little comments on the back of books that tell a potential reader, "Hey, buy this book; it's good." The real fact of the matter is that most readers must have new writers validated by someone else before they will "pick up" or read the work. As such, word of mouth is always the best advertisement. It can make or break a writer. These comments that one will be receiving from various members of the writing community will help to propel one's work to a larger reading audience.

Yet, it must be realized early in one's endeavors that this validation sought by a self-published author will be difficult to find. Further, Martin confirms that "even if you self-publish, the general rule for reviews is that no organization will review the book unless it also came out in hard cover. Again, this is silly, but this is the current state of trying to get a book reviewed by most southern journals and any large media outlet" (Martin 1999). Also, most large or more notable journals and periodicals tend not to review unsolicited work. Most self-published authors must hope that their work makes enough noise in the smaller periodicals that larger, more noted journals will be called to the work's attention.

Again, when one is self-publishing, everything is one's responsibility. But no matter which road one chooses, always copyright one's work. If someone publishes one's work, one can give them permission to use one's work, but the copyright allows one to retain all the rights. I tend to copyright all my work about every six months. Others wait and copyright only their complete manuscripts. As a rule of thumb, I never submit work to anyone that is not copyrighted. One obtains a copyright from the Library of Congress, Copyright Office, 101 Independence Avenue, S.E., Washington, D.C. 20559-6000. Or, one can go online and print a form at http://www.copyright.gov/forms. It costs eighty-five dollars per copyright. That is eighty-five dollars to copyright one poem or eighty-five dollars to copyright a collection of poems. That is why every six months I copyright a collection of work. However, one can also complete an online registration to copyright one poem, or one short story, or one novel for thirty-five dollars. For more information about online, single application, go to http://copyright.gov/fls/sl04s.pdf.

One issue that always arises is when self-published authors submit or allow their work to be included in anthologies. Generally, when a publisher applies for a copyright of an anthology, one is applying for a copyright for the entire work in the name of the publisher. That copyright covers the work as a whole. That is, the publisher's copyright only covers the works inasmuch as they are collected and complied to create one cohesive work, allowing the author to retain all rights to present, submit, or sell that particular anthology or collection of works. The rule is: if one owns a copyright of a work and does not surrender or sign it away, then the work remains the writer's until the writer signs something giving that right to someone else. The only problem that can arise is if one does not already have the work copyrighted before the publisher applies for a copyright for the anthology. Yet, unless one signs something specifically surrendering, relinquishing, or giving the rights of one's work to someone, then one's rights are covered or protected. There can only be a problem if a publisher wishes to claim that one's work was done as work for hire. That is, the writer specifically produced a certain work to be used by the publisher for a particular publication. In this case, it will be best that one has one's work copyrighted. Here, again, as long as one does not surrender, relinquish, or sign away one's rights, then one is protected. The publisher's copyright covers the anthology as a whole, but the writer still retains the rights of one's work. Yet, publishing work in an anthology is a great way to earn or gain promotion for one's lager work. For instance, if one's poem, short story, or an excerpt from one's novel is published in an anthology, then a larger reading base will have access to one's work and may want to purchase the entire work.

Once one has secured a copyright and reviews or comments, it is time to put the work into book form. This means finding a printer and acquiring ISBN (International Series Book Number) and LCCN (Library of Congress Catalogue Number) numbers. An ISBN is the social security number of a book. It allows the book to be tracked and sold anywhere on the planet. The LCCN is the social security number of your book for the world library systems. It allows the book to be tracked and loaned through any library system on the planet. To receive an ISBN write to R. R. Bowker (U.S. ISBN Agency), 630 Central Ave., New Providence, NJ 07974-1154, Phone: 877-310-7333, info@bowker.com, or go to https://commerce.bowker.com/standards/cgi-bin/isbn.asp or https://www.myidentifiers.com/. Once can complete the form online or print the application and mail it. Ten ISBNs cost $275.00, and 100 ISBNs cost $575.00. For more

ISBNs contact the website for pricing. R. R. Bowker will assign the numbers to the entity one lists under company name. One cannot transfer or sell the numbers to anyone else. If one engages a joint project with someone, one's ISBNs must still be listed to one's named entity, or the two partners must apply for an ISBN jointly. Because most if not all retailers require that books have a bar code, there is a place to order a specific bar code for a specific ISBN on the ISBN application. 1 – 5 bar codes cost $25.00, 6 – 10 bar codes cost $23.00, and 11-100 bar codes cost $21.00. Also, as of January 1, 2005, the book industry began adopting the use of a 13-digit ISBN. This change aligns the ISBN identifier with other worldwide product numbering systems, helping promote an efficient global supply chain structure. All books must be compliant with the new 13-digit ISBN by 2007. If one already has an ISBN, one can get it converted for free at http://www.isbn.org/ISBN_converter. If one is applying for one's first ISBN, one will be automatically given a 13-digit ISBN.

After receiving an ISBN, one will need a library catalogue card number (LCCN), which is also referred to as the PCN. This number is free, but cannot be obtained without an ISBN and a title page of the proposed work. The form is very self-explanatory. Write to Library of Congress, Cataloging in Publication Division, 101 Independence Ave., S.E., Washington, DC 20540-4320 or go online to http://pcn.loc.gov/pcn007.html. Again, this number is free, but one needs an ISBN to gain one. They only ask that after one receives the LCCN and one's book is published, send two copies of the book to be filed there. Submit those mandatory deposits to Attn: 407/Mandatory Deposits, Compliance Records Unit, Library of Congress, Cataloging in Publication Division, 101 Independence Ave., S.E., Washington, DC 20540-4320. When one receives one's ISBNs, one will also receive a Pre-Publication form from R. R. Bowker. Six months before the publication of one's book, complete and return this form to R. R. Bowker. This allows R. R. Bowker to list one's book with all booksellers around the planet. So if I know a writer's name, or the book title, or the ISBN, I can walk into any bookstore and ask for your book. Even if they do not have the book in stock, they will have the ability to order the book directly from you. This is how I sell all of my books. It is pre-pay only. They send me a check, and I send a book. I still get at least one order a week for from Europe for *The Lyrics of Prince*. I have never been to Europe, and I am not planning to go. But as long as I remain updated with R. R. Bowker, people can order my books from anywhere in the world.

One must also be persistent with Amazon.com, Barnes and Noble, and the other large dealers about keeping one's books listed. Periodically, I go online and check to see if I can find my books. At the moment, all of my books are listed at Amazon.com, Barnes and Noble, and my website. Finally, when publishing a book, it generally cost about $1,800 for a quality printer to print 500 books. This is about $3.60 per book. For years I used a local printer, but it just became more feasible to use a national printer, such as Lulu.com or CreateSpace.com. I liked being in close contact with the local printer, but once on-demand printers began offering easy access through uploading and web chats it just made more financial sense to use them. Always check with several printers in one's area as well as with national printers. It will then cost about $150.00 to $300 in postage to send complimentary copies to journals, writers, and friends. Identify about 100 copies for promo. Book clubs are fine, but they generally only read and review fiction and essay. They tend not to read much poetry.

Writing is like all other professions. One must be a student of the trade. This means that one must obtain a subscription or two in order to know what is being published and what the current conversations/issues of the field are, allowing one to grow as a writer. One should also join some regularly meeting workshop. A good writing workshop stresses reading and writing activities and exercises that challenge one to work beyond one's comfort zone, which forces one constantly to evaluate one's skills and grow. There are several online workshops that can also be used to supplement one's local workshop. An excellent online workshop is deGriot Space, which is facilitated by Askhari. For information to join, contact her at deGriotSpace-owner@yahoogroups.com or http://groups.yahoo.com/group/deGriotSpace.

A good reference point for workshops, conferences, publications, and journals is a free listserve operated by Kalamu ya Salaam. He is an institution within the institution of writing. Kalamu ya Salaam is one of the driving voices behind the African American Southern Literary scene. Salaam's work includes his latest book *What Is Life*? (Third World Press) and his poetry CD *My Story, My Song* (AFO Records). To join, simply e-mail him at kalamu@mac.com. He has a cyberdrum network by which he sends e-mails to anyone on the list about magazines, book companies, journals, conferences, and other publishers who are looking for writers to submit their work. One will receive about ten daily e-mails on submissions and discussions around the country.

Next, subscribe to at least two literary journals. One should be very academic, and the other should be very culturally astute and wise so that one is exposed to the best of both worlds. Academic journals focus on the form, genre, and structure of writing. Culturally artistic journals focus on the amalgamation of form and culture. Subscribing to both types of journals allows one to grow in various areas. Do not worry if many of the articles look intimidating. One must know theory (elements of literature) to write well or effectively. I use *Callaloo* ($40 yearly, Johns Hopkins University Press, Journals Publishing Division, 2715 North Charles Street, Baltimore, Maryland 21218-4363, 410-516-6987) as my academic journal and *Mosaic Magazine* ($15.00 yearly, 314 W 231 St #470, Bronx, NY 10463, mosaicmagazine.org) as my cultural journal. *African American Review* (Department of English, Saint Louis University, Humanities 317, 3800 Lindell Blvd., St. Louis, MO 63108) is also a very well established scholarly journal. A final journal to which I subscribe is *Black Issues Book Review* ($19.95 yearly, 350 Fifth Ave., Suite 1522, New York, NY 10118).

I am not suggesting that one "rush out" a get all these journals. But, I want young writers to understand that writing is more than what we feel. One may feel or think something, but one must develop the tools to articulate specifically and effectively what it is that one is thinking and/or feeling. Even if one may have good ideas and tools, one must get to work developing them. No matter what road a writer chooses to follow, only well-crafted writing will get a writer where one wants to go.

There are four additional books that all beginning African American writers should have in their possession: *The Norton Anthology of African American Literature* edited by Henry Louis Gates, Jr., *Trouble the* Water and *Black Southern Writers* both edited by Dr. Jerry W. Ward, and *Call and Response* edited by Dr. Trudier Harris. These four anthologies provide a cohesive understanding of the African American literary cannon. They also provide an idea of how the publishing of African American literature has changed and evolved. Specifically, these anthologies show how self-publishing and small/independent publishing have always been a part of the African American publishing tradition and how it remains a necessary mainstay.

As for self-publishing, I am broke but happy. I own my work. I control my work. I work at my own pace, which is cool since I know that I will work harder at selling my books than anyone else. Nikki Giovanni began as a self-published author, riding around with books in her trunk. Third World Press, which is now an international publishing force, began with Haki Madhubuti selling single poems at a barber shop. Gwendolyn Brooks and Amiri Baraka both have been visible and consistent supporters of independent and self-publishing. Self-publishing has been a major vehicle for African American writers who have been and are still very much locked or excluded from the mainstream process. Self-publishing and independent publishing appeals to many African Americans whose voices and subject matters have been and remain contradicting to mainstream publishing. When African American writers have needed a tool to raise their voices about their situation in American and that voice was no longer en vogue, self-publishing and independent publishing remained as excellent vehicles, ensuring that all voices will be given the opportunity to be heard. Yet, self-published writers must always realize that "how" one says something is as important as "what" one says. Thus, all the people I have mentioned are not memorable because they self-published but because they self-published quality work.

Works Cited

Martin, Reginald. "Personal Interview." Spring, 1999.

What Is a Poem?—Part Two

A poem is a puzzle, which is designed to test or inspire ingenuity by having the reader to ascertain or reason a meaning based on the word clues given and any association that the reader can make on the words clues given. Accordingly, a poem is also akin to a riddle because the words used imply a deeper, figurative, or symbolic meaning, which must be uncovered by the reader. The primary goal of a riddle or a puzzle is to induce or create critical thinking. Thus, a poem is an excursion of mental exercise. The pleasure and point of a poem is to achieve or inspire thought. Therefore, poetry becomes an indicator of one's critical thinking abilities, which becomes an indicator of one's humanity. For thinking not only informs us that we are alive, but it is the impetus to our evolution because thinking allows us to make sense and meaning of our lives. With poetry, we purposely place and arrange words, like pieces of furniture or plotted points along a map, in order to reveal or expose the aesthetic beauty and meaning of life. Thus, whether one utilizes or engages rhythm and rhyme, the understanding of language's circular relationship with culture, the innate metaphoric nature of words, and the crafting of metaphoric/figurative language, these elements make it clear that a poem is a work designed or constructed to stimulate, inform, and force the reader to think more deeply or intricately about surface and undercurrent meanings, with the stimulation and informing both being equal forms of pleasure.

Poems are puzzles pieced together by "picture words" to make meaning of life. That is what a poem is. We should not confuse a poem with a limerick or a rhyme. These are techniques, forms even, but they are not poems. A song or a chant is not a poem if the emphasis is merely on rhythm and rhyme. However, if the utilization or placement of rhythm and rhyme is used as a trope or as a way to uncover or "hash out" meaning in or through language, then this work becomes poetic, if not poetry. If the rhythm and rhyme are used as a way to juxtapose language patterns to make a statement about some essence or significance that exist between differing language patterns, then the work becomes poetic, if not poetry. For instance, in Kalamu ya Salaam's poem "Words Have Meaning but Only in Context," he uses the device of strained rhythm when he states "I...love...you...was...said ...by...a...man...raping...his...wife." Salaam has stated that he has consciously never written the piece because he wants to draw the receiver's attention to the delivery of the words, which shows that how and when words are said/delivered has an impact on their meaning. So, by emulating the vocal strain (stuttering and irregularity of pitch and tone) that normally happens when one is having sex and then intensifying that strain to communicate the sound of violence/rape, the receiver is then horrified at the notion that some men truly believe that a married man cannot commit rape of his wife. The sound/rhythm of the "I...love...you" is impregnated with the rage of violence and not the tone of caring because just as the speaker is attempting to force these words from his mouth the receiver parallels that struggle with the struggle of the male to forcibly penetrate the female. The rhythmic delivery of the line, especially when he repeats the first part of the line "I...love...you..." indicates the tension, struggle, and force that is occurring at that moment. Salaam is demonstrating an understanding of the phonetic phrasings of traditional black music by indicating that sounds/phonemes have meaning, and we can manipulate these meanings by placing them in differing contexts. This is why artists such as the Ray Charles, Sam Cooke, and the Staple Singers could mix and match sounds/phonemes as a way to transfer imagery and meaning from the sacred to the secular and back to the sacred, allowing the intense emotions of spirituality to be substituted for and replaced by sexuality as well as political concern as evidenced by the work of Curtis Mayfield, Marvin Gaye, and Stevie Wonder. Thus, the blues is merely secularized spirituals.

Also, if one can show that the differing language (rhythm and rhyme) patterns are specific representations of different cultures, then the use of rhythm and rhyme becomes a literary device that signifies cultural meaning through language. For instance, the ambiguity of Louis Armstrong's "What a Wonderful World" and the haunting quality of John Coltrane's "My Favorite Things" are used to juxtapose how two different races see the world based on their socio-political context. The version from *The Sound of Music* or a Lawrence Welk version of "My Favorite Things" is more syncopated and upbeat because that is the world in which they live. In fact in *The Sound of Music*, Maria is making a list of things about which she thinks to move her from sadness to happiness. Coltrane's version is slowed and often simmers at points to articulate melancholy if not sadness. The list does not completely cheer Coltrane because he has more to surmount. Accordingly, the slow pace of Armstrong's "What a Wonderful World" adds a melancholy feeling to the lyric. This ambiguity has allowed the song to be co-opted by various people for their own agenda. For instance, in 2006 XM Satellite Radio has added the song to its Christmas list and Clear Channel added the song to a list of songs that might be inappropriate for airplay on September 11. However, films such as *Good Morning Vietnam* and *Bowling in Columbine* used the song as backdrop to violent scenes, which seems to signify that their directors recognized a more sarcastic tone/meaning in Armstrong's delivery. When using or examining the use of rhythm, rhyme, or any other device or technique, we should understand that a poem is about troping language, which is already tropical/symbolic, attempting to know if there is any meaning in the innate/organic tropical/metaphoric nature of language and if this, thus, says something about any innate/organic meaning of mankind. But, let us go back before we go too far.

Poems are *puzzles*. Language exists in a circular relationship with mankind. Thus, if we want to understand man's language, we must understand his circumstance that creates the use of language. Words are often coined or reshaped to fit a new, specific need. The question is, "Does this coining or reshaping, in and of itself, have any innate or organic meaning?" Of course it does. It means that language is a tool to the man and not *vice versa*. Man uses language as any other tool in his life—to build a world. As man's world changes, his language changes—often in a circular relationship. The question a structuralist will ask is, "Was not the idea or the concept here before man constructed *physical* words to make the idea or the concept tangible or manifest in his life?" In fact a structuralist could argue that "God" is merely a concept or an idea that, like language, is made physical in the replica, which is our life (Plato's Ideal and Copy theory). Although most religions and cultures accept the notion that in the beginning was the word, that the word existed before life, there is no empirical proof to support this. What we do know is that language and life exist in a circular relationship. The chicken or the egg debate, "What comes first—language or reality?" is an important debate that has been perverted to the point of obscure obtuseness because critical theory is moreso cultural warfare than an attempt to get at the true essence of life by understanding the true essence of language. Though Russian formalists, structuralists, and the new critics *did* cement the study of language as a science, its originators were so drunk with power and blinded by prejudice that even though their theories *do* cause us to look more closely at the work, it leaves the work like a dead flower, disconnected from its roots—the society or human circumstance. To study language detached from its creator(s) is the ultimate scientific flaw of replacing meaning with raw data. It is like studying digestion without understanding why we eat.

Poems *are* puzzles. Man wants to make meaning of his life, so he uses language to signify who and what he is and what his life means. This is what Aristotle means when he refutes Plato's notion of poets being merely liars by asserting that poets complete life because things in themselves are useless without meaning. Aristotle asserted that things are not real until they have meaning. Thus, a poet completes life by giving meaning to it through language. And every religion with a creation story places language as the nucleus of life by having God speak life into being. So even if in the beginning there was the word, there was also someone there to speak the word. Thus, to invoke Barbara Christian, language is the manner by which man orders his world. A poem is an attempt to make meaning by examining the tropical or metaphorical nature of life, which is best seen in language. Ironically, Plato proves in his *Cratylus* that language is arbitrary down to the phoneme and morpheme. That is—the word or signifier, "tree," has no innate/organic connection to the thing that we call or signify as "tree." So a word, in and of itself, is a useless thing when it is void of society or human context. This is affirmed when writer/social critic Kalamu ya Salaam announces that "words have meaning but only in context." Only when organized with other words for a particular purpose, can a statement or a sentence become a trope of something. In fact, the greatest flaw of language is that it only has the ability to be a trope, to be figurative. Thus, language, in and of itself, is tropical or metaphoric— i.e., poetic?

Let's understand that until just after the Middle Ages or just before the Age of Enlightenment, Age of Scientific Discovery, Age of Specialization, the term poetry was synonymous with all other forms of creative literature. For that was the goal of creative literature—to be poetic. The oldest surviving poem is the *Epic of Gilgamesh*, from the 3rd millennium BC in Sumer (in Iraq/Mesopotamia). Yet the epic reads like a novel, which shows that originally,

190

poetry simply meant all forms of creative writing. This is also shown in Aristotle's *Poetics* when he describes the three genres of poetry: the epic, comic, and tragic, and develops rules to distinguish the highest-quality poetry of each genre, based on the underlying purposes of that genre. We know that epic poems, such as the *Iliad* and the *Odyssey* employ narrative techniques as much as they employ poetic techniques. And the comedy and the tragedy, which he names as poetry we now study as plays. In both African and Greek terms, epic poems are narratives if not plays. And even with the rise of the drama in Athens during the Sixth Century BC, the goal of both the poem and the play is to cause a catharsis. Then by nature, the poem represents the construction of meaning by emphasizing, juxtaposing, and layering words and techniques with the final goal to make a person, act, or event more meaningful than we originally realize it to be. Hence, to be poetic is to be literary. This is what, as Reginald Martin shows in his book *Ishmael Reed and the New Black Aesthetic Poets*, demands that slave narratives be considered literature: their poetic nature—their ability to make meaning by troping language. In James Albert Ukawsaw Gronniosaw's *A Narrative of the Most Remarkable Particulars in the Life of James Albert Ukawsaw Gronniosaw, an African Prince*, which is the first full-length black autobiography, Gronniosaw makes a point to show that language, specifically English is something that must be mastered and navigated to give voice, (identity and humanity) to African people by creating "the trope of the talking book…"

> "[My Master] used to read prayers in public to the ship's crew every Sabbath day; and then I saw him read. I was never so surprised in my life, as when I saw the book talk to my master, for I thought it did as I observed him to look upon it, and move his lips. I wished it would do so with me. As soon as my master had done reading, I followed him to the place where he put the book, being mightily

191

delighted with it, and when nobody saw me, I opened it, and put my ear down close upon it, in great hopes that it would say something to me; but I was sorry, and greatly disappointed, when I found that it would not speak. This thought immediately presented itself to me, that every body and every thing despised me because I was black" (Gates and McKay xxviii)

Gronniosaw is being as much metaphoric as he is being literal; his point is to assert that African people need literature that speaks to them, and the way to create this literature is to master and reshape the language that has been forced upon them. "With Gronniosaw's *An African Prince*, a distinctively 'African' voice registered its presence in the republic of letters; it was a text that both talked 'black,' and, through its unrelenting indictment of the institution of slavery, talked back" (Gates McKay xxviii).

Thus, it is not the level or amount of truth or fiction that makes a story poetic or even fiction, but it is the use of language devices that force us to examine slave narratives as something more than literal prose. For instance, Shakespeare was a poet who wrote plays in couplets and sonnets. At the core of all his plays is the notion, the desire, to make meaning, to be poetic, to understand the metaphoric essence of life. He uses literary devices not as things of themselves but as tools or artifacts that make meaning once they have been arranged in some form or fashion. Thus, Hamlet's "To be or not to be" and "What a piece of work is man" declarations can be—must be—read as sovereign poetry capable to stand on their own. In fact Shakespeare's plays have survived because segments of the plays can be recited and enjoyed for their own truth and beauty as poetry much as the segments found in Ntozake Shange's *For Colored Girls Who Have Considered Suicide When the Rainbow Is Enuf*. In this same manner, slave narratives make use of language devices to make meaning of their lives. This is why black dialect must be considered literary. The fact that black dialect exists in couplets and other poetic discourses/devices shows that African Americans are thinking about how to use the language to say something about their lives by creating a rhythm and a form that is different than Standard English. They make a confusing life logical through the refashioning of language. Black dialect is *one* way of making meaning of themselves, of giving meaning to themselves through language. Thus, the creators of black dialect prove Aristotle's theory that things are not real until they have meaning, and African Americans give meaning to themselves by demonstrating their intellectual selves by committing what Walter B. Rideout calls "linguistic liberation" on white language— they free themselves and give themselves meaning through language. Let me be clear. African Americans do not give meaning to themselves by mimicking white language. They give meaning to themselves by refashioning white language. So, whenever African Americans create new words or refashion white language, they are proving Richard Wright's theory that "If black writers turned to their own vernacular tradition black literature could be as original and as compelling as black music and folklore" (Gates xxxiv). Black dialect reveals a people attempting to manifest themselves through language. And this is poetic because they are making meaning through language.

So, to extend the slave narrative and Shakespeare analogy, plays and fiction are a collection of couplets and poetic verses. Thus, the essence of a play/story is the metaphoric significance of language, which is the question of "What does our language reveal about us?" Accordingly, black plays are about the battle of language and culture, the attempt to juxtapose two languages, black and white, in an attempt to juxtapose two cultures, black and white. Black plays are about black people making a language that was supposed to oppress them now speak for them. It is about their beauty being shown by how they take an ugly world or an ugly language and piece it together, beautifully. The quilting that happens in black dialect exemplifies the quilting that happens in black culture. Additionally, this is seen in the use of the "be" verb by the black working class. This segment of society does not have the time to use all of the different forms or conjunctions of "be" because their time is limited due to the excessive amount of work that saturates their life. Even T. S. Eliot, in his essay, "Tradition and the Individual Talent," asserts that there is an innate relationship between man's creation of artistic/aesthetic artifact and the amount of time he has to do so. The more time a people have, the more artistic they become. The less time they have, the more utilitarian they become.

The beauty of black dialect is the mastery of the economy of language, which is an act of troping language. African Americans have learned to say more with fewer words and less time. And because this economy of time and language is at the core of their dialect, black art, when taken seriously, tends to be utilitarian because it has to justify some functional or purposeful existence because, again, black art has to compete with the notion that African Americans do not have as much leisure time. This is why black art, whether for seriousness or for folly, more times than not comments on the black existence under a white umbrella because the bulk of black time is spent dealing with or surviving the white umbrella. So, verb usage and sentence structures are shortened, not because of intellectual inferiority, but because of time. This act is then troped by the poet as a sign of defiance or as the ability of a people to make life and language become useful and meaningful to them. An example of this is when Ralph Ellison has his protagonist in *Invisible Man* assert, "I yam what I am" (260). The use of the "yam" is an example of economy of language, troping Popeye's notion of "I am what I am," which is a trope of "I think; therefore, I am."

Both Popeye's and Ellison's trope represents a cultural battle of one culture/generation grappling with the words/language of other culture/generation to identify their own, new world. Of course, Popeye's trope represents the battle between the formal culture of Europe and the informal culture of America. Likewise, the use of the "yam" by Ellison shows how Africans were forced to take African words and concepts and house them in European syntax. Yet, it is only when Ellison's protagonist accepts himself, his blackness, his African-ness that he finds happiness and peace in the midst of white oppression. So, the placing of the "yam" within the European notion of self-actualization shows the manner in which African people are forced to quilt an existence, and it shows that despite the necessity of quilting African people must always find an acceptance of who they are as African people to find peace in this European land. The yam, which is a black Southern staple, is similar to the cassava yam of Africa. The eating of the yam in public while up North is a direct rebellion against middle-class sensibilities that have been adopted by African Americans as a way to assimilate and ingratiate themselves to whites. From birth, most African Americans are taught that part of aiding in the progress of the race is not to embarrass the race. Thus, African Americans are often warned against engaging in activities or behavior that whites have identified or stereotyped as organically black and inferior. By eating the yam in public, Ellison has his protagonist reject the sensibilities of assimilation to embrace or accept a more positive notion of himself by accepting his heritage as positive or nothing about which to be ashamed. Literature, then, is wholly about the use and meaning of language— what language means, does language have some innate meaning, or is the meaning determined by context and a socio-political matrix? These questions are at the core of all creative works. What makes a work literature or literary is its emphasis on language's ability to articulate some meaning about life. Thus, the language of the work is merely a metaphor or a trope of life—either in general or of the characters' lives.

A poem represents a conscious attempt by a writer to make meaning of the world by piecing together the artifacts of our lives through piecing together the artifacts of our language. So when a song, such as Prince's "Dorothy Parker," is about more than the lyrical and rhythmic movement and feeling, but centers itself on what metaphoric meaning is being projected through the piecing together of semantic artifacts, then it becomes poetic, if not poetry. Also, a poem represents a conscious attempt of a writer to make us know something by de-familiarizing it, as to draw us in deeper to the thing or make us look at it or perceive it differently. "Dorothy was a waitress on the promenade. She worked the night shift. Dishwater blonde, tall and fine, she got a lot of tips. Well, earlier I'd been talking stuff, fighting with a lover's past. I needed someone with a quicker wit than mine, Dorothy was fast." Dorothy is the personification of server whose intellect (wit) is as equally important as anything else she has or uses. Is she a prostitute or a psychiatrist? The ambiguity of the wording creates multiple meanings, giving the piece both a literal and figurative meaning. This is literary because the emphasis of the text is the use ambiguity as a way to de-familiarize the receiver, causing the receiver to look for deeper, more figurative meanings. What also makes the work literary is that it is meta-textual in that Prince is speaking to or building on the work of poet Dorothy Parker and songwriter Joni Mitchell, who is mentioned later in the piece, whose use of metaphor in her own work caused her to be hailed as a lyrical poet. Prince is taking Parker's and Mitchell's body of work (specifically their semantics) and refashioning them for his own context and meaning. This is what Wordsworth means when he asserts that the job of the poet is to make the reader notice the tree and all of its infinite beauty by making the familiar unfamiliar. The poet has the job of removing the film or

196

cataracts of daily living from our eyes, making us see life "mo' better," "mo' realer," or "mo' clearer." The poet is always asking himself, "How can I make them see this better?" "How can I manipulate the language in a manner that makes them better understand the world in which they live?" This can be seen in Richard Wright's desire in *Black Boy* when he states:

> My purpose was to capture a physical state or movement that carried a strong subjective impression, an accomplishment which seemed supremely worth struggling for. If I could fasten the mind of the reader upon words so firmly that he would forget words and be conscious only of his response, I felt that I would be in sight of knowing how to write narrative. I strove to master words, to make them disappear, to make them important by making them new, to make them melt into a rising spiral of emotional stimuli, each greater than the other, each feeding and reinforcing the other, and all ending in an emotional climax that would drench the reader with a sense of a new world (280).

One of the most effective devices a poet uses is imagery, which is, of course, mental pictures based on the six senses. We include the sixth sense because the poet does work with the sense of balance and order. This sense of balance and order in the middle ear is merely an internal prism or link, which connects the individual with the sense of balance or order in the universe. Of course, this sense of balance and order is what governs our sense of right and wrong, which is universal. I do not mean universal in the sense of Russian formalism, structuralism, and the new critic aesthetic where universal is linked to some arbitrary notion of whiteness. I mean the universal notion that has existed in all cultures of "do unto others as you would have them do unto you." This statement or notion has existed in some form or fashion in all cultures. Thus, this proves that there is a universal sense of balance and order. Of course, another example is Nature's balance and order, which continues to govern the life of all mankind. So we must, as poets, make the sense of balance and order one of the senses used in crafting imagery that makes the world see itself better.

The poet uses imagery to make life more vivid or to de-familiarize the world. However, the poet must also be mindful not to make life too vivid as to dull the reader's senses—making peach soda more pleasurable than peaches, or causing all readers to look for or expect to be saved by Super Negro instead of Plain Negro. We must not make our colors, emotions, circumstances, or characters so vivid that the reader does not recognize the real thing in real life. For instance, black people are still looking to be saved by Super Negro because he is going to give the speech that changes the tide of humanity or declare open warfare on all evil white governments. While the black race is looking for this dude, they are missing all of the real revolutionaries among them—the mothers and fathers, janitors, and just plain ole' boring, good hearted people who think that success is living in the womb of a whole family. For all of his good, this is the one tragic flaw of Ralph Ellison's unnamed protagonist in *Invisible Man*. While he eventually is able to reconcile himself to himself, he, throughout the novel, misses the metaphoric essence and significance of the character types who will lead the black movement because he is looking for a specific heroic type. In *Critical Memory*, Houston Baker asserts that Ellison completely misses, misunderstands and marginalizes the "black figures that, in fact, propelled the United States toward a crisis of race matters during the 1950s and 1960s and bid fair to call our country to an honest account of its relationship to black majority in the 1970s" (Baker 36). To avoid missing these or the full spectrum of significant "black figures," the poet must hone a skillful eye for detecting the beauty that might be beneath our radar of sensationalism or own personal, subjective reality. A skillful poet, such as Margaret Walker Alexander, is able to not only show the titanic, heroic essence of men like Martin Luther King, Jr., and Malcolm X, but she is also able to show the human qualities of figures, such as Papa Chicken, thus giving human qualities to a segment of society that is often seen as inhuman by the larger, white society and all too often by themselves. In fact the beauty and power of Alexander's "For My People" is that she deals with the complexity of black struggle by showing that even though African Americans are limping and stumbling, they are still moving and progressing, and that is what makes them great.

> "For my people...lost disinherited dispossessed and happy people filling the cabarets and taverns and other people's pockets needing bread and shoes and milk and land and money and something all our own; For my people walking blindly spreading joy, losing time being lazy, sleeping when hungry, shouting when burdened, drinking when hopeless, tied and shackled and tangled among ourselves...For my people blundering and groping and floundering in the dark..." (Gates and McKay 1573).

Yet for all of their faults, Alexander shows perpetual motion and progress by a people who are "trying to fashion a better way from confusion, from hypocrisy and misunderstanding, trying to fashion a world that will hold all the people, all the faces, all the adams and eves and their countless generations." This means that the poet must commit linguistic liberation as a manner to redefine greatness and humanity in his subjects and heroes. Mercer Cook, in *The Militant Black Writer in Africa and America*, adds to this definition of linguistic liberation: "Taking the white man's language, dislocating his syntax, recharging his words with new strength and sometimes with new meaning before hurling them back in his teeth, while upsetting his self-righteous complacency and clichés, our poets rehabilitate such terms as Africa and blackness, beauty and peace." Linguistic liberation allows the black poet to deconstruct words from their center that oppress them. This is the opportunity to take words such as black and white and reshape their negative and positive connotations, fulfilling Alexander's notion of "trying to fashion a world that will hold all the people, all the faces, all the adams and eves and their countless generations;"

Poems are puzzles whereby we piece together word pictures known as images to explain, make, or show meaning to life. For instance, the Shine tales are poems because they exist as tropes or metaphors of black intellect and black survival. At the core of the story is a meaning that tropes not only language but the reality of that language as viewed by the white owners of that language. Shine not only survives, but he outsmarts white people. The very existence of this type of story or character type reshapes the meaning/reality of life. Slave narratives are poems because they are allegories (tropes) that make meaning of black life, black circumstance, and black people. With the slave narratives, black people are re-writing themselves back into meaning, into a meaning from which their oppressors attempt to erase them. And at a structuralist level, the mere act of their giving life to themselves is an act of making meaning—about language and about themselves. The act of a slave writing has an innate meaning. The act, itself—the work, itself, lying on the page, makes meaning by refuting the meaning/reality of the world created by white slavers, which is founded and centered on the perceived intellectual impotence and inferiority of the African. Thus, for the salve to write is poetic. This act of writing makes meaning by merely being. Yet it is the devices used by these writers that make it literary.

We must understand that poetic devices, such as

foreshadowing, alliteration, and imagery (All creative devices are poetic devices.), are merely tools (paint) to craft the picture that the poet wants to show. Thus, poetry, fiction, and drama are all essentially and fundamentally the same. They are all poems in the deepest sense of the word. They are all poems because their essence is to make meaning by troping. We should view creative literature as the scientific hypotenuse—a question posed to answer real life issues or to lead us on some discovery of the society, the culture, or the self. "What happens if?" "What should we do if?" "What does this mean?" The central issue of poetry is "What does it mean?" The central issue of fiction is "What does it mean?" The central issue of drama is "What does it mean." Looking at creative literature as a hypotenuse allows us to remove the question or the incident being examined just far enough from the lives of those involved so that we can have an objective study to arrive at meaning. It is often easier to examine someone else's life because we are not intimately involved. So to fictionalize something is not to make up a lie, but to paint the picture of a real life incident in a manner that allows us all to detach ourselves enough from it to understand it and study it objectively. Toni Morrison's novels are clear examples that poetry, fiction, and drama are essentially the same. At the core of Morrison's work lies the poem or the poetic form of troping language to make meaning either through vivid imagery or through juxtaposition of people's characters, emotions, things, places, and events. At the center of her vivid descriptions and juxtapositions is her need/attempt to make meaning, to show the metaphoric meaning of something or someone. So, in regard to form, Morrison is a poet who writes extended tropes or metaphoric stanzas in prose form, but her tropes or metaphoric stanzas—descriptions of people, places, things, events or emotions—are also able to stand alone as whole, complete, and autonomous pieces of art. What moves the work into the novel form is that her poems are liner or connected by the same theme or motif. Often there are two central characters who represent some ideal or motif in the culture; often they represent a mainstream and counter-culture ideal, and there is the need to reconcile the ideals or motifs by reconciling the characters, such as in the novel *Sula* where Nel and Sula are set in contrast or in *The Bluest Eye* where Pecola and Claudia are set in contrast.. So the characters themselves are either metaphors or tropes or vehicles to carry and articulate some ideology. Thus, when the poems are placed into a collective, they become a novel.

Morrison's pieces are more than just revelations or insight. Her poetic sense allows her to create moments of microcosmic and metaphoric essence where the character, at any given moment of the movement, is a signifier for the meaning of the whole. By the end of *The Bluest Eye*, we realize that Pecola's self-hatred has caused her to go insane and that her condition is a critique of African people smothered in whiteness.

> "She spent her days, her tendril, sap-green days, walking up and down, up and down, her head jerking to the beat of a drummer so distant only she could hear. Elbows bent, hands on shoulders, she flailed her arms like a bird in an eternal, grotesquely futile effort to fly. Beating the air, an winged but grounded bird, intent on the blue void it could not reach—could not even see—but which filled the valleys of the mind" (204).

Pecola is trapped if not smothered and drowning in that "blue void," what Hughes called that "urge toward whiteness." By trapping Pecola in the "blue void" she has made her a metaphor for African people smothered in white culture and sensibility. Accordingly, chapters of novels are viewed in the same manner. For instance the "Battle Royal" scene from *Invisible Man* is seen as a microcosm of the entire work. Hence, by its very nature, the scene is a trope, making it a poem. And the same technique can be seen in the altercations between Harrison and Wright the altercations between Bill, Brand, and Cook in *Black Boy* are tropes that become techniques used to symbolize black self-hatred as well as the historical battling of the eclectic ideologies of African people trying to fashion a solution to white supremacy. And of course, lying somewhere between the traditional poem form and the novel is the chorepoem, which has been mastered by Shange. Every line in *For Colored Girls Who Have Considered Suicide When the Rainbow Is Enuf* is in verse, and every verse is housed in a stanza, and every stanza is a monologue, and every monologue is tropical. The characters, themselves, are tropical if not allegorical in nature. Each character and each poem (monologue) can stand on its on as an autonomous piece of art. The chorepoem is a movement of poetry connected only by theme and motif, bridging the poem form to that of the play and the novel.

What separates all of these from prose is that their essential desire is to be figurative if not symbolic, and the essay writer's essential desire is to be literal. This does not mean that an essay cannot be literary or does not make use of poetic devices, but its core mission is to be literal. If it seeks to be anything other than literal, then it ceases to be prose. There are, of course, writers and works that cause problems for this characterization--James Baldwin, for instance. His prose is so poetic that one has difficulty finding the dividing lines. Is *Evidence of Things Not Seen* prose or poetry? Because we know that Baldwin's mission was to make us see the unseen and understand its metaphoric essence, we know that he was a poet. In all of Baldwin's work, he moves pass the mere dissemination of information to the act of finding the metaphoric essence of life by studying singular events, then connecting those singular events to other events, until meaning is found—not merely the meaning/definition of the specific thing/event being studied, but the thing's/event's metaphysical significance or metaphoric essence. The same inquisitive spirit that drives *Evidence of Things Not Seen* drives *Just Above My Head*. What does the thing or event say about humanity? In *Evidence of Things Not Seen* Baldwin is wrestling with the meaning of the Atlanta child murders and what these murders say about America and about Black America.

And yet this same wrestling can be seen in his novels, such as *Go Tell It on the Mountain, Giovanni's Room*, and *No Name in the Street*, where protagonists wrestle to find meaning from the events of their lives. How do we better understand ourselves and our reason for being by better understanding the significance or metaphoric essence of the thing/event? This holds true for a work such as Kalamu ya Salaam's *What Is Life*. The title tells you that this is not going to be prose, but an excursion into the deepest regions of language to get at the deepest meanings of human existence. The title implies that ya Salaam is about to do a cosmological and ontological study of life because life is physical and metaphysical. To come to and articulate this type of meaning, one has to be poetic because the scientist can tell you what makes the sky blue, but he cannot tell you "why" the sky is blue. That is—what is the meaning of the color "blue." In this, I again agree with Aristotle that poets become the deepest and most salient thinkers by attempting to give meaning to life— attempting to connect the metaphysical and the physical. A scientist may be able to dissect a frog, but he cannot give meaning to a frog. There is no better example of this than when ya Salaam attempts to bridge the semantic gap between male (a physical, biological thing) and man (an ideological concept), which Reginald Martin, author of *Everybody Knows What Time It Is, Dysfunction Junction*, and *Southern Secrets* also attempts to get us to do in some of his other work. In attempting a linguistic or semantic bridging of these two concepts, what ya Salaam shows us is that the words that we use and the manner in which we use them are directly related to our attempt to make meaning of ourselves and our existence. Even further, the meaning that we wish to make is based on our subjective desire to construct a positive sense of self, well-being, and power. The need to define these terms, even when we do not have an adequate or well-informed notion of them, is a clear notion that language is about our need to define ourselves and our world. The inability to master language, as in our inability to adequately or effectively define man and woman, signifies two truths: one, we will never understand ourselves if we never master language, and two, there may be forces, human controllers, who are working to ensure that only a limited number of people obtain full use of language because language is, of course, power. That is— those who have the power to name and define control reality, control life.

Once we understand the power of language, we can then address the question: How do you construct a good (useful) poem or piece of fiction? A poem is a riddle elevated to its highest forms. It is a three dimensional puzzle layered in form, imagery, and style. The core of a poem is its imagery and ambiguity. It is unlike prose or the essay in that its intent is to be both literal and figurative. When we say that a poem is a riddle or a puzzle, we mean this in the way of being a parable that needs to be deciphered in order to gain a deeper meaning of the subject matter. I agree when both Wordsworth and Dr. Jerry W. Ward assert that the job of poetry is to make the familiar unfamiliar. It presents everyday reality in a manner so sensational or subdued that it removes the film and cataracts of numbness from our eyes so that we may recognize, enjoy, and celebrate our existence. In our daily existence to survive, we lose sight of the beauty of life. It is like going to work every day. After a certain amount of time, we become desensitized or numb to the beauty of the objects and people on our path or route to work. The job of poetry is to describe that tree or individual in such a manner that the imagery causes you to rediscover its beauty. The same can be held for something that we perceive as being negative. The job of poetry is to describe that negative thing in such a manner that it reawakens in the receiver the imminent danger or negativity of the thing or occurrence. For example, in a line from my poem "[i] Hate Christmas," Christmas is described as "a sick deranged monster with rusty ass claws and dull crooked fangs, the kind that puncher the skin and soul, leaving a chewed hole in my essence" (McInnis 43). Or in Baraka's poem, "Black Art" he assaults us with imagery to articulate the purpose of art, especially poetry, "We want live words of the hip world live flesh & coursing blood. Hearts Brains Souls splintering fire. We want poems like fists beating niggers out of Jocks or dagger poems in the slimy bellies of the owner-jews. Black poems to smear…We want 'poems that kill.' Assassin poems, Poems that shoot guns. Poems that wrestle cops into alleys and take their weapons leaving them dead…" (Gates and McKay 1883).

The job of imagery is not to get you to agree with the poet's emotions, but to get you to understand what, to him, the thing is so that you will have a better understanding of the thing or his perception of the thing. Imagery helps you see the thing clearer by giving you something, a tangible image, by which to compare and measure. The same holds true for the critic. The critic's job is not necessarily to agree with the author's notion, perception, or view of something, but to inform the reader whether or not the author is effective in the articulation and communication of his emotion, perception, or view. Further, the author's perceived subjectivity of the described emotion, object, event, or person is not as important as the author's ability to convey effectively his notion or perception of the emotion, object, event, or person. Thus, the job of imagery is to get the reader to see or understand the "thing" being discussed in a different manner. In this, subjectivity is not only warranted but validated. With many well-crafted writers presenting many well-crafted views of a particular "thing," no matter how subjective their individual views, a universal or a consensus will eventually evolve, understanding that the "supposed" universal or consensus is always open to and influenced by the constantly shifting notion of reality and values. Nonetheless, the well-crafted image expands our knowledge and understanding of a "thing" and allows those of us from different cultures to begin to create a bridge of understanding, which is a bridge to that universality of humanity that the Formalists, Structuralists, and New Critics are always attempting to argue into existence.

Bad (ineffective) poetry is the poetry that is so complicated, vague, and interwoven on itself that no one understands it but the poet. Or, ineffective poetry is poetry that displays a lack of imagination and mastery of the language by a poet who often makes use of commonly used images and clichés. So, then, the poet must have a mastery of language, culture, and history as well as an understanding of how the three work in a circular relationship to influence each other. Not only should the poet master his native (I use the term native quite loosely here.) language, but should be well studied in at least one other language. "Languages are the tools of thought. Unless you know more than one language, you cannot think outside of the confines of that language" (Olugbala 1998). The poet needs this background to truly understand how words, terms, and phrases evolve. There is a science to coining a word or a term. The poet must also be knowledgeable of various cultures and how all cultures are somehow and in some way related because language and culture are inextricable. It is difficult to tell where one ends and the other begins. Truly, to take a man's language is to take his culture, for tied up in his language is who he is— his creation narrative, his community rituals, his ideologies, and his evolutions. So poets must be well read. They must study all of the masters: African, Asian, Native

American, and European. Through this, they will gain a better understanding of language and how it is a tool of man, to which man and his existence dictates.

This mastery of language and culture is what allows the poet to create the proper phrase and imagery which allows him to adequately and effectively articulate the message to the receiver. This is what determines good (effective) and bad (ineffective) imagery. It is based on the image's effective articulation of the thought or feeling from the poet to the reader. Effective and ineffective imagery is determined by how well the image works to etch the subject into the mind and soul of the receiver. A student once came to me in tears because an instructor said that her work presented vulgar and degrading imagery. After reading the piece I understood why the instructor felt that way but informed the student that I thought that the imagery was effective. In my paraphrasing of one of the lines, the student wrote, "Writer's block is like I am stricken with the worst form of constipation. The words and ideas in my head are crammed and squashed together at the point of explosion, but there is no exit hole. Reading is like an enema, allowing the bowels of my imagination to flow like liquid" (Gibson 1997). As explicit as that may be, I understand the feeling of writer's block. In the passage, the student demonstrated both a knowledge and understanding of imagery and culture. It seems that every other minute that I turn on my television there is a commercial for some form of laxative. The rise in the marketing and need for laxatives in America is in direct relation to our poor American eating habits. For the young writer, writer's block comes from an unhealthy reading diet, which is either a lack of reading or from reading works that are less than intellectually stimulating. When one reads stimulating work, his own work will flow like the Nile, stimulating or nourishing the minds of other readers and writers.

Imagery is the soul of the poem because it relates to the soul of a culture. When Sappho uses the image of Helen of Troy in her poem "To an Army Wife form Sardis," she evokes all of the emotions tied to the event of Helen and places them within the context of her poem. Thus, her readers empathize with her poem's protagonist because they know and emphasize with Helen. When Zora Neal Hurston writes in *Their Eyes Were Watching God* that Janie had "firm buttocks like she had grape fruits in her hip pockets," it is an image to which all African Americans can relate. The more rounded and fuller figure of the African American female touches the soul of African Americans. In this one line Hurston is attempting to wipe away centuries of negative imagery of African Americans by celebrating the beauty of the African American woman. This is also seen in Lucille Clifton's "Homage to my Hips," where Clifton uses the African American female anatomy as metaphor to discuss the pains and limits of white supremacy and the power of having a positive sense of self. "these hips are big hips…they don't fit into little petty places. these hips are free hips." In a Western and American culture that teaches women that thin is the only merit of beauty, Clifton is refuting that notion by showing the beauty and power of the typical African American female body: "these hips are mighty hips…these hips are magic hips. i have known them to put a spell on a man and spin him like a top!" So, an effective image can not only etch a thought or feeling into the receiver, it can also be used as propaganda. This is why the color black is never attached to anything negative in my work. In fact the color black is always associated with something positive or fertile, such as "the black fertile sky holds boundless gifts from God." This, then, means that the critic must be as well read and studied on different languages and cultures as are poets so that they can recognize the effective imagery of various cultures and not be limited by the narrow notions of their own culture.

Thus, we end where we begin. Language is a puzzle that we piece together to make meaning. Language, then, is innately and organically poetic. Poems are merely tropes of that poetic nature. The most a poet can do is study language as much as possible to bridge the gaps of communication. The most a poet can do is attempt to give himself as many tools as possible to build the best house of communication, which will house as many people as possible. But even greater than this, all poets are not for all people because language, in its innate arbitrariness, is innately subjective if not novel. Therefore, the truly useful poet and critic attempts to find universality by piecing together our novelty. As the poet begins with the subjective and personal "I" and moves to the collective "I," it is the job of the critic to show this transition. The truth is that we can only find that supposed "universality" by studying the "novel" or "subjective." There can be no universal if there is no novel or subjective. For if there is no novel or subjective—as the structuralist and new critics would have us believe, why do we need a term such as universal? You cannot have mainstream culture without a counter-culture, so you cannot have universality without novelty or subjectivity. This is the dilemma that lies at the core of the poet's work. What is the gap between the subjective, collective, and objective meaning of a word, how does the poet bridge the gap, and what, if anything, does the gap mean? How does the poet move pass his own, personal, subjective self to communicate with a collective? *Not* how does he marginalize his novel life, but how does he craft his work in such a manner that allows him to celebrate those things that are novel and universal. If he can do this, he has made meaning of his life. And this is what the poem seeks and wishes to do.

Bibliography

Baker, Houston. *Critical Memory*. Athens: University of Georgia Press, 2001.

Cook, Mercer and Stephen Henderson. *The Militant Black Writer in Africa and America*. Madison: University of Wisconsin Press, 1969.

Ellison, Ralph. *Invisible Man*. New York: Vintage Books, 1952.

Gates, Henry Louis Jr. and Nellie Y. McKay, eds. *The Norton Anthology of African American Literature*. New York: W. W. Norton and Company, 1997.

Gayle, Addison. *The Black Aesthetic*. New York: Doubleday. 1971

Gibson, NaTasha Ria. "..." an unpublished poem, 1997.

Hurston, Zora Neale. *Their Eyes Were Watching God*. New York: Perennial Classics, 1937.

Martin, Reginald. *Ishmael Reed and the New Black Aesthetic Critics*. Houndmills: MacMillan Press, 1988.

McInnis, C. Liegh. *Confessions: Brainstormin' from Midnite 'til Dawn*. Jackson: Psychedelic Literature, 1998.

McInnis, C. Liegh. "Writing as Theory and Art Form." *Prose: Essays and Letters*. Jackson: Psychedelic Literature, 1999, 2007.

Morrison, Toni. *The Bluest Eye*. New York: Plume, 1970, 1994.

Olugbala, Sawandi. "Lecture on Creativity and other Principles of Kwanzaa." The 1998 Jackson Community Kwanzaa Celebration. December 31, 1998.

Salaam, Kalamu. *What Is Life?? Reclaiming the Black Blues Self.* Chicago: Third World Press, 1994.

Walker, Margaret. "For My People." *The Norton Anthology of African American Literature.* New York: W. W. Norton and Company, 1997.

Wright, Richard. *Black Boy.* New York: HarperCollins, 1945, 1993.

The Importance of Teaching Cultural Diversity in College World Literature Courses

To say no to a multi-cultural education is to say yes to the perpetuation of the ideology of white supremacy. Literature is the element to which we point to know a people. When we study any race of people to discuss their worth and contribution to society, their production of literature is a major factor in how the world views them as intellectual beings. James Weldon Johnson asserts, "The final measure of the greatness of all peoples is the amount and standard of the literature and art they have produced. No people that has produced great literature and art has ever been looked upon by the world as distinctly inferior" (Gates and McKay xxxv). Henry Louis Gates, Jr. goes on to affirm, "Writing stands alone among the fine arts as the most salient repository of genius, the visible sign of reason itself" (Gates and McKay xxxv). The reason we point to literature to study a group of people is because art represents the soul of a people. It is all of who they are: their physical, metaphysical, social, political, and religious being. It reflects their achievements, short comings, dilemmas, and evolution. So, if we do not study the literature of all the people on the planet, we have a limited view of humanity. Then history becomes one person's story. For too long world literature courses across the country were taught this way. Classes would be given the title of "A Study of the Great Masterpieces" and ninety-five percent of the works would be by dead white males. This is dangerous because in doing this we were engaging in cultural warfare on all peoples of color. By ignoring or denying the achievements in literature of other races, universities were perpetuating the notion of white superiority to white students and students of color who will continue to perpetuate this notion to their students. The Civil Rights Movement created many associated movements, including the push toward diversity or multi-culturalism into the American classrooms. The dream of this notion or movement is two fold, to teach and nurture respect and appreciation for scholars of color as well as for white scholars. By exposing students to the craft and achievements of writers of color, we are nurturing a respect for those writers in the students who will become the scholars of the next generation. Once these students gain a respect for these writers as valid tacticians, there is a natural evolution of admiration or fondness. In order to achieve this, the university must complete four basic steps. The university must begin showing writers of color as critical thinkers. The university must begin analyzing the problem of subject matter as it relates to perception and culture. The university must realize and address the issue that perpetuating the notion of the inferiority of writers of color perpetuates the notion of white supremacy. And finally, the university must understand that teaching diversity is celebrating the humanity (worth) of all peoples.

When during the European Renaissance the German philosopher Hegel utters "Africa had nothing to do with civilization," he is acting as an educational agent for white supremacy by denying the truth of Africans and all peoples of color as critical thinkers. We must understand that literary criticism is used more as a tool of cultural warfare than as a tool for understanding specific works of literature as it relates to that work's organic relationship to its culture. So, when we affirm a particular writer's work, we affirm him, his culture, and the tradition of writers who produced him. The American academies and universities have been slow to affirm the craft and talent of writers of color, especially when these writers of color tend to write from their particular experience which, of course, creates a particular form or style. To affirm a writer is to affirm his form or style. This issue is addressed in detail in *The Empire Writes Back: Theory and Practice in Post-Colonial Literature*. It seems that only those writers of color who write in the European tradition of language, form, and subject matter are valued as critical thinkers. And yet

Amiri Baraka, Richard Wright, and Chinua Achebe have all affirmed that this act of taking on the clothing of European literature is not an act of critical thinking but is more akin to teaching an animal to do some tricks where his actions are merely reactions to some type of stimuli. That is, the true critical thinker does not merely mimic someone else's culture and tradition. A true critical thinker finds a way to articulate who he is to the world. V. F. Calverton, a Marxist critic, puts it this way, "the Negro's music and folk art were never 'purely imitative' and that black vernacular cultural forms were 'definitely and unequivocally American' the only 'original American forms culture yet created'. Wright too, would repeat this claim. "If black writers turned to their own vernacular traditions, he concluded, black literature could be as compelling as black music and folklore" (Gates and McKay xxxiv). Both Wright and Calverton are speaking to the notion of the creative intellect of African Americans. This speaks to two larger issues about people of color, their ability to create civilization before European colonization and their ability to refashion an existence of their own under the umbrella of European colonization. Both cases speak directly to the notion of writers of color as critical thinkers. So if we consider that some of the earliest known writings date to the Sudan area of Africa around 6000 BC, then Hegel is absolutely false. Africans as well as all peoples of color did have something to do with civilization because it is from their oral poems, myths, and riddles that Greek literature evolves. In fact, the Greeks did not have an alphabet until 5,000 years after the Africans first wrote. When we exclude people of color from a class of "World Masterpieces," we are perpetuating the lie of white superiority and simultaneously excluding people of color as critical thinkers. Creative literature is not merely the art; it is also the critical theory governing the art. There can be no art without theory. Therefore, if these ancient civilizations of people of color from the Far East to Africa to Latin America created ancient art, there was also ancient

215

theory. Thus, they were critical thinkers. When we do not say this in our universities, we are perpetuating the myth of peoples of color not being thinking beings.

The major problem of not including peoples of color in the university literary curriculum has been the problem of subject matter. People generally fear what they do not know or understand. When the British, French, and Dutch began colonizing Africa, their lack of understanding caused them to dismiss the African's culture. When one does not understand a particular writer's culture, one will dismiss that writer's art, which, of course, springs form the bowels or the viscera of that culture. The theory of Negritude addresses this notion by affirming that African works will always be misunderstood and labeled as being marginal as long as they are critiqued by European writers who only have an understanding of European culture. For instance, if a critic or scholar has no notion of the concept of polygamy or comes from a culture where polygamy is viewed as a negative concept, he is likely to give an Achebe work a negative critique merely because of his sheer lack of knowledge of Achebe's culture. Negritude allows us to understand that if art is organic to culture, then we must understand specific cultures to understand specific works of art. Therefore, we not only need to teach diverse literature, we also need a racially diverse English faculty to help bridge the gaps of understanding.

Yet, the problem of subject matter is not just an issue of understanding or exposing oneself to another culture. The primary issue or conflict of subject matter is the problem that writers of color face when they discuss the problems of their people incurred because of white supremacy and colonization. If we are truly going to get at diversity, we must get at truth. Nikki Giovanni has a poem entitled "For Saundra" where she states, "my neighbor who thinks i hate asked -- do you ever write tree poems -- i like trees so i thought i'll write a beautiful green tree poem peeked from my window to check the image noticed the school yard was covered with asphalt no green -- no trees grow in manhattan ... so i thought again and it occurred to me maybe i shouldn't write at all but clean my gun and check my kerosene supply perhaps these are not poetic times at all" (Gates and McKay 1983). The issue here is reality and perception, the axle on which the Plato and Aristotle debate turned. Writers of color are often asked to write outside their reality experiences because their reality or sensibility is often offensive or threatening to the realities or sensibilities of whites. A neighbor asks Giovanni to write a poem about trees because tree or nature poems are pleasing and safe to the neighbor, yet a poet, a person, such as Giovanni has other more pressing issues with which to deal than the beauty of trees. Additionally, there were no trees outside her window. So, writing about trees, for this poet, would be to write outside of her cultural experience. Whites, who control publishing all over the globe, have manipulated writers of color by manipulating what they write. And if what they write is not palatable to white sensibilities, writers of color are ignored or marginalized. This is because nobody wants to hear that they are the cause or root of someone else's troubles. However, if writers of color are going to adequately and effectively address the problems of their people, they must address white supremacy and colonization. Yet, the truth is that no white publisher will regularly or consistently publish or celebrate literature that demonizes them or their tradition. White scholars want writers of color to write tree poems because it covers up the lie of white supremacy and colonization and lets them off the hook for their responsibility to aid in undoing the wrong that engineered the money for a Random House to exist. Langston Hughes affirms, "The Negro artist works against unintentional bribes from whites. Be stereotyped, don't go too far, don't shatter our illusions about you, don't amuse us too seriously. We will pay you" (Gates and McKay 1270).

The job of the university scholar is to solve problems not to cause or perpetuate them. By refusing to teach diversity in world literature courses, universities are perpetuating white supremacy. This, in turn, is perpetuating self hatred in people of color. Again, Hughes recounts of a promising young African American poet saying to him, "I want to be a poet -- not a Negro poet, meaning subconsciously, I would like to be a white poet, meaning behind that, I would like to be white" (Gates and McKay 1267). Obviously, this young African American poet was using the history and tradition of Europe as his model for becoming a good or celebrated writer. There is nothing wrong with studying writers of different races. Indeed, I owe a great deal to Keats for my whole understanding of being a philosopher poet. Yet, to study Shakespeare just because he is white is a detriment to literature and his talent. Is Shakespeare an effective writer? Of course, he is. Should Shakespeare be studied? Of course, he should. Have other writers of other regions and other races been given the same opportunity to be celebrated? No. Unless we ensure the diversity in teaching world literature, we will continue to create writers of color who want to be white because they see themselves and their culture as being inferior. A prime example of this is Phillis Wheatley, who was a skilled poet. Yet, because her educational and religious training were merely tools for white supremacy, Wheatley is able to excuse the crime of slavery as a minimal means to a justifiable end. In her poem "On being brought from Africa to America" Wheatley writes:

> "It was mercy brought me from my pagan land, Taught my benighted soul to understand That there's a God -- that there's a Saviour too; Once I redemption neither sought nor new... Remember, Christians, Negroes black as Cain May be refined, and join the angelic train" (Wheatley 12).

Wheatley was taught that everything of Europe is good, and everything of Africa is bad. In doing so, she was taught to internalize her own inferiority and her own culture's inferiority. In doing this we are able to teach children that the massacre of peoples of color for the perpetuation of colonialism, capitalism, and religion is a part of human history to be celebrated. Although Wheatley does, in her own very subtle manner, speak against slavery, it is always with the notion of Europeans accepting Africans on European terms. Because Wheatley has no real knowledge of her culture or of her people's contribution to the development of all global civilizations, i.e., humanity, she is unable to celebrate her people or herself. The most she can hope to achieve is to cloak herself in the clothing of European culture and gain some semblance of acceptance by ingratiating herself to Europeans by denying and marginalizing her people's culture. Or as Hughes affirms, in an attempt to integrate into European society African Americans have been taught to internalize "this urge ... toward whiteness, the desire ... to be as little Negro and as much American as possible" (Gates and McKay 1267). So then a lack of diversity in world literature courses helps to perpetuate the self-hatred in people of color that is given to them by the ideology of white supremacy.

At the center or core of any discussion about multiculturalism is power, especially in literature. Publishing is power because reading and writing have long been accepted as the most salient representations of thinking, higher intelligence, and humanity. To publish a person is to say that he and his culture represent the highest forms of intelligence and humanity. Therefore, publishing is one of the most dominate tools in cultural propaganda and cultural warfare. Amiri Baraka asserts this.

The "competition" in grants and the arts is essentially Class Struggle! It is ideological, finally, and determined by the judges' political ideological orientation. That's why "Homo Locus Subsidere" can get a "Genius Award" and don't even know enough not to be ugly. If its one thing I do know, after being dissed over the years—grant-wise, production-wise—is that all classes put their politics first. Look at who gets the huge grants, the big publishing contracts, the bourgeoisie's ink...and why?!? The "people making those decisions," as you say, have not "forgot" anything. To think that there is a wasting away of sensitivity or taste or information or intelligence by such agents is not to think it through. *They* are "those people making decisions" because *they* represent the values of *that* class which got the power, dough...*They* are not empty headed enough to give resources to their enemies! (Baraka 2001).

Reginald Martin, in *Ishmael Reed and the New Black Aesthetic Critics*, adds that "[Ishmael Reed] again asserts that those who oppose Afro-American aesthetic motifs in writing are those who are trying to uphold the white, Christian, Western way of maintaining a socialized order" (Martin 80). If we allow for the benefit of the doubt, we can accept that Russian Formalism, Structuralism, and the New Critics were all created as a reaction to WWI and II. This new world of chaos needed a new religion, a new theory, a new science that would ease the chaos. Yet from a political and economic standpoint, both of which compose the matrix of publishing, we understand that Russian Formalism, Structuralism, and New Criticism are a reaction to the growing number of non-white peoples coming into the Western academies as proven both by Martin in his article, "New Criticism and New Black Aesthetic Criticism: Debts and Disagreements," and by Raman Selden in his book, *Contemporary Literary Theory*. This growing number of non-whites not only upset the balance of power with their numbers (increasing

220

population), but also because they bring a differing sensibility that challenges, if not voids, the established truths of Western thought. In echoing Foucault, Selden asserts "discourse is always inseparable from power, because discourse is the governing and ordering medium of every institution. Discourse determines what is possible to say, what are the criteria of 'truth', who is allowed to speak with authority, and where such speech can be spoken." (Selden 129). The battle over literary theory is the battle over who has the right to speak and whose voices will be authenticated. Formalism, Structuralism, and New Criticism were all attempting to validate one language structure to gain one reading, which would enforce one truth—the Western truth. Being bombarded with new cultures, new ideas, and new ways of seeing the world, the Western academies needed a way to remain in control. They achieved this by asserting that a literary work can have but one "reading." This one "reading" affirms that there can be but one aesthetic—the white, Western aesthetic. By asserting this notion of one way of "reading" a work, the white professors are able to retain power by retaining the dominate culture—the only culture, with all cultures of color being merely appendages of white culture.

The dangers of cultures of color and their literature being categorized as merely an appendage of white culture is that people of color are not seen as human beings but as clones of white ancestry. Further, then, we must understand that the battle for multiculturalism is not just about black and white, but about people of color being able to study, celebrate, and express their human totality and diversity by expressing the wide array and full spectrum of their writers. Often, in reaction to calls for more ethnically inclusive syllabi, the academies often opt to include a writer of color who is easily assimilated into their aesthetic canon or easily identifiable as differing from their aesthetic. Although this inclusion is positive, on its face, it is often more detrimental. This type of flat, stock categorizing of writers of color flattens their literary canon, which, of course, minimizes and marginalizes their literary talents and concerns, which minimizes and marginalizes their humanity. For instance, the writers of the Black Arts Movement are often taught and celebrated for their rebellion against the Western academy. Their subject matter is noted more highly than their mastery of language and their contribution to the evolution of the form and aesthetic of American literature, which is the most important aspect of literary theory. The same is true of any period of black literature. Western academies often ignore the literary or scientific skill of the black writer, never understanding that his thematic liberation is tied to his linguistic liberation. Black writers who are syncratic in their approach, who amalgamate African and European styles at their own accord are often ignored or flattened, like Reed and Baraka have been flattened. White academicians want black writers they can pin down, categorize, and assimilate easily. Black writers who are syncratic in their approach destroy the Western academy's myth of the inferiority of black intellect. The same holds true for any discussion of a black aesthetic outside the confines of a "Black Literature" course. At the core of the Black Power Movement and its cultural arm, the Black Arts Movement, was the discussion of what a black aesthetic is. Addison Gayle, Baraka, and Reed represent various points and poles along the spectrum of Blackness. Al Young's poem, which asserts, "Don't nobody want no nice nigger no more/ these honkies man that put out/ these books & things/ they want an angry slib/ a furious nigrah/ they don't want no bourgeois woogie/ they want a militant nigger..." is a perfect bookend to Houston Baker's notion that Frederick Douglass and Ralph Ellison, while writing to largely white audience, were sure to emphasize those values in the black middle-class that related directly to the values of the white middle-class. In presenting differing notions and aspects of black literature, Gayle, Baraka, Reed, Young, and Baker are presenting differing notions and aspects of black culture, which affirms humanity. By adding to the pot the existence of Carolyn Rogers and Barbara Christian, we get an understanding of Clarence Major's assertion that "Total life is what we want." If writers of color are not able to explore the totality and diversity of their varying and constantly evolving aesthetics in the same nature as white writers, then they can never achieve humanity.

This gets us to our final notion that teaching diversity is teaching humanity. I love the challenge of teaching *Antigone* to African American freshmen. They generally approach the work as another dull piece of literature written by some dead white guy whose existence was nothing like theirs and could not possibly write something related to their existence. A work like *Antigone* is the perfect piece to convey to my students attending a Historically Black College or University (HBCU) that the best art is art that is able to break past those arbitrary and physical boundaries that man has erected and articulate the souls of a people to any reader. So rather than approaching the text in a manner of "It is good because Sophocles, a dead Greek, wrote it," I go to the text, uncovering the issues of humanity at play: the question of the rights of individuals verses the rights of the state, the supremacy of man's law verses God's law, and the notion of Antigone being a Christ-like figure. In all of us this, I am able to cite people like Malcolm X and Martin Luther King who were both willing and did die for their beliefs as did Antigone. By doing this, the students begin to understand that literature is about people's lives, which brings cultures closer. They begin to empathize with Antigone's plight. Also, Antigone's plight and circumstances as a woman are always noticed and engaged by my female students. In all of this, they begin to understand that literature is not merely about memorizing lines or names of characters. They realize that literature is about people: who they are, what they want, and what they need. Through our informed discourse about literature, the students realize that all people want the same things. By teaching diversity in world literature, we are teaching humanity. We are teaching students first to identify with all people on a human level and then celebrate the beautiful bouquet of humanity that we create. When we do this, we are teaching future scholars, as James Baldwin asserts, that "our birthright is to love each other," not to conquer each other (Baldwin 42). To not teach diversity in world literature courses is to teach white supremacy, is to give students a license to use scholarship as a means and a tool of global oppression.

Works Cited

Asante, Molefi Kete and Abu S. Abarray, eds. *African Intellectual Heritage: A Book of Sources.* Philadelphia: Temple University Press, 1996.

Ashcroft, Bill, Gareth Griffiths, and Helen Tiffin. *The Empire Writes Back: Theory and Practice in Post-Colonial Literatures.* London: Rutledge, 1989.

Baker, Houston. *The Journey Back: Issues in Black Literature and Criticism.* Chicago: University of Chicago Press., 1980.

Baker, Houston. *Critical Memory.* Athens: University of Georgia Press, 2001.

Baldwin, James. *Evidence of Things Not Seen.* New York: Henry Holt and Company, 1985.

Baraka, Amiri. "Slam Dialogue: Response to Responses." E-Drum: Kalamu@aol.com. (Online Posting) Moderated by Kalamu ya Salaam. July 26, 2001.

Gates, Henry Louis Jr. and Nellie Y. McKay, eds. *The Norton Anthology of African American Literature.* New York: W. W. Norton and Company, 1997.

Martin, Reginald. *Ishmael Reed and the New Black Aesthetic Critics.* Houndmills: Macmillan Press, 1988.

Reed, Ishmael. *19 Necromancers From Now.* New York: Doubleday, 1970.

Selden, Raman and Peter Widdowson. *A Reader's Guide to Contemporary Literary Theory.* Lexington: University Press of Kentucky. 1993.

Wheatley, Phillis. *Poems of Phillis Wheatley: A Native African and a Slave*. Bedford: Applewood Books, 1995.

Which King Is on the Postage Stamp?:
Evaluating Martin Luther King's Legacy
Presented at the 2003
Middle-Tennessee State University King Day Celebration

Which Martin Luther King is on the postal stamp? This is a very important question because it speaks to how we remember him, how we teach his legacy, and how we develop strategies to gain our sovereignty and first-class citizenship. So, I ask again, "Which King is on the postal stamp?" What we must understand is that what makes an oppressor great is his ability to co-opt the talents and skills of the oppressed. And what continues to happen to King's legacy is that those who wish to continue to oppress his people have been able to manipulate King's philosophy by removing the teeth of it, which he used to bite into the most complex of American problems. Or to put it another way, they want to celebrate King's vision (dream) without doing the real and difficult work of making it a reality. For instance, everybody wants to celebrate the dream of black folks and white folks living together in harmony, but very few want to deal with the check marked "insufficient funds" that has been continually written to Africans dislocated in America. And when we allow this to happen, we allow King's legacy to be defiled. So, again I ask, "Which King is on the postal stamp?" It depends on which King we choose to celebrate. We cannot allow King to be turned into a flat, one-dimensional caricature that makes the oppressor feel all warm and gooey inside. In fact, this is the antithesis of King's work. King was the griot of his time, constantly reaching his hands into the bowels of America's injustice, holding it up for us to moved by the filthy smell of it all. So, as we stand on the verge of another war in the Middle-East, we must ask which King is on the postal stamp because it is this King that will guide our actions. As we seek to address King's legacy in relation to how we make decisions on our present and future, we must understand that King's Legacy is one of

227

unity, selflessness, critical thinking, courage, and righteousness.

Unity

The Civil Rights Movement was a joint movement of various people with eclectic ideas. There is this misconception that downtrodden Black people were saved by the few Black leaders and the benevolent white liberals from the North. National media, including films such as *Mississippi Burning*, has perpetuated this false notion. However, if you read books, such as *Local People* by John Dittmer and *Coming of Age in Mississippi* by Anne Moody, or talk to the people who where there, you will find that the Civil Rights Movement was constructed on the backs of everyday common people, such as Fannie Lou Hamer. The reason why Hamer's statement of being sick and tired of being sick and tired is so powerful is because it was the articulation of the collective mind-set of an entire people. Hamer was a sharecropper who, as so many others, had grown weary of being chattel for plantation owners. It is folk like Hamer who were joined by folk like Medgar Evers, Aaron Henry, Annie Devine, and Hollis Watkins who then joined others to construct what became the Civil Rights Movement. So in truth, neither King nor Malcolm X led the movement. They were merely manifestations of the work of others before them as well as manifestations of the will of the people to become the voices of the Movement, along with others. This is an important issue because the "holy leadership" fallacy continues to hold Black people stagnant, waiting on a Messiah to be born of a virgin and deliver them. When in fact, Africans dislocated in America have the same tools and resources, in fact they have even more tools and even more resources, yet we still languish in the ocean of second-class citizenship. That is because instead of studying the work of King, we have decided to make a deity of him. What makes King a great man is that he was able to accomplish goals while dealing with varying concerns and issues. And one of those concerns was finding a way to form a coalition of the fragmented Black mass. This may be King's greatest feat; for one of the highest compliments paid to King is that he was just as comfortable in a cafe' as he was in the White House. So when you talk about King, you must talk about a man who was respected by almost every aspect of black society—the accommodationists, the integrationists, and the Black nationalists. Examples of this are his relationships with Stokely Carmichael, Malcolm X, Asa Phillip Randolph, and Bayard Rustin. King spent his life reaching out to diverse individuals with diverse backgrounds and ideas because he understood that black strength is black unity, but black unity only has value when each group is allowed to participate. Thus, King's ability to create coalitions was driven by his acute perception of the power of collective forces and his selflessness to lead by service.

Selflessness

It is a shame that we now live in a time when Negro leadership is getting rich doing nothing when Dr. King died broke for something. There was a nice check that came with winning the Noble Prize for Peace. But King invested the majority of his earnings back into the Movement and not into a house or a car. Yes, economically, King came from middle-class means, but ideologically King never had nor perpetuated the bourgeois, elitist attitude as many do today. Condoleezza Rice asserted that the sit-ins, protests, and marching in the streets were unnecessary overkill, and that if left alone segregation would have died out or ended on its own. Evidently, Ms. Rice was not watching the same movie that the rest of black America was watching. And while I disagree with Ms. Rice, I also understand that her perception was handed to her by her middle-class background. Class diversity or class fragmentation has been a major part of the African American struggle since the development of the first house slaves. Yet, for the most part, house slaves understood that even though they enjoyed better circumstances than the field slaves, they were still slaves. Thus, they understood that it would be in their best interest to work with the other slaves to end their oppression. Today, middle-class blacks must continue to understand that to whom much is given, much is expected. King could have very easily used his background and education for self-reward. This is one of the primary issues addressed in "Letter from a Birmingham Jail," when King chastises the other ministers for not using their positions of power to effect social and political change. Unlike most of them, King's life was about substance over symbolism. King was not required to go to Alabama and participate in the bus boycott to make his way in life. His father had already pulled strings to jump start his career. King did not have to go to Memphis in support of the sanitation workers' strike. He had already made his mark on Civil Rights. By this time in his life, he could have resigned his life to that of lecturing, book deals, and consultant work. However, King lived his life by the credo, "If I can help somebody along the way, then my living will not be in vein." King understood that a man's legacy should not be based on what he does for himself, but on what he does for others. As he asserted, "Everyone can be great because everyone can serve." To this he often added Jesus' remarks to his disciples, "He who is great among you shall be your servant." So, if you wonder why black people do not vote as they should, it is because their self-appointed leadership does not serve them. We must stop sending Negroes to office who vote their self-interest and not the interest of African people. If we are serious about living up to the legacy of King, we are forced today to ask, "What have we done to make this world a better place?" Only when we ask this question are we continuing the legacy of King. Asking this question gets us to the true purpose for being and helps us better to understand what it means to be educated. See, an educated man is not one who can regurgitate information or can be trained to perform a task. An educated person is one who can use resources and information to construct a better life for himself, his community, and the world. Innate and organic to the definition of education is improvement—self and community. Thus, it is the selfless man who will achieve the greatest heights of leadership because the selfless man understands that leaders ultimately serve the people.

Critical Thinking

The one point that is often missed about the Civil Rights Movement is the issue of strategizing and critical thinking. Most people think that Rosa Parks was just some tired woman who sat down on the bus. Although that is romantic (and Americans love their epic romanticism), that is not true. Ms. Parks and her actions were strategically birthed as a part of the planned movement. Not only had Parks been a member of the NAACP since the forties engaging in many of the NAACP's training and workshop sessions, she had also taken part in training and workshop sessions at the Highlander Center, which was founded in 1932 to serve as an adult education center for community workers involved in social and economic justice movements. When you deny this fact, you are denying the critical thinking abilities of Africans. And when you deny the critical thinking abilities of Africans, you are saying that they are sub-human. Thus, King's role of critical thinking and being a poignant orator is more evidence of African intellectualism. However, we never seem to celebrate this because to celebrate King as an intellectual is to refute the lie of white supremacy and to acknowledge the true barbarism of America in its enslavement of human beings. Look at it this way. If King is an intellectual, and he is a representation of African people, then what does it say about the people who would enslave intellectuals?

King's critical thinking was most evident in his last

days when he, like Du Bois, who had been a champion for integration, began rethinking his position and agenda, asserting, "I may have integrated my people into a burning house." Like Du Bois who eventually denounced his U.S. citizenship and moved to live his last days in Ghana, King may have become disillusioned in the ability of integration to provide sovereignty and first-class citizenship to Africans. And whether or not King became disillusioned about the complete or entire path of integration, it is true that as a critical thinker King never stopped evaluating himself, his ideals, and his philosophy. The two best examples of King always challenging himself and his ideals are his notions on "temporary segregation" and on "Black Power" as a slogan.

We should all find it interesting that the two biggest proponents for integration, Du Bois and King, both found themselves questioning the validity of integration, especially in relation to education. In an article entitled, "Does the Negro Need Integrated Schools," Du Bois asserts that it would be better for a black child to remain at a segregated school where the teachers care about him than for that child to be forced to attend a white or integrated school where the teachers hate him. In affirmation to this very same sentiment, King would assert that often "the Negro is integrated without power. We don't want to be integrated out of power; we want to be integrated into power...[so] there are some situations where separation may serve as a temporary way-station to the ultimate goal" of freedom. Now I am not here to tell you that King completely denounced integration. But King in no way believed that blacks should be in the presence of whites merely for the sake of being in the presence of whites. In fact, his statement clearly asserts that integration that breeds no sovereignty or power for blacks is just as bad as segregation, Jim Crow, and slavery. I bring this to your attention merely so that you can understand that King was a complex and complicated man who did not shy away from dealing with complex and complicated issues nor did he ever seek to over simplify the problem as some many try to over simplify him and his legacy so that he can be fitted neatly on a stamp. Yes, the critical King did have a dream for all of us to be united as one, but he also understood the complicated work it would take for us to achieve this dream and never did he shy away from the complex issues because the job of the critical thinker is to engage the difficult questions of the people. For what good is intellect and scholarship if it is not in service to the evolution of the people? King was clear that his dream was not merely about putting white people and black people in a situation together unless we were also going to create a plan where they both share the power, the wealth, and the decision making. This is the type of integration for which King dreamed. It is now sad that we allow people to mis-represent King's words to attack diversity by limiting educational and economic opportunities to Africans dislocated in America, which is turning King's dream into a nightmare. And this is being allowed to happen because we are raising black leaders who are dreamers, but they are not critical thinkers. Or to put it another way, we are raising black leaders who have memorized much of King's speeches, but they have not internalized his ideologies. With the question of integration, with the question of affirmative action, with the question of school vouchers, with the question of standardized test, with the question of "high stakes" testing, with the question of mis-used zero tolerance, King's critical legacy demands that we ask the question, "Why is America willing to invest in incarcerating African Americans, but she is not willing to invest in educating African Americans?" And if you understand King's legacy of critical thinking, then you must go back to 1662, when the first law was passed to perpetuate the second-class status of African people. The law that legally created a free class and a slave class was the prohibition of reading and writing by blacks. And it is this law to which Du Bois and King were reacting as critical thinking men, and it is this law to which we are all still reacting, even in the affirmative action case at the University of Michigan. The primary battleground for black first-class citizenship is education, and Du Bois and King understood, as critical thinkers, that placing black children under white control should not be viewed as the saving grace of black people.

A second example of King's critical thinking legacy is his disagreement in the use of the phrase, "Black Power" as a slogan for the Civil Rights Movement. King did not disagree with the term "Black Power" as he understood the meaning that Carmichael applied to it. However, King felt that those two words, combined together, would have a negative connotation for far too many people. Although I may disagree with King's notion of whether or not "Black Power" should have been the slogan for the movement, there is no denying that King approached this issue as all others, as a critical thinker. He said of the phrase "Black Power,"

> "...Black Power was a cry of disappointment...a call to black people to amass the political and economic strength to achieve their legitimate goals...and a psychological call to manhood...One must not overlook the positive value in calling the Negro to a new sense of manhood, to a deep feeling of racial pride, and to an audacious appreciation of his heritage. The Negro had to be grasped by a new appreciation of his heritage...He could no longer be ashamed of being Black" (King 323, 324, 326).

So, it is King, the critical thinker, who understands that the greatest hurdle for the African dislocated in America is not physical enslavement, but psychological enslavement, and psychological enslavement is not just a condition of the African but of whites who have been enslaved to the cancerous notion of their own supremacy. Unfortunately, we live in a time when too few want to address this issue of psychological enslavement as well as having the courage to live the life of King's legacy. Additionally, King could have taken the easy way out and merely sided with Carmichael because it was the popular thing to do. But, King understands that critical thinking is not about being right for the sake of being right, and critical thinking is not about being popular. Critical thinking is about problem solving, and he was willing to lose some cool points because his research and insight lead him to a different conclusion. More importantly, he had the courage to stand by his convictions.

Courage

In all cases, King's critical thinking skills were driven by his desire for righteousness and by his courage. In the *Souls of Black Folk*, W.E.B. Du Bois asserts, "Negroes must insist continually, in season and out of season...that color discrimination is barbarism, and that black boys need education as well as white boys." When hearing Du Bois' quote, most of you probably concentrated on and agreed with the statements, "color discrimination is barbarism and that black boys need education as well as white boys." However, that was not the most important phrase in Du Bois' statement. The most important statement is "Negroes must insist continually, in season and out of season." Theodore Draper asserts in his book the *Rediscovery of Black Nationalism* that Black Nationalism becomes en vogue about every seven years. This is Du Bois' point. There cannot be a time or a season for righteousness and courage. Righteousness and courage must be unceasing, unchanging, and unwavering through all of man's endeavors. More specifically, Africans dislocated in America cannot allow anyone else to dictate to them when they should address their issues. King understood this, and this is why he had the courage to speak against the Vietnam War. King stopped being the "Darling

235

of the Movement" when he spoke out against Vietnam. King stopped being the "Darling of the Movement" when he went to support the sanitation workers in Memphis. King understood that the moment that he filled his ideological dreams with tangible polices he had signed his own death warrant. That is why he declared "Tonight I'm not fearing any man." He understood that a man's life is meaningless if he has not the courage to stand by the principles that he claims. And this is echoed loudly, when King proclaims "I submit to you that if a man hasn't discovered something he will die for, he isn't fit to live."

When King takes his stand on Vietnam, he simultaneously demonstrates his critical thinking, his courage, and his righteousness. When King first began to address the Vietnam War publicly, many blacks and whites stated that King was "getting out of his depths." Why was King said to be "getting out of his depths?" Was it because Vietnam was an international issue and not a black issue? If so, is not the black issue a national and international issue? Did not the Europeans transport Africans all over the globe as chattel? Or maybe, King was getting out of his depths because as a black man he had not the intellectual prowess to engage such issues? Sadly, both reasons where why King was said to be "getting out of his depths." Africans have never been and still are not considered intellectual equals to their white counterparts. If you do not think that it is true, check the reading lists of your world literature, history, and philosophy courses. I am still amazed that ninety percent of an anthology's pages can be filled with dead white males and the course is still called world literature. So, you cannot tell me that the African is considered an intellectual equal to the white man when we continue to marginalize the African's history and art, which are the most salient representations of man's intellect. So it holds that King, great thinker that he was, found himself being hushed by the white power structure because he did not have the perceived intellectual depth. Yet, it is at that moment, more than any other, that he exemplifies the characteristics of courage, critical thinking, and righteousness. King declared, "I realized that Martin, you have to stand up on this no matter what it means...I didn't rush into it. I asked questions...I came to the conclusion that there is an existential moment in your life when you must decide to speak for yourself; nobody can speak for you" (King 335). Exemplifying and exercising his right to self-determinism, King strategically used his religious convictions as a catalyst for his courage and his critical thinking when he used the words of Paul to move him forward in the face of white resistance to black intellect. "Be ye not conformed to the world, but be ye transformed by the renewing of minds" (King 337). With the desire for righteousness as his guide, King then unleashes the whole of his courage and critical thinking on the issue of Vietnam.

> "There is a very obvious and almost facile connection between the war in Vietnam and the struggle I and others have been waging in America...[I have come to the realization] that America would never invest the necessary funds or energies in the rehabilitation of its poor so long as adventures like Vietnam continue to draw man and skills and money like some demonic, destructive tube...Perhaps a more tragic recognition of reality took place when it became clear to me that the war was doing far more than devastating the hopes of the poor at home. It was sending their sons and their brothers and their husbands to fight and to die in extraordinarily high proportions relative to the rest of the population...So we have been repeatedly faced with the cruel irony of watching Negro and white boys on TV screen as they kill and die together for a nation that has been unable to seat them together in the same schools" (King 337-338)

This is a very important critical point by King. It

seems that the black body is only of use to America when it is serving and dying as labor in service to the perpetuation of white wealth, but in all other endeavors America seems to have no use for the black body. And that "extraordinarily high" disproportion of black deaths is not just related to Vietnam or any other war. Black people commit only sixteen percent of the crime in America, but they represent sixty percent of the incarcerated population. Additionally, about thirty percent of black children are not exposed to college preparatory courses while in middle and high school. Yet, while we have refused to properly fund the education of black children, we continue to make a larger investment in the prison industry, where in many states prison guards make more than teachers. So while addressing the Vietnam issue, King was critically deconstructing the war in a manner that showed Vietnam, and any war, as merely a metaphor or a symbol for a country's capitalistic gluttony. King drives this home by stating,

> "The war in Vietnam is but a symptom of a far deeper malady within the American spirit...A true revolution of values [as opposed to the fake revolution of values waged by Newt Gingrich and the religious right] will lay hands on the world order and say of war: 'This way of settling differences is not just.' This business of burning human beings with Napalm, of filling our nation's homes with orphans and widows, of injecting poisonous drugs of hate into the veins of people normally humane, of sending men home from dark and bloody battlefields physically handicapped and psychologically deranged, cannot be reconciled with wisdom, justice and love. A nation that continues to spend more on military defense than on programs of social uplift is approaching spiritual death" (King 339, 340, 341).

So to address the war in the Middle-East we must be guided by the same critical thinking and courage that led King. We must ask of America, "Why are all our enemies people whom we funded and trained?" We funded and trained Castro. We funded and trained Saddam Hussein. We funded and trained Osama bin Laden. And in the words of Malcolm X, each time we suffer from our own chickens coming home to roost. In the legacy of King, we must understand that our own injustice and evil ways is what causes injustice and evil to continue to visit our doorsteps. If we want evil and injustice to stop visiting us, then we must stop perpetuating evil and injustice throughout the world.

Righteousness

Most times when we think of righteousness we think of Job or Jesus or Mother Teresa. We think of people who lived a life of no sin. However, when we think of Jesus, we must remember that even Jesus suffered from doubt. (Praying in the Garden and on the Cross). To suffer from doubt is to doubt the power of God. Even Jesus suffered this human failing. When we think of a righteous person, it should not be of one without sin. When we think of a righteous person, if should be of one who refuses to allow their own inequities to keep them from doing the will of God. When FBI Director J. Edger Hoover attempted to blackmail King to keep him from fighting against America's oppression, King asserted, "Mr. Hoover, you must do what you must do, and I must do the will of God." In the face of loss of life, loss of reputation, loss of family, King understood that doing the will of God was more important than being love by man. Like Jesus, King understood that the price for the riches and favor of Satan is too high to be considered. What, then, is righteousness? Righteousness is man's ability to do right even when it means that right will bring him bodily harm. It is now a sad day that all of these educated Negroes are too scared to stand against the terrorism of the Governor, the college board, or even the President because they are afraid that they won't be able to make their car note payment. It is a sad day that our children die from the poison of the "Bling Bling" mentality because their elders—their teachers, administrators, preachers, and politicians—are more concerned about moving to a better neighborhood than moving their people to sovereignty and first-class citizenship. King's life affirms that righteous men only fear God and that righteous knees only bow before God and can stand in the face of mayors, governors, college boards, and U. S. Presidents who wish to create policy that perpetuate the second-class citizenship of his people. So, on this celebration of King's legacy, I will leave you with this question, "Which King is on the postal stamp?" The answer lies not so much in King's life as it does in how we choose to celebrate and perpetuate his legacy with our lives.

Works Cited

King, Martin L. *The Autobiography of Martin Luther King, Jr.* Clayborne Carson, ed. New York: Warner Books, 1998.

The New Afro-Mississippi Writers

I was once asked by a non Mississippi literary critic *if I were from somewhere else, would I be a more noted or popular writer?* My immediate answer was a simple no. It is not your region that causes you to write well or be a good writer. It is your skill. As I began to probe a bit deeper into how I felt about the question, I realized that it was a question that I truly could not answer because it is, for me, too inconceivable to fathom. I am a Mississippian. That, and that alone, makes me a Mississippi writer. You do not have to be born in Mississippi to be a Mississippi writer. To be a Mississippi writer, some of your time and work must be invested into discussing Mississippi from the standpoint of someone who has lived there. In short, if what happens in Mississippi has an immediate and definite affect on you and your work on an organic or innate level, you are a Mississippi writer. If I were to move, I would still be a Mississippi writer. I would just be a displaced or traveling Mississippi writer for my sensibilities would be the same. I would merely be practicing those sensibilities in a different location or commenting on how those sensibilities make me different from others indigenous to my visiting areas. Furthermore, if we were to change history all together and have me born somewhere else, I would be a different person and a different writer. If this is too literal a translation and discussion of the question, allow me to answer in this way. America's perception of Mississippi writers is two fold. America has a vision of Mississippi that the Meccas of mass media (New York, Los Angeles, Chicago, and now Atlanta) have been unwilling to change because it is easy and lucrative to continue to hold Mississippi as a backward, poorly educated, and technologically inferior region so that any time is needed a movie or a book or some three minute news spot about country towns, they can come to Mississippi. Also, to hold Mississippi to his history allows places like New York, Los Angeles, Chicago, and now Atlanta to feel better about its progress. However, Richard Wright shows us in the "American Hunger" section of *Black Boy* that the rest of the country is not that much better than Mississippi; their smoking mirrors allow them to clean up better than Mississippi. And as then Senator Theodore Bilbo asserted to newly elected congressman Adam Clayton Powell, Jr., Washington DC is a southern town if you gauge it by its policies. Given, then, the unique and essential role that Mississippi has played in the development of the nation, I do not think that it would be possible for me to live, think, act, and write in the same manner if I lived else where. That is the beauty of regional art. That is the beauty of reading writers who do not live where and how you live. It is the good (useful) artist who can articulate the uniqueness of his existence and still encase it in the realm of universal humanity.

The Mississippi writer's biggest problem is the problem of forced identity. I was motivated to write my first collection of fiction because I had not read any fiction dedicated to the lives of Mississippians twenty-five and under living during the nineteen-eighties and nineties. Most, if not all of the fiction and poetry being published from the South, especially Mississippi during the nineties, save the writers of Atlanta and possibly some of North Carolina, was still discussing the nineteen sixties and earlier. Even *Satisfied with Nothing*, a wonderfully insightful and entertaining book by Earnest Hill, was quite impressionistic when it came to being placed in a certain time frame. It has been dubbed the *Native Son* of the nineties because it employs excellent literary techniques and was written in the nineties. But, it is not a particular or certain reflection of the ideologies and changes of the nineties as *Native Son* is of the nineteen-forties. This is true for far too many works by Southern writers because too many literary critics tie all literature of the South to *Black Boy's* evolution to *Native Son* after the experience of living the *Ethics of Living Jim Crow* which, of course, emerges directly from *Jubilee* by Margaret Walker Alexander. Yet, no one seems to want to read the new South's *Outsider* which is not surprising when you understand that nobody wanted to read or face *Native Son*'s evolution to the *Outsider*. And all of this is to make little mention of Etheridge Knight, the famous prison poet, about whom Henry Louis Gates, Jr. in his *Norton Anthology of African American Literature* states that "[Knight's] *Belly Song and Other Poems* (1973) is one of the most significant volumes to emerge from the Black Arts Movement. Knight was an inspiration to all those who felt poetry should be a functional and communal art with a strong oral artist in the middle of the circle" (Gates and McKay 1867). Yet, I did not know Knight's work as a student at Jackson State University, the urban university of the State. It is probably because Knight's work removes from the presence of Wright's and Alexander's work those editors who made their work palatable to whites and upper class Negroes. We must remember that "American Hunger" was originally omitted by the editors from *Black Boy*. Knight should have been the bridge from Wright and Walker to my generation, but his voice was silenced even by Mississippi literary scholars for being too dark, greasy, urban, and raw, making Mississippians realize that the civil rights movement, which my have begun in the South, had not given African American Mississippians the right to their own voices. Additionally, the other bridge from Wright and Alexander to my generation is Dr. Jerry W. Ward, poet and critic. His poem "Don't Be Fourteen in Mississippi" is exactly the kind of combining of historical foundation with new urban rage that marked Knight's work. The problem for Ward became his immense success and notoriety as a critic as well as his lack of post-seventies vernacular. The insight and the anger are beautifully combined in Ward's work, but the Black Arts Movement was often sensationalized by white critics for its associating anger with profanity and condemnation of a Eurocentric world. Ward's work is more retrospective in that it laments more the eroding of

244

Black culture than it does condemn white America for causing that erosion. In this Ward becomes more of a nationalist than any of us. His focus is on African American life rather than the outside influence. Yet, his largest hurdle is that he is a Mississippi writer in a State that refuses to teach courses on African American Mississippi writers. Dr. Ward is an accomplished, well published poet, editor, and critic to whom I was not introduced until I had left Jackson State University and studied at the University of Southern Mississippi. Why was his work not taught to me a JSU? I was told that is was because we want to give our students the same standard information that the world has. When will our writers become standard information? This is the problem for the new African American writer's of Mississippi.

There are generally four boxes into which African American Mississippi writers of the nineties are placed. Some Northern writers want to read Mississippi writers when they feel a need to reconcile their Northern existence with their inherited but forgotten Southern sensibilities. Secondly, other Northern writers read Mississippi writers purely for history. They look not for art, only documentation. The two are different in that the former is allowed to be a bit more philosophical than the latter which is resigned to being merely literary science no matter how much artistic training and imagination the author has. Thirdly, there are the Southern writers and readers who so desperately want to be a part of the African American Mississippi cannon that they spend their time copying and mimicking their Mississippi ancestors, thus producing nothing new, imaginative, or timely. Finally, there is the Mississippi writer who is so ashamed of being a Mississippian that he submerges himself in the culture of other places so much that no one knows what he is saying. It reminds me of young brothers from Clarksdale or Crawford or Bobo or Hot Coffee or any other one gas station, former plantation Mississippi town who speak with a New York accent after spending the summer watching Black Entertainment Television's *Rap City* or MTV's *Yo' MTV raps* on the piped in cable. Young writers such as the Martin triplets who, with their combined collection of poetry, attempt to breathe new air and life into that down home Mississippi sensibility of God, religion, and family. Because a work such as this speaks to those sensibilities which have been etched into the hearts and minds of most African American Mississippians, it is obvious that the work and the brothers will garner popularity. The negative affect is that not only will the Martin brothers be rewarded for their craft and accomplishments, a book of this nature by such young writers will be used to stifle the alternative young voices of those African American Mississippians who are not "church" folk, do not turn the other cheek, and frequent the speak easies, juke joints, cafes, and coffee houses of their generation. The new African American writers of Mississippi are not out to purposely distance themselves from the heritage of Mississippi. They merely wish to address the new-old ills. They want to refashion the verse, vernacular, imagery, and icons to address the old ills which have been refashioned. Mississippi is still the worst State on civil rights, education, health care, and economics. The new African American writers of Mississippi merely want to address the new tricks of oppression as well as celebrate and condemn the successes and failures of the "New Negro" of the South. The works of Charlie Braxton, Jolivette Anderson, David Brian Williams, Marcus "Uganda" White, and myself best escape the above mentioned four categories and exist as African American Mississippi literature of the nineteen-eighties and nineties. This is not to say that we ARE the African American Mississippi writing scene. This is to say that we have freed ourselves from the shackles and limitations of the past and are now focusing our energies on articulating our present existence as opposed to merely wearing the clothes of our ancestors.

Charlie Braxton, a graduate of Jackson State University (JSU), the school where Dr. Margaret W. Alexander taught and developed the humanities courses, is the most accomplished writer of the group. A native of McComb, Mississippi, he is a published poet, playwright, and one of the most noted Hip Hop journalists in the country, as well as having studied directly under Dr. Jerry W. Ward. In the work of Charlie Braxton you have the well traveled Mississippi writer who has influenced writers from other areas and has, himself, been personally and directly influenced by writers from other areas, such as Amiri Baraka, James Baldwin, Haki Madhubuti, Kalamu ya Salaam, Toni Media, and Kevin Powell. Yet, Braxton has managed to balance his inherited Mississippi lineage and heritage from Wright, Alexander, Knight, and Ward with his love for the work of African American writers from other areas. Braxton is and remains a Mississippi writer. The first example of Braxton's ability to bridge the urban and rural worlds of Mississippi is through his two plays, *Bluesman* and *Artist Doesn't Live Here Anymore*. *Bluesman* on the surface is a traditional, Mississippi, rural piece. Underneath, it is a piece about traveling distances, which is taken from the metaphor of the traveling bluesman. The traveling bluesman was in search of urban America, a place where he could sing his blues and get paid. *Artist Doesn't Live Here Anymore* abandons the rural setting to discuss the class conflicts between rural people dislocated to the urban areas of Mississippi to find work. Artist and his wife are torn because their ideologies are torn between the rural and the urban. And, just as the reality of the so called new Mississippi, a permanent barrier exists between Artist and his wife.

His poem, "Torn between two Worlds: Jesus at the Crossroads," is undeniably black as well as it shows the evolution of young African American Mississippians frustrated with the whole notion of the inertia of the Black Southern Church and its inability to address the concerns of

African Americans falling prey to the urbanization of the State. "And it came to pass that the son of man was called down to the crossroads where the Loa of the dead and the spirit of the undead meet in the sweet by and by" (Speyer and Park 72). This first line sets the mood not only for this poem but for Braxton's work and the evolution from the rural to the urban of the poets who follow him. The whole notion of the crossroad has always been a heavy icon in the blues and for Mississippi. The literal crossroad is the intersection of Highways 61 and 49 which intersect in Clarksdale, Mississippi, the mythical and historical home of the Blues. This intersection is important because it is the place where the old meets the new. It is the place where you leave the plantation and head into the city. Both 61 and 49 run from Delta to urban, 61 runs from Cleveland, Mississippi to the heart of downtown Memphis, Tennessee, and 49 runs from the heart of Clarksdale to Jackson, Mississippi. Braxton continues this transformation in the final lines of this poem with "...yes, Jesus went down to the crossroads to dance between two worlds his holy body breaking to the beat of a music loud enough to shake awake the black saints of old" (Speyer and Park, 72). This line is laced with symbolism of the duality of Mississippi and its transformation. The "dance between two worlds" echoes what Ray Charles has always said about secular and spiritual music, "The only difference is that they say 'Lawd, Lawd,' and we say 'Baby, Baby'" (Charles 1996). The two worlds are not just spiritual and secular, they are urban and rural. When Braxton has Jesus' "holy body breaking," he is obviously referring to break dancing, a form of dance indigenous to the Hip Hop culture. This is meant to be representative of the influence of urban America on Southern beliefs and sensibilities. Above all, we must ask why is Jesus at the crossroad. Man is typically seen at the crossroad. What decision must Jesus make? Braxton alludes to this by using African icons such as Orishas and Elegba. The decision is one that African American Christians must make, particularly in

248

understanding that Mississippi culture is soaked with African culture. As Braxton, himself, addresses the issue, "There is more retention of African culture in the State of Mississippi than anywhere else in America beside the Carolina islands. Yet, African American Mississippians have been so Christianized and, more specifically, Europeanized that we act more African than anyone else but don't realize it for our denials. Our conscious denials are killing us because subconsciously we attempt to reconcile ourselves to it even though we don't know what it is. We are looking at a dirt road on a paved city street" (Braxton, "Personal Interview," 1998). He follows "Jesus at the Crossroads" with "I Dream of Jesus." "Last night I dreamed I saw Jesus pimp strolling peacock-proud down Crenshaw Blvd., looking for lost souls in the valley of the damned" (Wideman and Preston 273). This is not traditional Southern literature. It has always been acceptable for African American Mississippi writers to take on white oppression, but it is not acceptable for African American Mississippi writers to question the role of Christianity in that oppression or the failures of Southern African Americans to take Christianity to the streets in the manner of the Nation of Islam. With these two poems, Braxton is giving voice to a section of African American Mississippians not heard since Knight. Also, Braxton further attests that Sterling D. Plumpp's *When the Mojo Calls I must Come* should be given the credit for unearthing the African layers of African American Mississippi Culture. "Many of the Mississippi writers of my [Braxton's] generation think that I removed the veil of African American Mississippi culture to reveal the African foundation in our work. But, it was Plump who first voiced this African-Mississippi connection in a real and consistent sense" (Braxton 1998). Braxton is, in affect, rebuilding the bridge back to Wright and Alexander through Knight, Plump, and Ward, but doing so in a manner that addresses the issues of his time and not of theirs.

David Brian Williams was born in Jackson, Mississippi but spent his middle-school and high school years in Gary, Indiana because his father relocated to the North to become a principle. Yet, after his urbanization, he relocated to Mississippi in order to attend a Southern, historically black college or university (HBCU), JSU. A poet, actor, lawyer, lighting and sound man, Williams was able to make a smooth transition because his family, namely his father, mother, and uncle (the late poet, Otis Williams) held firm to their Mississippi roots and sensibilities. Along with Braxton, Williams represents the urban expression of the deep South. He is a Northerner who, after graduation from JSU, attended law school in Boston and then returned to the South to practice law and write. His poems "Say Blood" and "Still They Come" speak directly to the left over problems and issues of the civil rights movement. "I heard you say while talkin' among the brothers that the sixties wuz coming back. I say you're wrong. You implied that we are ready to re-pick, re-afro, re-dashiki, re-boycott, re-sit in, re-burn, re-do, what you Colored people keep trying to forget. What you pseudo intelligent nanonitwit superspade klansman in disguise who act like you don't know that Ole Miss still don't want yo' black ass...why fight with old stale Malatov Cocktails when fresh lasers burn even hotter" (Williams, *Mirages*, 3-4). In "Still They Come" Williams is both questioning and calling a current generation to take up the call of the struggle of African Americans. "And still they came, in boats on foot to the notion that freedom was just around the corner or over the creek. And without fax or cell phone or beeper the word got out that freedom was just around the corner or over the creek. And with all of our technology, we do not come" (Williams, *Mirages*, 77).

Of the group, Williams is the most balanced with one foot firmly planted in Mississippi's blues poetry tradition and one foot striving in Mississippi's new tradition. His poems, "Simple Love," "Check One," and "I

Want to Have Church," speak the universality of the traditional African American experience. Williams is, as his uncle was, a juke joint poet. He has the ability to take a poem such as "Hootchie Coochie" and rework it in a manner that it speaks to African Americans of the nineties and beyond. When he does a poem such as "Birdland," which is an ode to the club, The Crystal Palace, which is located in the historic Farish Street district of Jackson, Mississippi where great artists as Duke Ellington, Count Basie, and others performed. Even with the arousing "Be Afraid," which contains sexual imagery that Mississippi poets have traditionally viewed as taboo for their work, he is simultaneously paying homage to the juke joint culture of the past and defining his generation. Finally, as one of the babies of the Shop Poetry Readings of the seventies which boasted regular and special appearances of such names as Dr. Jerry Ward, Leo Kayam, Cassandra Wilson, Richard Brown, Sonia Sanchez, Terri McMillan, Furahah Saba, Chinua Achebe, Amiri Baraka, Brian Ward (actor on the television series *Sea-Quest* and was a founding father of the Shop), Teddy Edwards, the late Freddie Waits, Al Fielder, as well as many of the students and products of Dr. Tommie Stewart of *In the Heat of the Night* and *A Time to Kill*, Williams' re-establishing of the jazz and poetry readings at the Birdland Cafe in the historic Farish Street district is taking poetry and jazz to those whom the academicians have forgotten. An area of drugs, homicides, and theft, Williams has established a weekly Sunday night reading where young men, who would at any other time and place attempt to kill each other, can come and enjoy the music and literature of their people.

Marcus "Uganda" White is a native of Grenada, Mississippi (a Delta boy) and, like Charlie Braxton, a student of Dr. Jerry W. Ward, having studied at Tougaloo College. White is representative of so many of the good Tougaloo poets in that his work weaves the rural and the urban in such a manner that it effectively shows the complexity of being a Mississippian from walking on urban streets that at any turn may run into cotton or soybean fields. White's work speaks of the new juke joints which, in truth, are not really that different from the old juke joints, but he delivers his characters in such a manner that you understand that what is happening in their lives was put into motion by a Civil Rights Movement that was left unfinished and died from a lack of attention. As a poet, he is probably the most polished and academically sound of the group. He can do in four lines for Mississippi poetry what it takes most several pages to say. His poems "As Black as They Are" and "Problem 54" are able to epitomize the new Mississippi in a way that informs us that the rage of the new Southern Negroes will not be quieted by spirituals. When the little boy in the playground of "Problem 54" wants the teacher to "come to the playground during recess so that he could teach her the words that Jimmy taught him like bitch and fuck," you understand that the irreverence that elementary children have for school and teachers is not because they are innately vile and wild but because they sense that they exist in a public school system that does not want to teach them. "She wasn't teaching me no math either. She was teaching me racism, the hands on approach."

Along with White there are several other emerging Tougaloo and Jackson State Poets, too many to mention here. But I would be remiss if I did not mention Michael "Diallo" McClendon, Colleen White, and Kamelia "Queen" Muhammad. Their combining of Afrocentrism with Mississippi tradition only works to bring home the work of a Jolivette Anderson. All these writers are definitely influenced by and motivated by W. E. B. Du Bois' notion in his essay "The Criteria of Negro Art" that "all art is propaganda" (Gates and McKay 757). It was McClendon, along with M. White, and Derrick Johnson who have established one of the most successful open mic poetry settings in Mississippi, Southern Vibes which has been renamed Mississippi Vibes. This setting takes place every Saturday night, currently at Highlites Fine Food and Drinks from 8:30 p.m. to 1:30 a.m. As much as it is the work and talent of all of the above mentioned writers, it may be their desire to maintain a writing community until both Mississippi and the Nation recognize and make room for these new voices which may truly be their lasing impact on their respective genres. Johnson, now the director of the State NAACP, puts its best when he states, "It was our intentions to develop a place that would be the center of a Mississippi Black Arts Movement. We wanted a place where young African American professionals could come and enjoy their culture, exchange ideas, and network. We didn't have this in Mississippi on a regular or consistent basis." (Johnson 1998). Johnson is right in understanding that artists need a home. Despite the lack of support and patronizing of the African American middle class, all of the artists mentioned in this essay have been dedicated to keeping alive the tradition as well as creating something that is uniquely their own. Yet, until the local African American middle class embraces the new expressions of their local artists, the voice of the African American Mississippi arts movement may never rise above a whisper. The reluctance of the local African American middle class to get behind these new writers speaks volumes to the local as well as national limited perceptions of what art is and what are produced by African Americans from Mississippi should be. This tension between the black middle-class and the black artists is nothing new. In his article "The Criteria of Negro Art," Du Bois' attack on Claude McKay's *Home to Harlem* must be seen as an example of how one's social sensibilities create the matrix for one's artistic/aesthetic sensibilities. For the most part, the Afro-Mississippi middle-class consists of laborers and not entrepreneurs. That is, even the black people in Mississippi with what is commonly thought of as wealth are beholding to whites for that wealth and are not willing to embrace artistic expression that may alienate them from the hands that feed them. Thus, as the writers have become more Africentric in their expressions, a wide gap emerges between the artists and the needed middle-class patrons. And to be sure, this movement needs these patrons because they are the ones who can purchase books and magazines. Without those patrons, writers are merely shouting into the wind. Even after a four year run of a Saturday night poetry reading that average about 250 customers a night, no local restaurateur or businessman wants to risk investing in the local literary scene. Even *Black Magnolias Literary Journal* which received rave reviews and subscriptions from university and city libraries all over the nation was not purchased by the local black middle class.

Howard Ramsey, II editor of *Spirits on High, Souls of Fyaah,* and *Black Thoughts* and co-founder of New Visions Press (TN), Nayri Miller, author of *Ascensions*, and NaTasha Ria Gibson, a Tennessean and two Northerners, are three writers who had a profound impact on the current Mississippi writing scene. They are mentioned here for two reasons, the quality of their work as storytellers disguised as poets, the manner in which their ghetto tales show their uncanny, organic relationship to plantation tales, and the manner in which they allowed their Northern tales to embrace their Southern heritage. Finally, they represent the urbanization of the South, the manner in which third and fourth generation Northerners, because of the prodding of their parents and grandparents, returned to the South to be influenced and to influence. Now that Ramsey, Miller, and Gibson have relocated to the North, they stand as ears and bridges to the North for emerging African American writers from the South.

Anderson is a Louisiana poet and actor who relocated to Mississippi to work with a local theatre company, New Stage Theatre. Her book and cd's *Love and Revolution, Past Lives, Still Traveling*, and *At the End of a Rope in Mississippi* fulfill the long awaited need of African

American women writers from Mississippi. Along with her Black Nationalist aesthetic, Anderson brings to the table the influence of and competition with popular culture. An instructor at Tougaloo College and with Civil Rights icon Bob Moses' the Young People's Project, Anderson understands the need and ability of a poet's work to entice, attract, and recruit young people whose ears and eyes are filled with Hip Hop. With the incorporation of a full-time band when she travels, Anderson, as Braxton and Williams, makes no apology for going after the younger generation. Having opened for Patti LaBelle and Brian McKnight, Anderson is taking her Southern literature to the masses with no hang-ups or apprehensions. Yet, Anderson is also a scholar of African and African American culture. This is her biggest asset. She is that shade of black revolution on which African Americans in Mississippi have been waiting to reach them since the death of Malcolm X even if most of them did not embrace that shade.

When I was an undergraduate student at JSU in the late eighties, I asked Dr. Ivory Phillips, professor of social science, did he remember where he was, what he was doing, and how he felt when he was told that Malcolm had been assassinated? This was when I gained my first lesson of the wide divide between the South and the North. He said, "I did not feel much of anything." Noticing the look of concern and confusion on my face he continued. "You must understand that because of the media and our own Southern prejudices, Malcolm was not seen as one of us. Mississippi was a Martin Luther King, Jr. State, as was most of the South. The common feeling of most African American Southerners was 'that X boy got the violence that he espoused'" (Phillips 1989). Later that afternoon I asked my father who had been so radical during the sixties and seventies that the police would arrest him on the charge of carrying a pencil as a concealed weapon, "Cause ya' kno' niggers don't write." I was surprised when he affirmed Dr. Phillips' sentiments.

"Not only was there not much emotional outpouring, many of us Southern African American Civil Rights People felt a sense of relief on hearing of Malcolm's death because we did not have to deal with him. He was asking the children of the plantation to leave the plantation. King was merely saying integrate into the plantation. Can you imagine what Malcolm sounded like to those of us who had spent our lives trying to eat in the 'Big Kitchen' of the plantation?—break away from America, become self sufficient, be responsible for your actions. That is a lot for those of us with plantation mentalities to handle. We didn't understand Malcolm until about '67. He scared us. You must understand why turning the other cheek appealed so much to us. Most African Americans of the South couldn't raise a hand to strike a white person in self-defense let alone kill one. And furthermore, 'what dem white folks gon' do to us if we practice this stuff?' You have to understand that lynching was a Southern institution not a Northern institution. Lynching was indigenous to the South and was primary in creating and developing what has become known as the slave/plantation mentality. Southerners lived lynching on a daily basis. By the time the sixties roll around, it is firmly etched into our psyche. It was difficult for the mass African American populous of Mississippi to get pass the physical and emotional fear of lynching. And on top of all of that, they had names like "X" and weren't Christian, oh, hell no!!! Finally, many Southerners did not know that Malcolm had split from the Nation or why he split. We just got sound bites. I had to go to college to understand Malcolm. But, by that time, it was too late. I believe that most of us love Malcolm because we have a false sense of the grand success of integration and are now thankful that we didn't have to do what he told us to do" (McInnis, Sr. 1989).

As a student of Egyptology and other African and African American cultures, Anderson is that poet who, through the icons and imagery of her work, celebrates African American culture. He work affirms Malcolm X's statement, "You can not be concerned about what's happening in Mississippi if you are not concerned with what's happening in the Congo." She weaves Mississippi and African culture so well that it is difficult to tell where one ends and the other begins. African American women flock to hear her tales of broken hearts, female sexuality, and the black woman as the mother of the Earth. Her lyrical and poetic *Cane*-like piece *Past Lives*, with introduction by Haki Madhubuti, succeeds as *Cane* succeeds by equally combining several forms and genres and becoming a bridge for the past and the present. Its use of traditional spirituals with icons of the sixties all undercut by her life story as a metaphor for the present danger and evolution of African Americans is both masterful as well as acts as a "talking book" for the lives of African American Mississippians under thirty. Her other pieces call on various ancestors and Egyptian Gods to give her the strength to tell the stories of her Mississippi. And as host of the very popular Saturday night open mic reading, Mississippi Vibes, she incorporates educational sections/discussions throughout the readings. She, as all of us, feels the constant pressure from many of the academicians to reject and leave the juke joint and the cafe and run into the university. But until the Mississippi university becomes better enabling of the celebration and promotion of modern African American writers, she is inclined to stay in the streets and deal with the current issues of her people.

As for myself, I am a nineteen-eighties and nineties African American Mississippian in every way possible. I am that chicken grease, café Negro that both sides would like to shut up, but I somehow I keep placing poems, short stories, and essays in journals and newspapers across the country. Additionally, because many other upper class African Americans consider themselves too important to teach at HBCUs, I am able to teach the legacy of Wright, Walker, and Knight to a new generation of onyx writers. Also, if some of the older African American scholars do teach at HBCUs, they are so busy jumping through hoops of the State board that they produce little if anything that is of any significance to the nurturing of new African American writers. Inasmuch as I am a Delta boy who likes salmon patties, biscuits with molasses, and going to the juke joint on Saturday night and sleeping in church on Sunday morning, I am also a cable ready, national programmed radio listener who grew up having himself and his Mississippi defined by cable, Reaganomics, free agent baseball, Prince, and a story or two from his father. I guess what makes my work different is that I grew up with a nationalistic father and an integrationist for a mother and was left to weave my way between the two worlds, constructing an identity that suits me first. Of this mentioned group, I am probably the poorest writer but add myself to the list because of my publications and the fact that both Mississippi writers and readers state that I say things that they would like to say. I guess insanity runs deep. I have watched how a Mississippi audience which oft times deplores profanity in their poetry, begins to sit more and more upright as I keep repeating the phrase, "If you ain't never picked cotton, you can't tell me shit," as if to some that is all the justification they need for staying in the State. Or when I recite a poem like "The Evil of Integration" or "Mississippi Like..." and people my age and a bit older come up to me just to shake my hand. Or when I do a poem like "Ghetto Issues," they can relate because "Mississippi's got ghettos too." I know that I am not the appropriate person to talk about my work. I will end this section by saying that I have chopped cotton, been denied funding for college, and been car jacked. For me not to talk about all of these issues is to deny the totality of my Mississippi experience.

The new African American Mississippi writer has to find a way to deal with urbanization, the recruitment of more white folks to get the "new" jobs, the migration of crack to Mississippi, the attack of the State on HBCUs, and the worsening of rural areas which were in the dark during the fifties and have continued to deteriorate over the past fifty years. What makes this difficult is that the Mississippi writer knows that every time he picks up the pen, African Americans across the Nation are both consciously and unconsciously looking to Mississippi writers to show that the foundation of Southern sensibilities are still there. Everyone else wants the Mississippi writer to affirm the illusion that although "slow" and somewhat "backwards," we are still the soul of black America. This hypocrisy and limitation is what is driving the new African American writers of Mississippi to take some of the most profane stances against this illusion, to say, "Hell no, everything ain't all right. Crack is as lucrative as cotton. Your Northern and Western gangs have infiltrated the minds of our Southern gentlemen. We now have men who refer to our women as bitches and whores. We ain't happy, and we don't want our blues to make you feel good." The African American Southern sensibility that pre-dates the Civil Rights Movement is an outdated illusion. We are no longer gentile because our reality and the expectations of the East Coast and the West Coast have sucked us dry. We have spent the last thirty years publishing stories that everybody else wanted to hear. Now we have withered and dried from not telling the stories that we need to express about our existence, which has been seen as less important than everyone else's modern stories.

As new African American Mississippi writers emerge, they are too greasy, too urban, too angry, and too far removed from the perpetuated stereotype of Mississippi writers. Even the soothing summer night's air imagery and lyricism of Marcus "Uganda" White is too "non-cotton" for the rest of America to place in Mississippi. The stories of Highways 49 and 61 are being replaced with the stories of Interstates 55, 20, and 220. The Delta blues lyric in now laced with urban couplets and imagery. Front porch stories are now street corner updates. This is not to say that these new African American Mississippi writers have no connection to the past. Those elder African American Mississippi writers such as Dr. Jerry W. Ward, Dr. Hillery Knight, Dr. Wanda Morgan, and Dr. Marie O'Banner Jackson are still a foundation for their work. Yet, it is sad to say that I can only mention these few as elders who are taking an active, participating role in the workshops and open mic venues across the state.

The largest problem is that African American Mississippi writers were never allowed to address the diversity of their existence throughout the entire state. Contrary to popular belief, Mississippi is a very fragmented State with three very distinct regions: the Delta, Central Mississippi, and the Coast. The Delta is and always will be farm land, despite the boom of casinos throughout the region. Gambling is not new to the Delta. Now you just stand a better chance of not being cut after winning. The Delta is the home of the blues as evidence of the National Blues Museum being in Clarksdale, Mississippi and the University of Mississippi having one of the largest holdings of blues artifacts. Events like the rise in legal gambling and legal battles on the redistricting of certain farm lands such as Hog farms have created new problems for the writers of the Delta. Central Mississippi (Jackson to Hattiesburg) has always been the urban area. It is where African Americans went for urbanization if they could not make it to Chicago. It is also where they came to attend college at either Alcorn in Lorman, JSU in Jackson, or Tougaloo in Jackson. These were your progressive black scholars as Mississippi Valley State University and Rust College students of the Delta areas were more conservative. We must remember that the sit-ins, marches, shootings involving JSU and Tougaloo students on the JSU campus took place the same year as Kent State. Where are their stories? Also, Central Mississippi, namely Jackson with its Farish Street District of African American professionals, was the Mecca of African American professionalism of the State. This is not to exclude the fact that the Delta had its hub of African American autonomy and economic prosperity, namely Ruleville, Mississippi. The difference is that although it was an all black town it was mostly a rural existence where as the Farish Street District was an urban, professional existence. South Mississippi or the Mississippi Gulf Coast has always been an amalgamation of races where the transient mixed races could migrate from New Orleans to Florida and back, often extending as far as California. Where are their modern stories? There is an abundance of neo-mulatto and false casino salvation tales on the Mississippi Gulf Coast. The distinction in the three regions is great and can be easily seen in the migration patterns. African Americans fleeing the Delta were more likely to go North and East. African Americans fleeing South Mississippi were more likely to go West. And coming full circle, these migrations away from Mississippi would eventually become migrations back to Mississippi by a new generation of African Americans, seeking the peace of Mississippi and not finding it. We can not deny the influence of those later generations returning to Mississippi from the West Coast, Chicago, and the East on modern Mississippi. They are still the old problems of race, class, and caste with the struggle of white Mississippians attempting to garner all of the profits and benefits, but they have new names and titles which call for an evolution in the genres.

African American Mississippi literature never has been allowed to deal with these distinct issues in any real or tangible sense. It seems that African Americans from Mississippi suffer from the regional affliction that affects the national mentality of far too many African Americans, the inferiority complex. Since the black Exodus, African Americans who stayed behind suffered belittling and chastising from those African Americans who left the South. It is as though every Southerner has suffered because of Booker T. Washington's belief that the South was the place for the Negro as well as his being perceived as being soft on the issue of lynching and other injustices suffered by the Negro. In short, if you stayed in the South, the rest of the African Americans saw you as being "slow," "sorry," "cowardice," and "backward." After all, "How can you stay where they hate you?" This perception has been perpetuated by the national media. How many major films or television movies have been dedicated to Southern champions of the Civil Rights Movement? Malcolm has a major movie. Where is King's? Every time there is a major work about the Civil Rights Movement of the South, the heroes are either white or from the North. The African American Southerners are bumbling idiots waiting to be rescued by some intelligent Northerner or the good graces of Southern white folks. Check *Mississippi Burning*. Even in the feature film *The Ghost of Mississippi*, the central character is a white Southern attorney merely doing his job. When will there be a feature film about Medgar Evers?

It seems that Mississippi has taken the full brunt of this issue, shadowing the works of African American Mississippi writers. Because of these prejudicial notions, the world, including African Americans, does not want to hear about the subtleties and intricacies of African American life in Mississippi. So, African American writers have continuously adjusted their work to give the Nation what it wants. It is time to say that not every African American Mississippi story opens and begins in a cotton field or church. Where are the stories of African Americans relocating from the North back to Mississippi because Heaven was not found in the North? Where are the stories of the Jackson college students relocating to the Delta to teach? Where are the stories of the Delta citizens relocating to Central Mississippi and becoming urbanized? Where are the stories of the Gulf Coast transients and their blurred and exact world of the color line throughout different Mississippi regions? They are here, but no one wants to publish them because it changes our perception of Mississippi. I have often wondered if so many people like "Transitions," my short story tale of a sharecropper escaping from the Delta to Jackson, more than the other tales of the book because "Transitions" is something that they know, and a story like "Circle," which involves a group of college students deciding to kill a drug dealer a week, is something that they do not know in reference to Mississippi. Or, is it that "Transitions" reaffirms what most people know about Mississippi and "Circle" forces them to deal with a new Mississippi.

Progress has come to Mississippi, but it has come limited and isolated, often excluding Afro-Mississippians from that progress. Many people are looking to the new Nissan plant for Mississippi's future economic base, but we have forgotten that what was commonly practiced in the Delta is still being practiced throughout Mississippi. In the Delta there are counties and towns that are majority black but still have majority white county boards, city councils, or white city/county attorneys who use the position to impede progress. This is because most of the African Americans living in these areas are still beholding to white employers, such as plantation owners. And as long as sharecropping is alive and well in the Mississippi Delta, African American economic and educational opportunities will remain limited, and this is sure to affect the African Americans writers that the region is able to produce. It is not unusual for a plantation owner to send word to the local preacher that any church on plantation grounds is to be use exclusively for praising God and not any "socio-political mess." Even today, white plantation owners continue to have a great influence over the social, political, economic, and educational aspects of Afro-Mississippians, in the same manner that MCI-World Com and Capital City Inc. have control over the City of Jackson, even though the city's population is majority black. For instance, a major national company wanted to build a factory in West Tallahatchie County. The all white West Tallahatchie Board of Supervisors refused to give the permits to build the factory in the region because it would affect the wages that they paid their sharecropping tenants and other labor. Just as recently as 2000, the black citizens of Montgomery County had to file a lawsuit to stop whites who lived in Grenada, Mississippi form voting in the county separate schools election as a way to have county funds funneled into the mostly white Grenada school district. As long as white businessmen are able to limit the economic opportunity of African Americans, then African Americans will be limited in their progress. Where are these stories, and why can we not get them published? The African American community has not been able to produce enough writers to shed light on this issue of refurbished Jim Crow because there are simply no publishing opportunities. The Afro-Mississippi writer must be able to deal with both the Delta and the Capital City plantations. If the writers are not able to write about refurbished Jim Crow, then no one will understand the complexity of enduring *The Ethics of Living Jim Crow* in the new millennium. The same rings true with Nissan. We have already witnessed that the State of Mississippi has deliberately and systematically paid African American land owners less for their land in comparison to what they paid white land owners. And at the heart of this eminent domain issue is choice, which African Americans still do not have. White land owners were given blank documents and asked to write a price for their land in the blank space. Black land owners were given set amounts. This lack of choice shows a blatant disregard for African American citizens by the State of Mississippi. More importantly, if there had been more articles, short stories, novels, and poetry about the West Tallahatchie issue ten years earlier, then maybe the state would be less likely to work the same type of program with Nissan coming to town. When African Americans are not able, not allowed, or merely choose not to write about the evolution or transition of old issues into modern issue, the African American community is given no blueprint or voice to articulate or deal with their concerns.

Also at the heart of the West Tallahatchie and Nissan issues is the impact that economic opportunity has on educational opportunity and quality. No jobs means no tax base. No tax base means limited education. Limited education means second-class citizenship. Education is still the primary battle ground in Mississippi for African Americans. Thirty percent of African American children are not exposed to college preparatory classes. This not only means that they are being excluded from the college process, but they are also being made ready to take their places as a permanent labor class. Because of a limited tax base and discriminatory funding by the State Department of Education, majority black school districts are offering second tier education. Along with not being given the core tools for critical thing, which every generation of writers need, black children are exposed to black authors at a lower rate than the national average, which is, itself, dismal. Along with not receiving a proper, well-rounded education, African American children are being weeded from the education process all together with the discriminatory use of "Zero Tolerance" and the "Three Strikes and You're Out" mandate of "Senate Bill 2239." Under the new "Zero Tolerance" guidelines that Mississippi has in place, white children receive more counseling and "in school" suspension while the rates of suspensions, expulsions, and transfers to alternative schools for African American children have doubled. Also, the number of black children being referred to youth detention centers has also doubled. When you combine this information with the fact that the State's Attorney General, Mike Moore, has personally acted in a discriminatory manner in regards to how the "Zero Tolerance" laws are enforced, then you understand that the State of Mississippi is still selectively educating its children and directly targeting its black children as potential slave labor. Where in the past black children had to leave school to work the fields during harvest season, now they are being routed from school to become private, prison labor. Moore personally came to the aid of a white child who was being suspended for having a knife at school, but he remained silent when four black boys were suspended and threatened with federal charges of assault for throwing peanuts. It is, also, ironic, that as black children are being weeded from the education process, Mississippi has become one of the model states for the new prison industry, which profits by offering cheap labor to their states and to private companies. We can add to this scenario that white plantation owners in Tunica County attempted to use the new casino funds to build an all-white public school. In an area where the public school population is 99.9% black, and the private school population is 100% white, a coalition of plantation owners, which also controls the county school board and board of supervisors, attempted to use the new casino funds to build a new school in an unpopulated area, which is illegal, and then surround that school with housing that was to begin at eighty thousand and up. It is obvious that the overwhelming majority of the black citizens of Tunica, who work mostly as sharecroppers and other types of underpaid, so-called "unskilled" labor, would not be able to afford the new housing and would be, therefore, outside the district of the new school. This is merely a new twist of the old game of keeping the education system separate and unequal. The white children would attend the new school while the black children would continue to attend the old school, which was not scheduled to receive any finds for much needed repairs while this new school was being built. Again, it was Moore who was aiding the sharecroppers in this development plan, attempting to use his power to negate as much of the school desegregation law as possible. So it seems that Mississippi's next generation of African American writers are being displaced from public education into private incarceration. As such, there is a need for those African Americans writing today to shed light on this and all modern issues of enduring *The New Ethics of Living Jim Crow* in their various genres.

Working as a supplement to the public schools issues is the mishandling of the Ayers case by Negro leaders (politicians, professionals, and preachers). The twenty-six year old Ayers case was filed by Jake Ayers and other concerned Afro-Mississippians to increase and equalize the funding disseminated to HBCUs. What Jake Ayers wanted was for HBCUs to have the ability to cultivate leaders in every area and aspect of community and societal development. Unfortunately, the so-called Negro leaders have dropped the ball. Writing about the Ayers case provides an opportunity for all writers to deal with the issue of dual antagonists afflicting the African American community: the racist white system and the Negro leader who is more accountable to the white dollar than to the black community. This issue of the Negro leader's non-accountability is not a "cut and dry," black and white issue. This issue is one that opens itself to the discussion of Du Bois' notion of "Double Consciousness" and how double consciousness has manifested itself into the regional and State particulars of Mississippi. At the core of this exploration of double consciousness in Mississippi politics and culture is the notion of finding national universality through the exploration of regional novelty. The Ayers case was the test case for Tennessee and Louisiana just as Mississippi's zero tolerance and school safety laws were test cases for the rest of the nation. All of this shows the complexity of life in Mississippi and removes the film of stereotypical "good" and "bad" attributed to and forced upon Mississippi by the rest of the country. For while the Afro-Mississippi writer is concentrating on non-accountable Negro leaders, he must still keep one eye on white supremacy, which is the root of the Negro's self hate and greed.

By addressing the Ayers case, the Afro-Mississippi writer is addressing the inequality of life in Mississippi, which relates directly to the 1968 Kerner Commission Report. White racist officials, non-accountable Negro leaders, and the power of the *Clarion Ledger* as the arm of propaganda for the State have allowed cases such as Ayers to be stripped of their original directives to address and dismantle the racist atmosphere and institutions of Mississippi. No longer at the heart of the Ayers case is the notion of making a mends for the years of injustice and the notion of destroying a racist system of governance and funding and replace it with a more fair and equitable system which allows all of the State's institutions to create leaders for their particular communities. The absence of a bountiful amount of black writers and a journal in which to write has left the African American community voiceless and powerless to affect change by asking questions and articulating the injustice and inhumanity of discriminatory funding practices. Further, this discriminatory funding practice has limited HBCUs, which used to be the bastions of black literature, from evolving and growing at the rate that they should. It makes no sense that a school such as Jackson State University, which was home to Margaret Walker Alexander for over twenty years, has no creative writing program in memory to the legacy of Dr. Alexander and the contribution of Afro-Mississippi writers. Even when Alice Walker lived in Mississippi she taught at an HBCU, JSU. During the seventies, under Dr. Alexander's guidance, JSU was host to some of the most prolific and cutting-edge conferences of the day. Why has the State of

Mississippi failed to reward Dr. Alexander's efforts by developing a creative writing program to address the specific needs and aesthetic of Afro-Mississippi writers? Why has the State of Mississippi refused to continue Dr. Alexander's cultivation of new Afro-Mississippian writers? Added to this must be the notion that the State's white universities have continued to marginalize African American writers and the African American aesthetic. As late as 1994, the University of Southern Mississippi was still teaching an American novel class, which covered the period of 1900 to 1965, that had no African American writers in the syllabus. Anyone who knows anything about American literature knows that this particular time period is the apex of the black novel. To not teach African American writers during this period is to marginalize the best of what African American literature has to offer—is to say that the African American best is, at best, marginal. This one act does much to perpetuate the notion of African American second-class citizenship in the State of Mississippi. One of the State's centers for higher learning is saying that African Americans are not critical thinkers and are not worthy to be studied as equals with white critical thinkers. This is then perpetuated by all of the white and black students who take the course and continue to disregard and marginalize African American literature. When you disregard and marginalize African American literature, you are disregarding and marginalizing African American thinking. When you disregard African American thinking, you are disregarding African American humanity. New Afro-Mississippi writers, journals, and newspapers are needed to counter-act this perpetuation of African American second-class citizenship.

This marginalization of African American thinking and literature has a direct affected on the lack of a major literary journal designed to study and celebrate the Afro-Mississippi aesthetic, the community that is and produces that aesthetic, and the internal and external influences upon that aesthetic. By asserting that there is no major journal, I merely mean that there is no local literary journal that is created by, for, and about the Afro-Mississippian community to specifically cultivate young black writers and celebrate established black writers on a State-wide level. The greatest drawback of having no black aesthetic centered journal in the State is that there has been no literary voice to counter-act that of the *Clarion Ledger*, which as been acting as the voice of propaganda during the Ayers case and as a voice acting to undercut the majority black city council. Also, without a journal, the Afro-Mississippi community is not able to petition freely their own leaders nor thoroughly address the gap between the black middle-class and the black working-class. The *Clarion Ledger* or no other white journal will print letters and articles focusing on how and why African American leaders are not being accountable to African American communities because the *Clarion Ledger* is an arm of propaganda for the white community. This is not to say that the white community is a monolith. This is to say that the white community is the dominate, majority, and the *Clarion Ledger* is not going to do anything that compromises the white community's position of dominance. A counter-journal would also allow the masses of Afro-Mississippians, which are guided by middle-class white attitudes, to recognize and embrace Afro-Mississippians who have their best interest at heart. For instance, local Jackson attorney, Chokwe Lumumba is often ridiculed by middle-class Afro-Jacksonians for being too radial, too loud, and for using the jargon of black dialect. I am amazed that a man who has a law degree can be marginalized by his own people for speaking truth to power. When Lumumba is on television, I can feel the collective cringe of most middle-class Afro-Jacksonians who just want Lumumba to disappear for loving his black self, unconditionally, which allows him to combat white supremacy in any manifestation, whether it is in the form of a suited-up white man, a red neck, or a suited-up black man. Afro-Mississippians need a journal that celebrates their heritage and tradition in the same manner that white Mississippians have a Rebel Flag and thousands of museums to celebrate their heritage and tradition. Richard Wright is right when he asserts "If black writers turned to their own vernacular traditions, black literature could be as original and as compelling as black music and folklore" (Gates xxxiv).   In this case the emphasis is on "compelling."   The power of the black vernacular is marginalized by white middle-class standards. And as long as Afro-Mississippians continue to "desire to pour racial individuality into the mold of American standardization...to be as little Negro and as much American as possible," the race will continue to be powerless and limited in his human evolution. It is amazing that Faulkner was expelled from the University of Mississippi for using improper English, but Afro-Mississippians blindly accept Faulkner, his language, and his culture as superior to Lumumba, merely because Faulkner is white. We need black journals so that black writers may give black communities a knowledge of self, which I hope will manifest itself as self love and in the form of black politicians becoming accountable to the black community and not the white dollar. Black writers need to seek to inspire black leaders to pool their resources and nurture and develop black owned businesses that are accountable to the black community. This is a national issue but with regional indexes. If the Afro-Mississippi writer does not deal with all of these issue as a collective and as independent issues, then the canon of Afro-Mississippi literature is doomed to be stagnant and marginalized, which will doom the African American community of Mississippi to remain stagnant and marginalized. The goal of any writer or critical thinker is the forward evolution of his people. Getting jobs without any sovereignty merely makes the African American community high paid slaves. It will only be through black art that Afro-Mississippians can be given a sense of their wholeness and complete humanity. If the new Afro-

Mississippi writers do not take on this challenge, the work of those before them will have been for nothing.

To change our perception of Mississippi is to change our perception of the Nation. It is easy to blame America's race problem on Mississippi in one broad sweep, but difficult to deal with Mississippi and the complexity of her race issue. If Mississippi is not merely a black and white, two-sided, one dimensional race issue, what does that say about the Nation? Ultimately, this complexity and failure of integration demands for something that most African American integrationists fear, a call for Black Nationalism. If the happy-go-lucky Mississippians, who for so long just wanted a seat at a table, are questioning integration and its successes, then we truly have a problem with the complacency of African Americans. Mississippi could always be counted to support integration and Christianity in its art. Now, these new African American Mississippi writers shake the foundation which is sure to cause a rumbling through the Nation. Yet, by questioning the success of integration and Afro-Christian leaders, the new African American writers are also alienating themselves from potential middle-class patrons whom they do need to fund and perpetuate the local black arts movement.

I do not mind living in the State that has been the measuring stick for race relations of this country. I do mind that the Nation has glossed over the issue of Mississippi's failings in race relations while at the same time denying African American writers from Mississippi to deal with the complexity of who we are. Other African American writers might argue that their glass ceiling and artistic limitations are just as confining, but there is no evidence of other African American writers being as tied and limited by the past as African American Mississippi writers. This is the problem and issue of the new African Mississippi American writers. Their answer has been to go forward with their vernacular, their imagery, and their settings. It is up to the citizens of the State and the rest of the Nation to decide if it wants to listen.

It must be understood that the African American Mississippi writers of the next millennium will begin to produce works more in line with the Braxton group of writers. They will be, for all practical purposes, carrying on the tradition of Wright and Alexander as handed to them by Knight, Ward, and their socio-economic conditions. Not to judge them accordingly is to do a disservice to them, their work, African American writers, and American writers. They will be carrying it own by studying, writing, performing, and publishing. The best discourse about poetry is not the essay. It is the poetry created. It is the work that creates the cannon, not the discussion of it. Most importantly, we are forging ahead in the vernacular and imagery of our Mississippi time. In doing this we truly follow in our ancestor's footsteps.

Bibliography

Anderson, Jolivette. *Love and Revolution.* Jackson: SisterLove, 1998.

Anderson, Jolivette. *Past Lives, Still Traveling: Traveling the Pathways to Freedom.* Jackson: SisterLove, 1999.

Anderson, Jolivette. *At the End of a Rope in Mississippi.* Jackson: SisterLove, 2001.

Asante, Molefi Kete and Abarry, Abu S., eds. *African Intellectual Heritage: A Book of Sources.* Philadelphia: Temple University Press, 1996.

Braxton, Charlie. *Ascension from the Ashes* with introduction and forward by Amiri Baraka and Dr. Jerry W. Ward. Atlanta: Blackwood Press, 1990.

Braxton, Charlie. "Personal Interviews and Conversations." November and December, 1998.

Charles, Ray. *Brother Ray.* PBS/ETV Special. 1996.

Gates, Henry Louis and McKay, Nellie Y., eds. *TheNorton Anthology of African American Literature.* New York: W.W. Norton & Co, 1997.

Johnson, Derrick. "Personal Interview" September, 1998.

Miller, Nayri. *Ascensions.* (Self Published Manuscript)

McInnis, Claude L. (Sr.). "Personal Conversations." Spring, 1989.

Phillips, Ivory, Dr. "Personal Conversations." Spring, 1989.

Plumpp, Sterling. *When the Mojo Calls I Must Come*. Chicago: Third World Press, 1972.

Ramsey, Howard, II, eds. *Spirits on High*. Nashville: New Visions Press. 1996.

Speyer, Alex and Park, Mary, eds. *CutBank 44*. Missoula: University of Montana, 1995.

Thompson, Julius, ed. *The Anthology of Black Mississippi Poets*. Rochester: Frederick Douglass Institute/ University of Rochester, 1988.

Wideman, Daniel J. and Preston, Rohan B., eds. *Soulfires*. New York: Penguin. 1996.

Williams, David Brian. *Mirages*. Jackson: Desque, 1998.

Williams, David Brian. *Simple Love*. Jackson: Desque, 1998.

Letter to My Wife

Dear Monica,

Sometimes it seems that we are so far apart on my vision of being a writer. I am no longer trying to become a writer. I am a writer. This is what I have wanted to do all my life. I've wanted to write, educate, and entertain people. I love writing, I love critical discourse, I love entertaining. I know that when we first met, this wasn't the life I was leading. Maybe I was mis-leading as to what I wanted to do with my life.

I guess it scares me that I don't know what to say when you say that sometimes you feel like you are not first in my life. I will admit that sometimes I am driven madly and wildly to write, publish, and perform. All I can say is that it gives me something that makes me feel alive. It's the only thing that I have ever done with my life that gives me complete satisfaction. I love it. I don't know if that will ever change. I think that for the rest of my life I will be chasing this dream of living like a writer or like my notion of what a writer is. But, I feel blessed that people want to read my work or hear me read. I feel blessed that somebody asked me to read for them. As bad as I didn't want to go tonight, there was this voice in me, making me go. It kept saying, "Man, God has blessed you to be in a situation where somebody thinks enough of what you do to ask you to share it with them, and your egotistical ass isn't going. Don't get to big for yourself!" Every opportunity to share my work is an opportunity for me to live to the fullest. I cannot tell you how I feel when someone comments on something that I have published or when I am reading to an audience that is responding positively. It is like my life, me, I really matter. The problem, of course, is that when I don't do well, no matter the reason, I feel like I haven't produced much in the way of having a life.

Artists create for three reasons: for personal release/therapy, to inform or move people toward a particular direction, and to entertain. And I will admit that I enjoy entertaining people as much as I enjoy informing them. Whether in the written or in the oral, I want to give pleasure. I want people to see themselves in my work, especially when I'm beginning with my life. It means that I click with someone else. It means that someone gets it. Like tonight, even when my work is not received well by the majority of the people, a brother can say, "Man, you don't even know me, and you were talking about me in your poems. That's sholl how I be feelin'." That's worth more money than I could ever earn. I created something that means something to someone else. It touches them in a place that lets them know that they are not alone in the way that they feel or think. It lets them know that they are not crazy. And, I guess their response does the same for me.

To be honest, I was pissed at the poor response/ reception, especially since I didn't want to go in the first place. And, I know that my state of mind affected my reading, the delivery of my work. Therefore, most of them didn't like my work, but I didn't want to be there anyway. But, I can't use my not wanting to be there as an excuse because it is just a cop-out, a lame excuse. See baby, I pride myself on being a professional; I meet my publishing deadlines no matter what is happening in my life, and I give one hundred percent when I am sharing my work orally. Maybe I needed a humbling experience. Maybe the 'lectric Man was getting a fat head. But the real deal is that I'm pissed because I didn't want to read, and I wasn't able to overcome that feeling so that I could give my best.

So, why did I go? I went because I'll read anywhere, anytime, and anyplace. I went because Anita is always supporting what we do, and I felt a need to repay her for her support. This is what black people are supposed to do for each other, help each other. She didn't need me, but she was kind enough to ask. I felt honored that she would. And every opportunity is an opportunity to see if my work is improving. For me, it is about the work, the images. How well do my images paint a picture in the receiver's mind? This is why I push myself to create a better image, to paint a better picture. I don't write for sex or money or fame. That shit is lame. Besides, I know who and what I am. I'm a thick ass brother with a perm. And that's cool. I know who I am, and I am comfortable with that. What I want is for my work to move people, to inspire people, to make them want to be and do better.

As much as I love you, I don't see any change in the pace of my work. I don't want to live my life questioning whether or not I did my best to get my work to people. If they don't like it, then the customers are always right. But, I must try everyday of my life to get my work to them. I am having a difficult time balancing being married with being a writer. All I can say is that I'm trying.

It seems that so much has changed in our life. I know that it seems that the only places I want to go have to do with poetry. To be honest, those are the only places where I feel comfortable. I spent my whole life feeling uncomfortable, living by somebody else's rules, justifying everything that I do to somebody else. I promised myself that when I got to own my house, my own car, and my own life that I would never, ever again, go anywhere I felt uncomfortable. So, you are fighting two difficult flaws: the amount of time that I'm spending with my work and my inability to move in a social capacity outside the literary world. To be honest, I don't know how to solve it. I am who and what I am. I cannot apologize for that. But don't ever think that what I do is for glory or sex. What I do is driven by something deep inside me. I can't control it. I guess my problem is that I've stopped trying to control it, and I allow it to control me. But for the first time in my life I have something that gives me an identity and makes me happy. I'm a writer and a performer. It may or may not be good or useful or pleasing or money making, but it is what I do. It's what I do best. Besides teaching on the college level, I don't know if I could do anything else.

While I do realize our differences, I also realize how important you have been to my growth and development. For the past seven years, you have been right by my side. All of any good that is me is because of God and you. I love you and thank you for your love.

A Blessed Man

Of all the socio-political essays that I have ever written and published, of all of my harsh and unflinching critiques of racist whites and Negro leaders who have shirked their duties to gain white gold, this is the most difficult and scariest thing that I have ever had to write. But, I am, on this day, unable to hold my peace any longer. I must say that God is a good, just, and wonderful God who has blessed me more than I have ever deserved.

One Thursday, while giving a lecture on Carter G. Woodson's *Mis-education of the Negro* to an advanced high school history class at Forest Hill High School, I told the students that I agree with Woodson that African people are second-class citizens because we have been taught to hate ourselves and have been historically given an education that teaches us to be inferior. However, I wanted to tell them desperately that if we or any people align themselves to the will of God, no man has the power to oppress them. A proper education in God is as important as an education in all things worldly, especially since He created all things. The only power that white people have over African people is that which we give them. In fact, if we spent as much time trying to please and ingratiate ourselves to God as we do to gain material things, then we would have our liberation.

Why is this so difficult to say? I do not belong to any church, and I am not a man who lives by the Christian code. So, for me, it has always been difficult to say to people that Jesus is blessing me because I always felt that it would be hypocritical. And for those of you who know that I am a big Prince fan, this has nothing to do with his becoming a Jehovah's Witness. If you know me, you know that I ain't getting up that early on a Saturday morning to do anything, especially knock on somebody's door. And yet, it is difficult for me to continue to awake and look around me and not shout the praises of Jesus to the mountain tops or simply to the top of whatever the highest point of Jackson is. I think that it was Matthew who said that the word and joy of God is like a fire raging to be set free on the world. Try as I might to hold back my praises because of my fears and iniquities, the joy of the Lord must be set free from me. I am not blessed because of my house, my car, my job, or my mediocre writing achievements. I am blessed because the joy of Jesus lives in my heart, and I have a wonderful wife who reminds me on a daily basis what it means to love and be loved. I am blessed because I have finally realized that no matter what I do, or what others may say about me, or do to me, no man can shake the foundation of Jesus. Jesus provides a safe haven that ten thousand Katrinas cannot destroy.

One of my many conundrums is how can a man who once published a poem calling God a tyrant by comparing Him to Napoleon now do an about face to sing His praises. And yet, this is not my greatest crime. My greatest crime is having more desire to be an accomplished writer than an accomplished family man. I have spent too much time trying to craft literature that has a positive impact on society and not enough time helping my step-children grow into constructive and positive contributors to society. And yet, I thank God for the diligence of my wife that they have not turned out too badly.

Now, I don't want anybody to get me twisted. I still believe that Black Nationalism is the best theory for Africans dislocated in America. And, I will still wage war against the racists and Uncle Toms who continue to build and lock gates that separate African people from their freedom. But, I also know that the greatest freedom is the liberation provided by the blood of the lamb. I also believe that Jesus wants all of His people free and unburdened so that they can live a life that shines a path back to Him. On this day, however, I only want to sing, and shout, and dance for Him. I want tears to flow like rivers from my heart as testimony to His goodness and greatness.

God has given us all that we need, but we squander so much. We have enough food, yet we do not feed the hungry. We have enough land, yet people have nowhere to live. And, I contribute as much to these problems as anyone else. Even with all of that, I can no longer be afraid to call His name in public. I cannot leave this Earth without giving praises to the Master. I cannot not die without using my breath to sound to the world that He is life, the only life that we will ever need. And no, I am not dying. I mean we are all dying, but I have no illness or confliction that is speeding my death. I just can't bear the thought of leaving this Earth without acknowledging all that God has done for me.

For those of you who have joined this email listserve to receive cultural and political news, I apologize for having overstepped my bounds. Please send an email if you would like to be removed. Tomorrow, it will be business as usual. We will be posting cultural and political happenings. Tomorrow, we use our talents to make the world a more peaceful and beautiful place. And yet, I can only hope that tomorrow I feel as close to Jesus as I do right now, and that I am able to say to someone that Jesus is the greatest revolutionary of all time and the only valuable worth obtaining.

www.ingramcontent.com/pod-product-compliance
Lightning Source LLC
Chambersburg PA
CBHW030355020726
47493CB00003B/822